THE CIVIL WAR
AT SEA

Also by Craig L. Symonds

The Battle of Midway

Lincoln and His Admirals: Abraham Lincoln, the U.S. Navy,
and the Civil War

Decision at Sea: Five Naval Battles That Shaped American History

American Heritage History of the Battle of Gettysburg

Confederate Admiral: The Life and Wars of Franklin Buchanan

Stonewall of the West: Patrick Cleburne and the Civil War

Joseph E. Johnston: A Civil War Biography

Navalists and Antinavalists:
The Naval Policy Debate in the United States, 1775–1827

Gettysburg: A Battlefield Atlas

A Battlefield Atlas of the American Revolution

A Battlefield Atlas of the Civil War

THE CIVIL WAR
AT SEA

CRAIG L. SYMONDS

OXFORD
UNIVERSITY PRESS

OXFORD
UNIVERSITY PRESS

Oxford University Press is a department of the University of Oxford.
It furthers the University's objective of excellence in research, scholarship,
and education by publishing worldwide.

Oxford   New York

Auckland   Cape Town   Dar es Salaam   Hong Kong   Karachi
Kuala Lumpur   Madrid   Melbourne   Mexico City   Nairobi
New Delhi   Shanghai   Taipei   Toronto

With offices in

Argentina   Austria   Brazil   Chile   Czech Republic   France   Greece
Guatemala   Hungary   Italy   Japan   Poland   Portugal   Singapore
South Korea   Switzerland   Thailand   Turkey   Ukraine   Vietnam

Oxford is a registered trademark of Oxford University Press in the UK
and certain other countries.

Published in paperback in 2012 in the United States of America by
Oxford University Press
198 Madison Avenue, New York, NY 10016

First published, in a slightly different form, in hardcover in 2009 by
Praeger, an imprint of ABC-CLIO, LLC.

Library of Congress Cataloging-in-Publication Data
Symonds, Craig L.
The Civil War at sea / Craig L. Symonds.
p.   cm.
Includes bibliographical references and index.
ISBN 978-0-19-993168-2 (pbk.)
1. United States—History—Civil War, 1861–1865—Naval operations.
2. United States. Navy—History—Civil War, 1861–1865.
3. Confederate States of America. Navy—History—Civil War, 1861–1865.
4. United States—History—Civil War, 1861–1865—Blockades. I. Title.
E491.S96   2012   973.7'5—dc23   2012006688

1 3 5 7 9 8 6 4 2

Printed in the United States of America
on acid-free paper

CONTENTS

AUTHOR'S NOTE

THIS VOLUME COVERS the operational history of the Civil War navies—on both sides—in America's great national trauma from 1861 to 1865. Rather than present a simple chronology of the war at sea, however, I have instead addressed the story of the naval war topically: the dramatic transformation wrought by changes in technology; the establishment, management, and impact of the blockade; commerce raiding and commerce defense; and combined operations, especially at Charleston, South Carolina. In this book, I sought not merely to tell a great tale, but to emphasize the salient issues of the naval war so that those issues did not get lost amidst the detail of events. At the same time, I have tried to illuminate and characterize many of the leading personalities in this fascinating story. If some get more coverage than others, it is not because I think the others historically unimportant, but because the figures I discuss help me cast light on the central issues of the naval war. The chapters are arranged more or less chronologically as well as topically and can be read independently or sequentially with equal benefit.

I want to thank John David Smith, who invited me to undertake this project, Robert Hanshaw, the photographic curator at the Naval Historical Center, who helped me obtain the illustrations in this book, and Tim Bent, Keely Latcham, and Joellyn Ausanka at Oxford University Press, who brought this edition to press. In this, as in all of my work, I owe an enormous debt to my wife, Marylou, who has read every word of this book more than once and offered her usual cogent advice.

THE CIVIL WAR
AT SEA

I

The Ships and the Guns

Civil War Navies and the Technological Revolution

IN DECEMBER OF 1862, sixteen-year-old Alvah Hunter watched from shore as one of the U.S. Navy's newest ironclads, the *Passaic*-class monitor *Nahant*, steamed slowly back to its berth at the Charlestown Navy Yard near Boston. Having spent months trying to convince naval authorities that he was old enough, and responsible enough, to serve as a ship's boy, young Hunter had finally been assigned to the *Nahant*, and now he watched with a mixture of pride and apprehension as his designated future home crept toward the wharf. It was nothing at all like the commodious ship-of-the-line *Ohio* on which Hunter had spent the last several days while awaiting assignment. For one thing, the *Nahant* was much smaller than the *Ohio*, which, in its heyday, had required a crew of more than a thousand men to load and fire the 104 guns arrayed on its three gundecks, or to set the sails on its three towering masts that rose so high above the waterline that crewmen at the main top could look down on the roofs and steeples of Boston. Stripped now of its guns and much of its rigging, the *Ohio* was being used as a receiving ship, essentially a nautical barracks, to house the thousands of new recruits, like Hunter, who were joining the greatly expanded U.S. Navy. Though no longer considered a combat vessel, the *Ohio* dwarfed the little *Nahant*, which had no masts or spars, carried only two guns, and whose principal design feature was a stubby armored turret, only 23 feet across, topped by a small round conning tower, giving it somewhat the appearance of an iron wedding cake.

In spite of that, Hunter was thrilled to catch this first glimpse of his new ship, and he pointed it out to a veteran sailor who was loitering nearby. The veteran snorted dismissively and unleashed a string of profanities at the stubby little ironclad—"the bloody old tub," as he called it. "Them new-fangled iron ships ain't fit for hogs to go to sea in, let alone honest sailors!" he declared. Then he turned to Hunter and offered a prophesy: "You'll all go to the bottom in her, youngster, that's where you'll all go!" The old salt's warning did not deter Hunter from his decision, nor in the end did it prove accurate, but just as the physical differences between the *Ohio* and the *Nahant* were a metaphor for the revolution in naval warfare that took place before and during the American Civil War, the old sailor's reaction to the *Nahant* measured the impact of those changes on the culture of the pre-war navy.[1]

FOR ALL HIS BITTERNESS about changes to the Old Navy, the veteran sailor who cursed the *Nahant* as a "bloody old tub" must surely have seen those changes coming, for the harbingers had been evident for at least a decade. The Civil War marked the culmination of an era of technological innovation that had a dramatic impact on the way Americans lived their lives, and eventually how they fought their wars. The Civil War did not cause these changes; they were evident years before, the consequence of a revolution in the American economy. A few statistics bear this out. Between 1820 and 1840, capital investment in American factories grew fivefold from $50 million to $250 million, and in the 1850s, the number of patents granted by the U.S. Patent Office jumped from 5,942 to 23,140. Though the value of agricultural products in the United States more than doubled in those years, for the first time in American history the value of manufactures surpassed them. A modern scholar cites the 1850s as "one of the most rapid periods of industrial growth in United States history." One clear manifestation of this national transformation was a revolution in transportation and communication: A boom in canal building in the 1820s gave way to a boom in railroad construction in the 1830s, both of which sped transportation, and the advent of the telegraph in the 1840s dramatically accelerated the spread of information. It is one of history's many ironies that even as canals, turnpikes, railroads, and telegraph lines knitted the country together, the inability of Americans to agree upon the future of chattel slavery in the West drove the sections apart.[2]

This technological revolution impacted the U.S. Navy as well. In 1843 the United States launched USS *Princeton*, the world's first propeller-driven steam warship (though the British *Rattlesnake* was only a few months behind). Designed by the Swedish immigrant John Ericsson, who also fashioned its 14-foot, six-bladed propeller (then called a screw), the *Princeton* was both faster and more efficient than any paddlewheel steamer of her day, and for a brief moment it looked like the United States had stolen a nautical march (to use a mixed metaphor) on its principal maritime rival, Great Britain. The moment did not last. Though the design features of the *Princeton* were widely adopted by both France and Britain, it did not mark a turning point in U.S. Navy warship development. For one thing, the explosion of one of its experimental, large caliber guns, dubbed the "Peacemaker," during a public relations cruise in 1844 killed the Secretary of State and Secretary of the Navy among others, and cooled the ardor of Congress for naval experiments. Though that gun had been designed by the *Princeton*'s captain, Robert Stockton, and not by Ericsson, the principal blame for the catastrophe attached itself to Ericsson. As a result the navy temporarily shut out the inventive Swede from further projects.[3]

Even without that consequential mishap, however, it was difficult for American naval planners to justify a full-scale commitment to steam-powered warships of any kind in the 1840s because of America's strategic geography. The United States was three thousand miles from Europe, a comforting isolation that was a great blessing to the adolescent United States, providing it with a cocoon of protection from the great powers. Nor was there serious competition from North American rivals. When the United States went to war with Mexico in 1846, its foe had such a small navy that the Mexican government sold off its few warships at the outbreak of hostilities to prevent them from being captured by the Yankees.

The Mexican War also demonstrated that steam-powered vessels had severe logistical difficulties when operating on distant stations, for they were prodigious consumers of coal. U.S. Navy steam ships blockading Vera Cruz on Mexico's Gulf coast operated at a distance of more than 900 miles from the nearest friendly coaling station at Pensacola, Florida. Since those warships had a steaming range of only about 2,500 miles, a round-trip to Pensacola and back burned up almost three quarters of the coal most of them could carry, and the United States had to establish a coaling base at Anton Lizardo south of Vera Cruz to keep its steamers supplied. Given that logistical reality, showing the flag at remote sites from the Mediterranean to the South China Sea—the primary duty of the pre–Civil War navy—made steam ships impractical. Consequently, even as the British, French, and other European powers whose rivals were close at hand, forged ahead with steam propulsion, the United States clung to a dependence on sail power for its peacetime navy. By 1850, when the British had 150 steam warships, and the French had 70, the United States had only six.[4]

Change was coming nonetheless. Despite their self-evident logistical limitations, the tactical superiority of paddle steamers in the Mexican War led Congress in 1847 to approve three new side-wheel steamers (the *Susquehanna*, *Powhatan*, and *Saranac*), and one with a screw propeller (the *San Jacinto*), all of which would play prominent roles in the Civil War. Like all steamers of that era, each of these ships carried a full suite of masts and spars and were labeled "auxiliary steamers" because they were expected to navigate under sail at least as often as they did under steam. They were, in fact, transitional vessels that straddled the age of sail and the age of steam. The principal reason for including the *San Jacinto* in the program was to compare a screw-driven vessel with a paddlewheel vessel, a comparison that was marred by the fact that the *San Jacinto* had a number of engineering flaws—including a propeller shaft that was twenty inches off the centerline.[5]

Despite that, it soon became evident that the side-wheel steamers were inferior to screw steamers. When the *Susquehanna* was dispatched to the Far East by way of Cape Town and the Indian Ocean in 1851, it took her eight months to steam 18,500 miles, burning 2,500 tons of coal en route. Simple division shows that this yielded an average of 7.4

miles of forward progress for each ton of coal burned. Since coal cost an average of about $10 a ton in 1851, it cost the government about $1.35 (more than a full day's pay then) for every mile that passed under the *Susquehanna*'s keel. Moreover, the lengthy transit time was a product not only of her relatively slow speed (8–10 knots), but also the fact that the *Susquehanna* had to stop eight times en route to refuel, spending 54 days in port re-coaling. Finally, all of those coaling stops were necessarily at foreign ports since the United States had no overseas bases in the mid-nineteenth century. Even after the *Susquehanna* arrived—finally—on station at Hong Kong, she remained dependent on foreign sources of fuel to stay there. Obviously, for a navy with far-flung responsibilities and no overseas coaling bases, steam power continued to have significant limitations.[6]

A second problem with side-wheel steamers like the *Susquehanna* was that those enormous paddlewheels on each side obscured much of the ship's broadside, thus limiting the number of guns it could carry, and those big paddlewheels also made very inviting targets. If one of them became damaged by enemy fire, the ship's mobility would be dramatically affected, and the helmsman would need great skill to prevent the ship from yawing off course, or even steaming in a circle. Navy Lieutenant W. W. Hunter suggested that the solution was to turn the paddlewheels on their sides and place them below the water line thus putting them out of the line of fire and restoring an uninterrupted broadside. Dubbed the Hunter's Wheel, this seemed to offer a technological and tactical solution. But in practice the Hunter's Wheel proved stunningly inefficient. In 1842 the USS *Union* was engineered to operate with Hunter's Wheels, but while they dramatically churned up the water and burned extravagant amounts of coal, the ship made no better than 5 knots, and in 1848 its engines were removed and it was employed as a receiving ship. In the end, the best solution proved, after all, to be Ericsson's screw propeller, and in the mid 1850s during a burst of naval expansion, the U.S. Navy returned to it for a new generation of warships.[7]

IT IS A COMMONPLACE to assert that the U.S. Navy was dramatically ill prepared for the outbreak of war in 1861. Virtually every history of the war notes that the U.S. Navy had fewer than 90 ships at the outbreak of war, only 42 of which were capable of active service, and that in 1861 most of those were overseas showing the flag on distant stations from Brazil to China. Soon after he was inaugurated, Lincoln asked his new Navy Secretary, Gideon Welles, what kind of naval force could be made available in case of war, and Welles named only twelve ships that could "at once" be put into service. Clearly this was a Navy that was completely unprepared to command the coastline, impose an impervious blockade, pursue rebel commerce raiders, and do the other jobs that would be assigned to it in the forthcoming struggle.[8]

And yet such a conclusion is only partly accurate, for the U.S. Navy was far better prepared for war in 1861 than it had been for any previous American war. This was because in the five years between 1854 and 1859, the Navy underwent a dramatic transformation characterized by the construction or purchase of no fewer than twenty-four major new combatants, all of them propeller-driven steamers, and all of them armed with the latest and most sophisticated naval ordnance. It was the largest peacetime naval expansion since the Naval Act of 1816 that had authorized the *Ohio* and her sister ships. This building spree was not undertaken in anticipation of civil war—or war of any kind—but simply to modernize an aging and outdated fleet in a time of technological change. Even so, it took place simultaneously with the well-known series of sectional crises that marked the country's descent into fratricidal war.

In 1854 Congress passed the Kansas-Nebraska Act, a fateful piece of legislation that provoked violence on the Kansas plains, tore the Democratic Party in half, and foreshadowed the coming rift in the Republic itself. That year also witnessed two other events that together marked a tipping point in the technological history of the U.S. Navy. One was the launch of the USS *Constellation*, the last U.S. Navy warship ever built without a steam engine plant. The other was a Congressional appropriation for the construction of six new propeller-driven steam frigates. The *Constellation*'s link to the past was self-evident. Named for one of the Joshua Humphreys–designed frigates first authorized back in 1794, it even used some of the timbers from that iconic warship in its construction. With this bow to its heritage, however, the Navy said goodbye to the era of the sailing navy, for if the *Constellation* looked to the past, the new steam frigates (often called "screw frigates" in recognition of their two-bladed pro-pellers) looked to the future.[9]

All of the new screw frigates were named for American rivers. The first of them was christened USS *Merrimack* for the river that flows southward through New Hampshire and into the Atlantic at Newbury-port, Massachusetts.* Launched on June 14, 1855, it was destined to become famous in the war to come. The *Merrimack* was a large vessel for its day (at 257 feet, it was 60 feet longer than the old *Ohio*), displaced 3,200 tons, and was powerfully armed with fifty heavy guns. Aware that the United States could not build as many ships as its traditional rival Great Britain, American planners had from the beginning sought to endow each of its ships with a larger battery than other vessels of the same nominal class. When the *Merrimack* visited English ports in 1856–57, her powerful broadside battery so impressed the British that they began planning a new class of steam warships of their own.[10]

In spite of that, the *Merrimack*-class screw frigates did not quite constitute a full-scale naval revolution. Their tenacious grip on the past was evident in the fact that all of them carried the three masts and full rigging of sailing-era frigates. Indeed, but for the single telescoping smokestack between the foremast and mainmast, they could easily be mistaken for them. Like the *Susquehanna*-class paddlewheel ships, they were effectively "auxiliary steamers," and in recognition of that, their propellers and drive shafts could be lifted from the water to reduce drag while under sail. Moreover, the *Merrimack*'s great size, combined with her undersized engines, made her, and the other ships of her class, very poor steamers that averaged only about 5 or 6 knots under steam, and only 7.6 knots when under both steam and sail. Moreover, the fuel effi-ciency of these new frigates was no better than that of the *Susquehanna*, and they remained just as dependent on foreign coaling bases.[11]

---

*The other ships in this class were *Wabash*, *Minnesota*, *Roanoke*, and *Colorado*. USS *Niagara*, also authorized at this time and sometimes lumped in with the others, was constructed with sharper lines and was quite different in both appearance and perfor-mance. It was both longer (328 feet between perpendiculars) and faster than its sister ships. Her size and speed were factors in her selection to lay the first trans-Atlantic cable in 1858.

The USS *Merrimack* as it appeared soon after its launch in 1856. Labeled an auxiliary steamer because it was expected to use its engines sparingly, it is shown here the way it generally operated: under full sail with the engines shut down. Nevertheless, the steam-powered, propeller-driven *Merrimack* marked the beginning of a prewar modernization for the U.S. Navy. (Courtesy of the Naval Historical Center)

Moreover, impressive as they were, the *Merrimack*s were wholly inappropriate for the tasks that traditionally befell American navies in time of war: defense of the coast, protection of trade, and raiding enemy commerce. Indeed, because of their 23-foot draft, there were a number of American ports, especially along the southern coast, that these ships could not even enter. Consequently, in 1856, while the *Merrimack* was still on its shakedown cruise and violence was exploding across Kansas, Franklin Pierce's Navy Secretary, James C. Dobbin, went back to Congress to urge the construction of another new class of warships: somewhat smaller, shallower-draft steam sloops, and the first U.S. Navy warships to have twin screws. The lame duck Democratic Congress passed an appropriation of a million dollars for five such vessels on March 3, 1857, the day before James Buchanan took the oath of office as the fifteenth president, and three days before the Supreme Court handed down its decision in the Dred Scott case.[12]

The new sloops of war, often called screw sloops, were named for American cities. The first of them, and the namesake of the class, was the *Hartford*, which during the Civil War became famous as the flagship of David Glasgow Farragut. (The others in this class were *Richmond, Brooklyn, Pensacola*, and *Lancaster*.) Launched in 1858 during the Lincoln-Douglas debates, the *Hartford* drew only 18 feet of water, which allowed her and her sister ships to enter most southern ports where the bigger *Merrimack*s could not go. Indeed, during the Civil War the *Hartford* would steam up the Mississippi to Vicksburg, and fight her way into Mobile Bay. Ironically, however, in 1857, southerners were among the strongest supporters of the appropriation. Convinced that slavery either had to expand or begin to wither, they sought to extend American influence—and eventually American sovereignty—into the Caribbean and Central America, and they hoped that these new screw sloops would be instrumental in achieving that goal. Instead, of course, they became instruments for suppressing the southern bid for independence. Along with the big *Merrimack*s, the *Hartford* class screw sloops gave the United States eleven new steam warships of the most advanced type.

Nor was that all. The same year the *Hartford* was launched, Congress appropriated money for yet a third class of new steam warships. These screw steamers were all named for Indian tribes, and the first of them,

USS *Mohican*, was launched only a year later in 1859. (The others were *Tuscarora, Iroquois, Dacotah, Seminole*, and *Narragansett*.) Though these smaller ships also carried masts and spars, their sail pattern was much reduced, and they were the first warships in American history to be classified as genuine steam warships rather than as auxiliary steamers. They were also the first to be armed with large caliber pivot guns rather than guns arrayed in broadside. In both respects they pointed the way toward the future of warship design.[13]

Thus it was that between 1854 and 1859—that is, between the Kansas-Nebraska Act and John Brown's raid on Harpers Ferry—the U.S. Congress authorized funds for three new classes of steam powered, propeller-driven warships. These timely appropriations enlarged and modernized the U.S. Navy so that, as noted above, it was better prepared for war in 1861 than it had been for any previous war. The six *Merrimack* class heavy frigates, the five *Hartford* class screw sloops, the six *Mohican* class sloops, plus other screw steamers purchased by the Navy in this same period, gave it two dozen new and powerful warships that had not existed five years before. All but one of them remained in the arsenal of the U.S. Navy after secession, and all of them played crucial roles in the war to come.[14]

THESE NEW WARSHIPS marked a technological milestone not only because of their more efficient engine plants and screw propellers, but also because they carried newer and deadlier guns, for along with the revolution in propulsion, the 1850s also witnessed a revolution in shipboard ordnance. For nearly a thousand years, naval gunnery meant using black powder to fire iron balls from muzzle-loading iron gun tubes. To be sure, the cannons had become larger, the gun tubes stronger, the balls heavier, and the powder more reliable. But a sailor from the navy of Sir Francis Drake would have recognized the 24- and 32-pound guns that had made up the armament on the *Ohio*, and after a moment or two of observation, could have slipped efficiently into one of its gun crews. Then in the mid-nineteenth century, a number of important innovations dramatically changed the character and efficiency of naval ordnance.

The first of these innovations was the use of explosive shells as well as solid shot. In the 1820s, a Frenchman named Henri-Joseph Paixhans began to experiment with powder-filled shells that had a fuse built into the shell's casing. The fuse was ignited by the initial powder charge and burned while the shell was en route to its target so that the shell would explode after impact. For wooden ships of war, this dramatically increased the amount of destruction that could be caused by a single hit. Prior to the advent of Paixhans' shell gun, the greatest danger to wooden ships in battle was that a solid shot might weaken or wreck the standing rigging, which could make a ship unmaneuverable and encumber the gundeck with the impedimenta of fallen spars and rigging. The danger to sailors from solid shot was not so much that a cannon ball would take their head off or cut them in half (though such things did happen), but rather that a solid shot smashing into the wooden bulwarks would generate giant splinters that flew across the deck like so many javelins. Most injuries in battles at sea in the age of sail came from these splinters rather than from direct hits by a solid shot. Despite the heavy casualties that often resulted, a wooden ship could absorb literally scores of hits by cannon balls and still continue to fight. The advent of explosive shells changed all that. Now a single well-aimed shell could blow a hole in the side of a ship and send it to the bottom. The United States began to adopt some shell-firing guns as early as 1850, but an important turning point came in November of 1853 when Russian ships armed with Paixhans guns utterly destroyed a Turkish fleet in the Black Sea at the Battle of Sinope. That example accelerated the adoption of shell-firing guns, and by the time the Civil War broke out, cannon that could fire shells as well as solid shot had become commonplace.[15]

In addition to firing explosive shells, many of the new naval guns were rifled. That meant they had spiral grooves cut on the inside of the barrel that put a spin on the projectile so that it would hold its trajectory for a much longer distance. Since the projectiles for smooth-bores (either shot or shell) had to be slightly smaller than the gun tube itself in order to prevent jamming, they exited the muzzle with an imperfect and often uncertain trajectory. Beyond a few hundred yards, no one could be very sure of their ultimate destination. This made aiming a naval gun in the age of sail more of an art than a science, and explains why the fighting instructions of that era called for the combatants to get as close as possible before wasting valuable powder and shot. Before the 1840s, the ideal distance for naval combat was "a half cable's length"—about 100 yards. Some captains preferred to get even closer and waited to open fire until they were within "half pistol shot" (about 60 yards). What mattered in such engagements was less the accuracy of the fire than the discipline that kept the men at the guns, loading and firing as fast as possible. Now, with the widespread adoption of rifled cannon prior to and during the Civil War, the effective combat range of warships multiplied dramatically, from 100 yards to 2,000 yards or more.* Because of this, there were very few engagements in the Civil War that were conducted at "half pistol shot" simply because ships seldom got close enough for a genuine hull-to-hull exchange.[16]

The guns were also much bigger. Indeed, naval guns grew so large that they were no longer categorized by the weight of the ball they fired (e.g., 24-pounders) but the diameter of their bore (e.g., 6 inches). In the United States, a navy lieutenant named John Adolphus Dahlgren, who was destined to become a Union admiral in the coming war, experimented with very large caliber guns. The problem was that the explosion of the larger charges of black powder needed in such heavy guns exerted additional pressure on the cast iron gun tube. The explosion of the "Peacemaker" on the *Princeton* back in 1844 was evidence that using too much powder could fracture the iron of large gun tubes with catastrophic effect. Thickening the entire gun tube to withstand the pressure would make the guns so heavy as to render them impractical. Dahlgren attacked the problem by carefully measuring the amount of pressure at each point along the length of the barrel and shaping the gun to be strongest where the pressure was greatest. The result was a gun that was fat at the breach, narrowed dramatically halfway down the tube, then flared out again at the muzzle. The resulting Dahlgren gun looked for all the world like a giant iron soda bottle turned on its side, and was consequently nicknamed the soda bottle gun. Dahlgren produced a successful 8-inch gun, but his 9-inch gun, which weighed

---

*One severe limitation to firing shells from rifled guns at such great distances was that most long-range firing was done by ricochet. That is, the shells were fired at a flat trajectory and skipped across the water toward the target like a flat stone. The problem with this for rifled guns was that the first skip usually disrupted the spin put on the shell by the rifling and threw the projectile off course.

just under 5 tons and fired a 100-pound projectile, became the Navy standard, and eventually some 1,185 of these were cast and sent to the fleet. Later, Dahlgren also made 11-inch guns, and after the war began, he produced a number of larger and heavier 15-inch guns. He even produced a 20-inch gun, the largest naval gun ever forged, though it was never deployed aboard ship.[17]

An alternate solution to Dahlgren's solution of thickening the breech of naval guns was to strengthen the breech by placing iron bands around it. To do this, a red-hot band of wrought iron was slipped over the breech of a conventional cast iron gun tube. When it cooled in place, it gripped the gun tube, strengthening it precisely where greater strength was needed. Sometimes two bands were slipped over the tube, one on top of another, creating a "double-banded" weapon. In 1861, on the very eve of the war, Robert P. Parrott, an ordnance specialist who worked at the Cold Spring Foundry near the Military Academy at West Point developed a particularly effective double-banded and rifled weapon, and over time rifled Parrott guns of up to 10 inches in bore began to appear in the Navy's arsenal, though the Dahlgren 9-inch smoothbore remained the most common piece of naval ordnance for both sides during the Civil War.[18]

At about the same time that Parrott introduced his rifled gun, Thomas Jackson Rodman, an 1841 West Point graduate who worked at the Allegheny Arsenal in Pittsburgh, attacked the problem of strengthening the new larger gun tubes in a different way. Instead of casting the cannon as a solid mass of iron and then drilling out the bore, which was the usual practice, Rodman guns were cast as hollow tubes and cooled by circulating water through the bore of the tube so that it cooled from the inside out making it strongest where it was likely to be most stressed: along the inside of the bore. This made 6-, 8-, and even 10-inch Rodman guns more reliable and less likely to fracture after prolonged use.[19]

All these changes—steam propulsion, the screw propeller, larger and more powerful rifled guns that could fire explosive shells as well as solid shot—made warships of the 1860s significantly more maneuverable and much deadlier than ships built only a decade earlier. After hostilities began, there would be more innovations, including armor plate and the revolving turret, both of which were evident in the *Passaic*-class monitor *Nahant*, which boasted two large-caliber guns, including a 15-inch Dahlgren gun. By the time young Alvah Hunter stood watching the *Nahant* steam slowly back into its slip at the Charlestown Navy Yard, it had become evident that, for better or for worse, these innovations marked the end of the sailing era—represented by the stately but now archaic *Ohio*—that had dominated naval warfare since the days of the Spanish Armada. It was the passing of that era that so antagonized the grizzled old sailor on the wharf at Charlestown Navy Yard and provoked him to warn Hunter of the perils of going to sea in a "bloody old tub."

IF THE UNION WAS BETTER PREPARED for a naval war than ever before, the Confederacy began its bid for independence with no navy at all. As the southern historian J. Thomas Scharf put it in his 1886 history of the Confederate Navy: "The timber . . . stood in the forest, and when cut and laid was green and soft; the iron required was in the mines, and there were neither furnaces nor workshops; the hemp required for the ropes had to be sown, grown, reaped, and then there were no ropewalks." If it was not quite as bad as that, it was grim enough. At the outset, the only ships to which the fledgling government could lay claim were those that were seized by local authorities immediately after secession: four revenue cutters, an ancient side-wheel steamer (the *Fulton*), and a few small tenders and tugs, ten altogether. Confederate authorities urged southern-born U.S. Navy officers "to bring with you every ship and man you can" when they returned to their native States, but those who did resign to serve the Confederacy first turned their commands over to national authority before making their way south. As Scharf noted, perhaps ruefully, "not a [single] United States vessel was delivered up by a Southern officer."[20]

From the outset, Confederate authorities recognized that their bid for independence was to be primarily a land war. They acknowledged that "any very extensive naval preparations in time to meet the dangers that threaten us are impracticable," and as a result, a committee of four former U.S. Navy officers who pledged themselves to the new Confederacy recommended that southern naval efforts be restricted to the construction of small flotillas that "might serve as auxiliaries to forts." From the start, therefore, the Confederacy planned to rely mainly on fortifications, supplemented by small gunboat squadrons, to defend its coast. Alas for these plans, the Civil War took place precisely at the time when steam-powered ships armed with heavy rifled guns had shifted the historical balance of power between ships and forts. Though historically forts had proved stronger than ships, the new technology overturned that assumption. Lacking the ability to produce modern warships of the newest type, the Confederacy was at a severe disadvantage.[21]

One proposal, sponsored by Matthew Fontaine Maury, known as the "Pathfinder of the Sea" for his pre-war work in charting the ocean's currents, was to construct a swarm of small wooden gunboats each armed with two heavy guns. Maury borrowed both the concept and its rationale from Thomas Jefferson who had championed a gunboat navy a half century earlier. Undeterred by the fact that Jefferson's gunboat navy had not lived up to expectations during the War of 1812, Maury insisted that "the true naval doctrine for these times is . . . 'Big guns and little ships.'" He argued that the increased firepower of large rifled naval guns meant that it was no longer necessary to spend vast sums of money on massive sea-going warships. It would cost less to put two hundred of the new heavy guns afloat in small open boats than it would to build one steam frigate that might carry only ten of them. He succeeded in getting the Confederate Congress to appropriate $2 million—its single largest naval appropriation—to build a hundred of these small double-enders in December, 1861. Soon afterward, however, the remarkable debut of an experimental ironclad warship in Hampton Roads caused a revolution in naval strategic thinking on both sides of the Potomac River.[22]

That remarkable ship was the *Merrimack*, and to tell its story requires some backtracking. When Virginia seceded in April of 1861, the steam frigate *Merrimack* was in the Gosport Navy Yard near Norfolk for an overhaul of her weak and unreliable engines. Gideon Welles ordered the commander of the Yard, Commodore Charles McCauley, to prepare her for sea at once and send her out of port as soon as possible lest she fall into the hands of the secessionists. Instead, intimidated by a mob that was more noisy than dangerous, McCauley panicked and ordered that the *Merrimack* be scuttled. Concerned about McCauley's reliability in this crisis, Welles sent Captain Hiram Paulding in the USS *Pawnee* to stiffen the old commodore's resolve, but by the time Paulding arrived, the *Merrimack* was already resting on the bottom of the Elizabeth River.

Paulding thereupon concluded that it was too late to attempt to defend the Yard, and he ordered his men to finish what McCauley had started. They set fire to the masts and upper scantlings of the *Merrimack*, still visible above the water, and burned eleven other, less valuable, ships. They also fired most of the workshops and other buildings in the Yard. Only the sailing frigate *Cumberland* was salvaged from this self-inflicted disaster, towed to safety by the little steam tug *Yankee*. In time, of course, the South's acquisition of the damaged but not destroyed *Merrimack* would prove fateful.[23]

The Federal abandonment of the Gosport Navy Yard was equally consequential in terms of naval ordnance since McCauley and Paulding left behind a total of 1,195 naval guns. Paulding had ordered his men to sledgehammer the trunions off some of them, but this proved futile, and in the end they were simply abandoned. To be sure, many of them were older 24, 32, and 64 pound smoothbores. But the haul included 52 Dahlgrens, and this windfall was crucial because at the time the South lacked both the raw materials and the industrial infrastructure to manufacture its own artillery in large numbers. In time, the South would supplement these captured weapons with modern heavy ordnance imported from Europe and, in a testimony to American (in this case southern) ingenuity, it would eventually develop the ability to manufacture its own modern weapons.[24]

The most important site in the Confederacy for the manufacture of naval ordnance was the Tredegar Iron Works in Richmond, which was supplemented by the Bellona Gun Foundry a few miles down the James River. Over the course of the war, the Tredegar Works produced over a thousand heavy guns for the South, most of them for the army, but some for the navy as well, including 173 heavy guns. Another important source of heavy naval guns was the Naval Gun Foundry at Selma, Alabama. It is a measure of the extent to which Confederate decision makers focused on the land war that this important facility began as a private enterprise by Colin J. McRae who had trouble convincing officials in Richmond that establishing a naval gun foundry two hundred miles from the sea was a worthwhile investment. Eventually this site produced more than 100 heavy naval guns, many of them double-banded 7-inch and 8-inch rifles designed by John Mercer Brooke.[25]

Because the South suffered from a dearth of ships, it had few assignments for those southern-born naval officers who resigned from the U.S. Navy to serve their native states. There were, interestingly, fewer of these than there were army officers who resigned. While more than two thirds of southern-born *army* officers went south, less than half of southern-born *naval* officers did so. In large part this was because, as one of them (James Waddell) noted, naval officers "were generally employed on foreign stations, and more than the officers of the other branch of the National defence, had lived under the flag as the visible embodiment of their country," giving them a stronger sense of nationalism. In addition, some southern-born officers may have remained by the old flag simply because it was evident that the Confederacy had no meaningful jobs for them. Even with a limited number of officers, there were more than the Confederacy could meaningfully employ. In March of 1861 (before Fort Sumter), Confederate law established a naval officer corps consisting of four captains, four commanders and 30 lieutenants. By then, however, there were already twelve captains, twenty-four commanders, and 53 lieutenants who had resigned their U.S. Navy commissions to come south, and by July, there would be fifteen captains, 33 commanders, and 78 lieutenants looking for jobs in a navy that had plenty of officers but almost no ships. Many of them accepted positions as engineers and gunners in the Confederate army.[26]

The man whose job it was to create a Confederate navy virtually from scratch was former Florida Senator Stephen Russell Mallory who Jefferson Davis named as Confederate Secretary of the Navy. With his round avuncular face framed by a leprechaun-like fringe of beard, Mallory was less than heroic looking, but he possessed both the temperament and the expertise needed to preside over the thankless job of conjuring a Confederate navy. Born in the West Indies, Mallory's family had moved to Key West when he was ten years old, and he grew to manhood in that rough-and-tumble maritime community where the principal business was the rather ghoulish practice of salvaging the many ships that were wrecked trying to round the keys. Mallory developed his judicious temperament while adjudicating the conflicting claims of wreckers and ship owners. Elected to the Senate, Mallory served many years as chairman of the Naval Affairs Committee, which gave him a familiarity not only with naval administration but also with

Stephen Russell Mallory, the hard-working and competent Confederate Secretary of the Navy, advocated iron-armored warships to compensate for the Union's numerical superiority. He also championed laying the foundations for a permanent Confederate Navy, including the establishment of a Confederate Naval Academy. (Courtesy of the Naval Historical Center)

most of the personalities he would have to deal with during the war. A moderate Democrat during the run up to war, Mallory was a calm voice amidst the storm, but when Florida seceded, he went with his state. His ability to maintain his equanimity in the midst of squabbles was important to his lengthy tenure in Jefferson Davis's Cabinet where he was one of only two Cabinet members to hold his office throughout the war.[27]

Mallory had two overriding objectives as Navy Secretary. The first was based on his recognition that the South could not possibly match the Union ship-for-ship, and must therefore instead seek to overcome "inequality of numbers" with "invulnerability" by relying on armored warships. Mallory's other goal was to establish the infrastructure for a permanent standing navy, not merely an ad hoc fighting force. Consequently, he sought to develop shipyards, iron foundries, gun works—even a naval academy. He would pursue both of these goals throughout the war, and despite the lack of an existing infrastructure and the reality that the needs of the Confederate army invariably trumped the needs of its tiny navy, Mallory was remarkably successful.[28]

Barely three weeks into the war, Mallory wrote to the new chairman of the Committee on Naval Affairs to declare that "the possession of an iron-armored ship" was "a matter of the first necessity." Such a vessel, he declared, "could traverse the entire coast of the United Sates, prevent all blockades, and encounter, with a fair prospect of success, their entire navy." The problem was that the all but nonexistent southern industrial base was inadequate to construct a steam-powered, iron-armored warship from the keel up. Mallory's first hope, therefore, was to acquire such a vessel overseas. In 1855, the French had launched an ocean-going iron-armored warship named *Gloire* that was at the time the most powerful ship afloat. Mallory hoped to buy her, or a ship much like her. The French were not selling, not only because it would have been a flagrant violation of the neutrality laws, but also because the *Gloire* was the jewel of their fleet. It became evident early on that if Mallory wanted an iron-armored warship, he would have to find some way to construct one.[29]

Mallory was not the only one thinking of armored warships. He was still unpacking his boxes after the Confederate government's move from Montgomery to Richmond in June, 1861, when he received a visit from fellow Floridian John Mercer Brooke. Brooke was an 1847 graduate of the Naval Academy who had spent most of his career in scientific pursuits at the Naval Observatory and mapping the sea bed. His interest and expertise in naval ordnance made him a kind of southern counterpart to John Dahlgren. Now on June 3, he came to Mallory with a proposal for an armored warship. Mallory encouraged him to draw up some preliminary plans and do the necessary calculations, which Brooke did, and in only a few days he presented Mallory with the sketch of a casemate ironclad with a flat-bottomed hull. The shield of the casemate would consist of two feet of wood covered by three inches of iron plate. Impressed, Mallory sent for William P. Williamson, recently appointed as the Confederate navy's Chief Engineer, and John Luke Porter, its Chief Naval Constructor.[30]

As it happened, Porter, too, had been thinking about an armored warship, and he brought with him a plan of his own. It was very similar to Brooke's except that Porter's casemate covered the entire hull of his model while Brooke's plan had an extended bow and stern to provide greater buoyancy for the heavy iron shield, and to prevent the bow wave from washing up on the armored casemate. The problem with both plans was that they stipulated a steam-powered, propeller-driven, marine engine, and the Confederacy simply lacked the wherewithal to manufacture an engine powerful enough to drive an iron vessel through the water. Instead it would be necessary to cannibalize an engine from an existing vessel. Brooke and Porter visited Gosport to see if the engines from the recently salvaged *Merrimack* might meet the need. But those engines had been designed to fit inside the *Merrimack*'s deep V-shaped hull and could not be squeezed into the flat-bottom design the two men preferred. It was Williamson who suggested that perhaps an armored casemate could be built on top of the *Merrimack* itself.[31]

It was not an ideal solution since the *Merrimack*'s great size would limit her mobility, and her 23-foot draft would greatly restrict her ability to operate in coastal waters. Still, it was the one way the South could obtain an armored ship quickly, and Mallory seized upon it with enthusiasm. The scuttled *Merrimack* had already been raised from the muck of the Elizabeth River and placed in the granite dry dock that the evacuating Federals had also neglected to destroy. Workers now cut away the charred remains of the upper hull, and while Williamson worked to purge the salt water from its engines, carpenters began to erect a casemate atop the hull. Experiments conducted ashore proved that two layers of two-inch plate were more effective against solid shot than five layers of one-inch plate, and so orders were sent to the Tredegar Iron Works, the only facility in the Confederacy that could roll two-inch iron plate, to begin producing the needed armor.[32]

This proved to be the industrial bottleneck, for the plan called for the application of some 800 tons of iron armor, more than was available in all of Virginia. Consequently, the construction team had to scavenge iron from across the state, melting down old cannon, iron tools, even nails. Confederate authorities even ripped up sections of little used railroad lines to melt the rails down into molten iron for the Tredegar rolling mills (a fact that has led some to conclude, incorrectly, that the *Merrimack* was coated with iron rails). This was very nearly an act of desperation, for arguably the South needed its railroads for internal transportation at least as much as it needed an armored warship. Mallory, however, did not quail at the sacrifice, convinced as he was that iron-armored warships were the key not only to a successful defense of the coast but also to seizing control of the war at sea.

MALLORY'S COUNTERPART IN WASHINGTON was Connecticut-born Gideon Welles, who was as demonstrative as Mallory was reticent. Not one to remain in the background and bide his time, Welles was more likely to assert positions boldly, occasionally losing his temper in the process. Eventually, Lincoln came to rely on both his candor and his loyalty and, like Mallory, Welles would serve in his post throughout the war. Critics attacked his eccentric looks (a full white beard and an obvious brown wig which led others to refer to him as Father Neptune), and later they also bemoaned his apparent inability to track down and destroy rebel commerce raiders like CSS *Alabama* (see Chapter 3). But much of this criticism was personal or politically motivated, and for all his

Gideon Welles was the Union Secretary of the Navy. Lincoln appreciated Welles for his blunt candor and his loyalty, though that candor often won Welles enemies in the public press. This engraving by J. M. Butler only hints at the marked contrast between Welles' brown wig and his white beard. (Courtesy of the Naval Historical Center)

eccentricities, Welles' management of the unprecedented Union naval mobilization was both efficient and effective.[33]

Welles found out about the progress the rebels were making on the re-floated *Merrimack* in Norfolk simply by reading the newspapers, for there was no such thing as an industrial secret in those days. Veteran officers assured him that the U.S. Navy had nothing to fear from one experimental ship, even assuming the Confederates could successfully complete the makeover. But as the weeks passed, and news of rebel progress continued, Welles decided he had to act. He requested, and Congress passed, a bill authorizing $1.5 million to construct three iron-clad warships, and he formed a board of three senior captains to select a design. Some fifteen serious proposals made their way to this committee. One of them was from an entrepreneur named Cornelius Bushnell who was sponsoring a design by Samuel Pook for a sloop-rigged steamer with an exaggerated tumblehome covered with interlocking half-inch iron plates. The scheme called for several layers of this iron plating to a maximum width of 4 inches. When he pitched the design to the committee, however, someone suggested to him that with all that armor, the ship was unlikely to float. To rebut this assertion, Bushnell decided to verify Pook's design with the man that everyone told him was the world's foremost expert on such things, John Ericsson in Brooklyn.

Ericsson was still holding a grudge from the way he had been treated after the explosion of the "Peacemaker" gun in 1844. Nevertheless when Bushnell knocked on his door and asked him to evaluate Pook's design, Ericsson willingly did so, announcing after a brief examination that the proposed vessel would indeed float and that its armor was likely to repel shot of up to 6 inches in diameter. But then he asked Bushnell if he would like to see a plan for a floating battery "absolutely impregnable to the heaviest shot or shell," and he produced a model for the vessel that subsequently became the USS *Monitor*. Intrigued, Bushnell took Ericsson's plan first to Hartford, Connecticut, to share it with Welles, and then to Washington to show it to Lincoln.[34]

Lincoln was fascinated by new technology. He remains the only president to hold a patent, having invented a device for lifting river steamers over sand bars in the 1840s. The president was so impressed with Ericsson's plan that he went personally to the meeting of the

Ironclad Board the next day. When the captains expressed uncertainty about the queer little craft, Lincoln shared his own views in a characteristic way by declaring, "All I can say is what the girl said when she stuck her foot in the stocking: It strikes me there's something in it." Thanks in part to Lincoln's support, the Ironclad Board somewhat reluctantly adopted Ericsson's proposal along with Pook's design (which became USS *Galena*) and an armored frigate (which became USS *New Ironsides*). The contractual conditions for Ericsson's design were severe: he had to build the vessel for less than $275,000, and he had to do it in less than a hundred days. Moreover, he would not receive final payment unless and until the vessel proved itself. If it failed to perform as advertised, Ericsson would be out of pocket.[35]

Meanwhile in Norfolk, Confederate authorities were striving to finish their ironclad as fast as possible. Though the Tredegar mills worked at full capacity, the armor plate arrived with agonizing slowness. Not until the end of February 1862 was there enough iron on hand to complete the armor shield. Now rechristened CSS *Virginia*, the ex-*Merrimack* bore ten guns (a 7-inch Brooke rifle in the bow and stern, and four 9-inch Dahlgren guns along each broadside) instead of the fifty it had carried as a steam frigate. In addition, it also had a 1,500-pound bow ram, which made the ship itself a deadly weapon.[36]

Aware that he needed a confident and aggressive commanding officer for this costly and experimental vessel, Mallory dispatched Captain Franklin Buchanan to Norfolk. Buchanan was an old sea dog, a 45-year veteran of the navy who had accepted a midshipman's warrant as a teenager during the War of 1812. A Marylander by birth, Buchanan had been outraged back in April of 1861 when an angry crowd in Baltimore had clashed with a Massachusetts regiment that was passing through town en route to Washington. Sure that Maryland was about to secede from the Union, Buchanan made his way to Gideon Welles' office and submitted his resignation. But Maryland did not secede, and Buchanan soon had second thoughts. Rather sheepishly, he attempted to withdraw his resignation to which the judgmental Welles replied dismissively: "By direction of the president, your name has been stricken from the rolls of the navy." Buchanan saw himself as the victim in this scenario. He denied that he was a secessionist. "I am as strong a Union man as any in the country," he insisted. But Welles would have none of it. He had no time for "pampered officers who deserted their flag . . . when their loyalty should have upheld it." In a letter to his son, Welles acknowledged that this response might seem "ungracious," but he insisted that he had no alternative, for Buchanan, and others like him, had been "faithless to the their country in time of peril." Eventually Buchanan went south (though he waited until after the rebel victory at Bull Run to do so) and reported himself to Mallory as ready for duty in the Confederate Navy. Once the *Merrimack/Virginia* was ready for sea, Mallory decided that this pugnacious veteran was just the man he wanted to command her.[37]

Buchanan wasted little time. He reported aboard the *Virginia* on March 4, and four days later he took her to sea for her maiden voyage as an ironclad. It had been advertised as a shakedown cruise, but Buchanan was determined to seize the moment and attack the enemy at once. Consequently, the big rebel ironclad steamed slowly out of the mouth of the Elizabeth River at mid-morning on March 8 and steadied on a course for Newport News Point on the northern side of the roadstead where two Union warships, both of them wooden-hulled sailing vessels of the Old Navy, lay at anchor. One of them was the frigate *Cumberland* that had been rescued from the Gosport Navy Yard during the Union's hasty evacuation the previous April; the other was the *Congress*, a 20-year-old sailing frigate armed with fifty smoothbores. It would be ten guns against eighty, but it would also be iron against wood.

The quartermaster on the *Congress* hardly knew what to call the *Virginia* when he first spotted the black smoke from her stack that betrayed its approach that morning. Handing the telescope to a nearby officer, he declared, "I believe *that thing* is—acomin' down." For their part, the men inside the *Virginia* had a strong sense of isolation given that they were enclosed inside a floating iron fort with no view of the outside world. Because the ponderous *Virginia* had a top speed of only about 5 knots, the run across Hampton Roads toward the enemy warships seemed interminable. As one sailor recalled, "The suspense was awful."[38]

Buchanan's plan was to steam his big ship directly into the *Cumberland*, plunging the *Virginia*'s ram into the side of the wooden ship. He sought out the *Cumberland* first because he believed that it carried a rifled 10-inch Columbiad on its foredeck. Such a weapon had at least a chance of penetrating the 4 inches of iron armor and 2 feet of

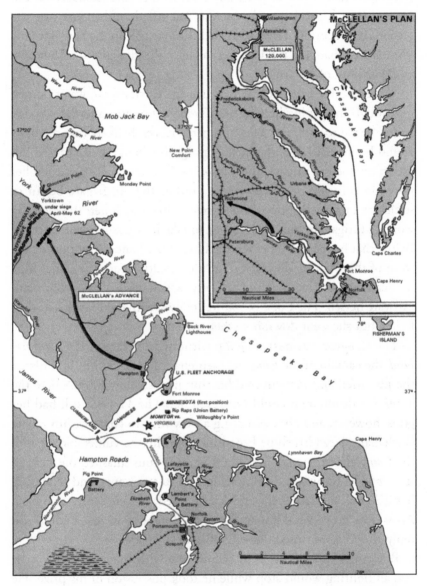

THE PENINSULAR CAMPAIGN AND HAMPTON ROADS, MARCH 1862. Map by Bill Clipson, reprinted with permission from *The Naval Institute Historical Atlas of the U.S. Navy* by Craig L. Symonds, © 1995.

wood backing that made up the *Virginia*'s casemate, and Buchanan wanted to take it out of the fight first. In fact, the *Cumberland* did have a 10-inch pivot gun, but it was not rifled, and in any case the second shot from the *Virginia*'s 7-inch Brooke rifle in the bow not only dismounted that gun, it killed every man in the gun crew—all but one, who lost both of his arms.[39]

When the *Virginia*'s bow ram struck the *Cumberland*, water poured in through the gaping hole in the *Cumberland*'s side, and the wooden frigate began to sink. For a few moments it seemly likely that the blow would be mortal for both ships. Though Buchanan had ordered full astern just before impact, the *Virginia*'s great momentum buried her prow deep inside the *Cumberland*, and as the old frigate began to settle she carried the bow of the *Virginia* down with her; the mortally wounded frigate seemed determined to take its assassin down with her. Before that happened, however, the flow of the James River pushed the stern of the *Virginia* downriver and the resulting torque on the ship's ram caused a section of it to break off, which allowed the *Virginia* to extricate herself. The *Cumberland* went down with guns firing and flags flying, but she went down nonetheless.[40]

The *Congress* was next. Having witnessed the fate of the *Cumberland*, the captain of the *Congress*, Lieutenant Joseph Smith, Jr., ordered the jib raised and maneuvered his ship into shallow water where the *Virginia*'s deadly ram could not reach her. The *Virginia* still had her guns, however, and after executing a slow turn to come within range, Buchanan placed his ship's broadside opposite the vulnerable stern of the *Congress* and opened fire. The *Virginia*'s guns smashed the stern of the *Congress* to pieces, dismounting its two stern guns and rendering her defenseless. Lieutenant Smith was killed, as were scores of others. After enduring several hours of bombardment to which it could not reply, the *Congress* raised the white flag of surrender.

Buchanan expected that in accordance with the traditions of the sea, all fighting would stop while he took possession of his prize. He ordered the *Beaufort*, one of the small steamers that was part of the Confederate James River Squadron, to go alongside the *Congress*, allow the survivors to escape to shore, and then set the abandoned ship on fire. But when the *Beaufort* approached the *Congress*, Federal soldiers on shore opened fire and forced her to retire. Buchanan sent a small boat under a white flag toward the *Congress*, but the Yankee soldiers fired at it, too, wounding the boat captain who was Buchanan's young aide. A sputtering Buchanan could hardly believe it! "They are firing at our white flag!" he exclaimed incredulously. Infuriated, he climbed out of the armored casemate, put a musket to his shoulder, and fired a shot at those dastardly soldiers on shore. They fired back, and he slumped to the deck when a bullet struck him high in his thigh near his groin. Realizing now that the Yankees on shore would not allow him to act in accordance with the laws of war as he understood them, Buchanan ordered that the surrendered *Congress* be set afire with hot shot. It was not an easy decision, for he knew that his own brother, McKean Buchanan, was paymaster on the *Congress*. Nevertheless, the *Virginia* fired two rounds of heated shot into the stern of the *Congress*, which was soon burning briskly.[41]

This iconic image of the naval battle between the CSS *Virginia* (*Merrimack*) and the USS *Monitor* in Hampton Roads on March 9, 1862, was painted by J. O. Davidson in 1886. (Courtesy of the Naval Historical Center)

Each side charged the other with inhumanity in this episode. Confederates complained that Yankee soldiers had twice fired on a white flag; Federals pointed out that the rebels had fired hot shot into a ship that had already surrendered, a ship with wounded men on board, some of whom subsequently burned to death. Just as the new technology of the mid-nineteenth century led to a new kind of war, the bitterness of fratricidal war led to a new harshness in its execution.

The *Congress* burned all afternoon and into the evening. As it burned, the *Virginia* made a half-hearted sortie toward another Union warship, the USS *Minnesota*, aground on a nearby shoal, but with Buchanan severely wounded and daylight fading, it seemed prudent to call it a day. The *Virginia*'s executive officer, Catesby Jones, took command and directed the big ironclad to an anchorage off Sewall's Point on the southern rim of the roadstead. Despite the confusion concerning the surrender of the *Congress*, the day had marked a signal victory for the Confederates, and Mallory would subsequently reward Buchanan by promoting him to the rank of full admiral. Two major warships with a total of eighty guns had been destroyed. Measured either in terms of lives lost or tonnage sunk, it was the worst defeat in the history of the U.S. Navy since its founding, and would remain so for eighty years more—until December 7, 1941. Mallory's investment in an experimental ironclad warship had paid off spectacularly.

The *Congress* was still burning at midnight, the flames reflecting redly off the inky surface of the roadstead, when the USS *Monitor* crept into Hampton Roads under its own power. It had been towed down from New York and nearly foundered in a storm off the New Jersey coast, but it cast off the tow upon entering the Chesapeake Bay. It tied up alongside the USS *Roanoke*, its arrival punctuated by the explosion of the *Congress* when the flames finally reached its magazine.

THE BATTLE OF IRONCLADS on March 9, 1862, is one of the great set piece stories of the Civil War. Both at the time and in the years since, each side portrayed the battle as one of David vs. Goliath. The Confederates emphasized the fact that their one ship took on the entire U.S. Navy in Hampton Roads, whereas the Federals noted that the fight pitted the much smaller *Monitor* against the larger and more heavily armed *Virginia* (which they continued to call the *Merrimack*, often spelled without the terminal "k").

The commanding officer of the *Monitor* was 44-year-old Lieutenant John L. Worden, a scientific officer who (like John Mercer Brooke) had spent much of his career in the Naval Observatory. He conceived of his primary responsibility as protecting the Union wooden ships in the roadstead, especially the still-grounded *Minnesota*, and like a nautical sheepdog, he intended to impose the *Monitor* between the *Virginia* and the *Minnesota*. He also planned to get as close as possible to his foe before opening fire. Though he had only two guns to the *Virginia*'s ten, he had three important advantages. First, his guns were bigger: The *Monitor* had two 11-inch Dahlgrens while the largest gun on the *Virginia* was a 9-inch Dahlgren, though the *Virginia* also carried two 7-inch Brooke rifles which, with their higher muzzle velocity, were also very dangerous. Second, Worden planned to use 175-pound solid shot (bolts, as they were called), which were best for piercing armor plate. Though Worden could not have known it, the *Virginia* had mostly explosive shells in her magazine for Buchanan had gone to sea the day before expecting to encounter only wooden ships. Finally, not only did the *Monitor* have thicker armor (8 inches in the turret compared to 4 inches on the *Virginia*'s casemate), but also its revolving turret allowed it to target its opponent regardless of the ship's heading, though the imprecision of the turning gears meant that the gunners generally had to shoot on the fly as the turret swept past the target.[42]

The battle lasted four hours, and because neither side was successful in inflicting a decisive blow, the confrontation clearly demonstrated the near-invulnerability of iron armor. At once point Worden broke off the fight and retired to shallow water where the *Virginia* could not follow in order to replenish the stock of ammunition in the turret. During that brief hiatus, Jones returned his attention to the *Minnesota*, but soon enough the *Monitor* was back, interposing itself between the *Virginia* and its prey, and the battle resumed.

The battle reached its decisive moment when a shell from the *Virginia* exploded directly against the pilothouse on the *Monitor*'s foredeck while Worden was looking out through the narrow slit. A "flash of light" lit up the tiny pilothouse and filled it with smoke. Worden staggered backward, his hands to his face. "My eyes," he cried out, "I am blind." The ship's paymaster and surgeon manhandled Worden down from the pilothouse to the deck of the passageway. The wound was not fatal, but clearly Worden could no longer exercise command, and just as Buchanan had been forced to turn command over to Catesby Jones, Worden turned the *Monitor* over to his second in command, Lieutenant Samuel Dana Greene. "Do not mind me," Worden told him. "Save the Minnesota if you can."[43]

The 21-year-old Greene had never been in combat before. Indeed, he had hardly been to sea since his only seagoing experience was the stormy trip down from New York in the *Monitor*. Perhaps because of that, his first decision was an instinctive one. He ordered the helm over and took the *Monitor* back into shallow water where the *Virginia* could not follow. Once he had an opportunity to assess the situation, however, he realized what his duty was and he ordered the *Monitor* back into the fight. In that brief interim, Jones had had a chance to assess his own circumstances. Having fired away several tons of ammunition, the *Virginia* was now several inches higher in the water and, intermittently, her unarmored lower hull became exposed. That, and the fact that he was low on both coal and powder, convinced Jones that he should head back to Gosport before the falling tide trapped him in the roadstead in a vulnerable state. Consequently, just as the *Monitor* was returning to the open roadstead, the *Virginia* retired up the Elizabeth River.

Historians have noted the revolutionary character of this first fight between ironclad warships. In the main, they have concluded that the outcome was essentially a draw because neither vessel managed to inflict any serious damage on the other. Indeed, no one, on either side, had been killed. In fact, however, measured in strategic terms, there *was* a clear winner, for by its very presence, the *Monitor* had succeeded in halting the rampage of the *Virginia*, and that allowed the Union Navy to remain in control of Hampton Roads and support the Peninsular Campaign of George B. McClellan.

Though the rebel ironclad returned to port to be met by cheering crowds, she had already fired her last shot in anger. The *Virginia* subsequently offered to renew the fight, appearing several times at the mouth of the Elizabeth River in mute challenge to the *Monitor*, but the *Virginia's* new commander, Flag Officer Josiah Tattnall, was reluctant to take her back out into the open roadstead where she might be run down by one of the Union's big steam frigates that had been hastily equipped with bow rams. Nor was the *Monitor*'s new commanding officer, Lieutenant William N. Jeffers, willing to accept Tattnall's implicit challenge since his was the only armored vessel (so far) in the Union arsenal. Sensitive to that fact, the Union Navy Department ordered Jeffers not to engage the "Merrimac" unless it threatened the Union fleet in Hampton Roads. William Keeler, the *Monitor*'s paymaster, wrote home that these orders reminded him of the way "an over careful house wife regards her ancient china set—too valuable to use, too useful to keep as a relic, yet anxious that all shall know what she owns & that she can use it when to occasion demands. . . ."[44]

As a result of these decisions, a kind of uneasy quiet settled over Hampton Roads, broken only in May when a Union amphibious landing on the southern rim of Hampton Roads forced the Confederates to evacuate Norfolk and the *Virginia* lost her base. Unable to reduce her draft to allow her to ascend the James River to Richmond, Tattnall reluctantly gave the order to destroy the vessel to prevent her from falling into the hands of the Yankees. This was a disaster for the Confederacy, one from which it would never fully recover. So much had been invested in this one ship that it was both materially and psychologically devastating to have to blow her up after she had seen a fighting career of only two days. It was as if a speculator had put all of his disposable money into a single stock and then the company went bankrupt. There would be other Confederate ironclads, and other successes against the Yankees, but the Confederate Navy would never have another day like it did on March 8, 1862.

BOTH SIDES sought to replicate the success of these inaugural armored vessels. The Union effort was better organized, better funded, better supported, and consequently more successful. Indeed, the *Monitor*'s perceived success in Hampton Roads led to what many have labeled "monitor fever" in the North as Welles quickly contracted with Ericsson for ten more monitor-type vessels. Congress had already appropriated $20 million for ironclads, but after the *Monitor*'s debut in Hampton Roads, it authorized an additional $10 million.

For this new class of monitors, dubbed *Passaic*-class monitors after the first of them to be launched, Ericsson made several improvements. At 200 feet from stem to stern, the *Passaics* were 30 feet longer than the original *Monitor*, and they had thicker armor (11 inches in the turret). They also carried bigger guns. From the beginning, Ericsson had wanted to use the largest caliber guns available in his armored turrets. He had designed the *Monitor* to carry two 12-inch guns, but since none had been available in the early spring of 1862, he had settled for two 11-inch guns. Now he wanted the *Passaics* to carry two of Dahlgren's new 15-inch guns. Once again, however, there were not enough 15-inch guns available and so each of the *Passaics* instead carried one 15-inch gun and either an 11-inch Dahlgren or a 100-pound Parrott rifle. One problem with such a battery (besides mismatching ordnance) was that the muzzle of the 15-inch gun was so large it would not fit through the bored gun ports of the turret. To prevent muzzle smoke from filling up the turret and asphyxiating the gunners, Ericsson designed what he called a "smoke box" around the muzzle that directed most (but not all) of the smoke outside the turret. The third important design change in the *Passaics* was self-evident after the fighting in Hampton Roads. On the original *Monitor*, the pilothouse was a square iron box on the foredeck. That proved to be inefficient not only because it masked the fire of the big guns in the turret so that they could not fire directly forward, but also because it physically separated the captain in the pilothouse from the gunners in the turret and made command and control more cumbersome. Moving the pilothouse from the bow to the top of the turret (which gave the *Passaics* their wedding-cake appearance) allowed the big guns to fire forward and allowed the commanding officer to give orders directly to the gunners in the turret below him.[45]

The ten *Passaic*-class monitors (including Alvah Hunter's *Nahant*) played important roles in the Civil War, though monitors never proved to be as decisive in the naval war as Welles envisioned. For one thing, their seakeeping capabilities were limited, which made them extremely uncomfortable for their crews during lengthy stays on the blockade. For another, despite their near invulnerability to hostile fire, they had very limited offensive firepower. With only two guns firing at an interval of once every five to seven minutes, they simply could not lay down the kind of steady fire that could compel gunners ashore to abandon their guns. They were very effective against other ironclads, a fact proved in June of 1863, when the *Passaic*-class monitor *Weehawken* compelled the surrender of the Confederate casemate ironclad *Atlanta* after firing only five shots. But they often proved a disappointment when fighting against well-built coastal fortifications (see chapter 5).[46]

Before any of that was fully evident, however, Welles contracted with Ericsson for another class of even larger monitors: the *Canonicus* class. At 225 feet, these were 25 feet longer than the *Passaics* (and 55 feet longer than the original *Monitor*) and they carried two 15-inch guns, each of them capable of firing a 440-pound iron bolt. (It is interesting to note that a full broadside from a 44-gun frigate armed with 24-pounders hurled just over 500 pounds at its foe while the two guns on a *Canon-icus*-class monitor fired 880 pounds.) In 1864, the Union began constructing double-turreted ocean-going monitors, five of which were eventually built, but only two of which saw service: the *Onondaga* and the *Monadnock*. The Union also built a number of double-turreted river monitors, two of which played an important role in the attack on Mobile Bay. The North even built one *triple*-turreted vessel, the USS *Roanoke*, though it proved so top-heavy as to be unreliable except as a guard ship.[47]

All in all, including light draft monitors and river ironclads, the Union built eighty-four ironclads during the war, and sixty-four of them were monitors. In hindsight, it is possible that the North's penchant for the monitor-type ironclad may have been misplaced. In the aftermath of the ironclad duel at Hampton Roads, the apparent success of the original *Monitor* closed out the field to most alternative designs, even though monitors were of dubious utility for the missions to which they were subsequently assigned. Many of them were committed to the blockade, where their slow speed, marginal buoyancy, and uncomfortable living spaces made them less than popular with both their commanders and their crews, and their slow rate of fire made them indifferent vessels for attacking the South's coastal forts, which turned out to be their principal job.

On the other hand, the monitor program led to the emergence in the North of a truly modern industrial system. Because the various components of the monitors had to be manufactured at different sites and then brought together to be assembled, the whole program provided an important boost to both metallurgy and fabrication, and allowed the U.S. Navy to create and maintain a stockpile of spare parts. In effect, the "monitor fever" that coursed through the North in 1862–63 allowed the nation to develop what economists call the second stage of a modern industrial system.[48]

THE CONFEDERACY ALSO TRIED to duplicate the success of the *Virginia*. Not long after the *Virginia*'s debut in Hampton Roads, the Confederate Congress cancelled the $2 million appropriation for Matthew F. Maury's tiny gunboats in order to spend the money instead on armored warships. The early loss of the South's two best shipbuilding sites at Norfolk and New Orleans was a severe blow to this ambition, but Mallory authorized new shipbuilding sites farther inland where he hoped they would be beyond the reach of the Union Navy. These included Rockett's Shipyard on the James River below Richmond; Columbus, Georgia, on the Chattahoochee River; Selma, Alabama, on the Alabama River; and Shreveport, Louisiana, on the Red River. At these sites and elsewhere, the South laid down eighteen ironclads in the fall of 1862, and by the end of the war, the Confederacy had begun a total of fifty ironclads, twenty-two of which were actually completed and placed in commission. Virtually all of these vessels were of the casemate design, not only in conscious imitation of the *Virginia*, but also because the Confederacy did not have steam presses powerful enough to stamp out curved iron plate.[49]

Indeed, iron plate was one of the key bottlenecks in the Confederacy's ironclad program. Mallory wanted his ironclads to be armored with 3-inch plate, but the South had no foundries that could produce it. Most had to settle for three layers of 1-inch plate, and even that was scarce; several southern ironclads had to be armored with interlocking T-rails obtained from the railroads. The other bottleneck was the scarcity of suitable marine engines. It took a powerful engine to drive an iron-armored ship through the water, and the South simply could not produce these. As a result most of the South's ironclad ships were severely underpowered, and many languished at the dock unused, or served as floating batteries, because they had no engine at all.

In addition to government efforts, several so-called "Ladies' Associations" raised money for ironclads as evidence of their patriotic commitment. The *Virginia II*, a slightly smaller clone of the original, though with thicker armor, was partially funded by the Richmond "Ladies Aid and Defense Society," and similar groups in Charleston and Savannah contributed to the construction of the CSS *Palmetto State* and CSS *Georgia*. Not all of these initiatives proved successful. The CSS *Georgia*, one of the ships armored with railroad iron, was entrusted to amateurs and proved a failure. In Alabama, the state government purchased the cotton lighter *Baltic*, turned the side-wheeler into an ironclad with four guns and a ram, then presented it to the Confederate Navy with the expectation that it would help defend Mobile Bay from a Yankee invasion. The Confederate Navy accepted the gift, but found itself saddled with a cranky, unmanageable, and unsuitable vessel.[50]

In spite of these handicaps, by 1864, the Confederacy had assembled small but still dangerous ironclad squadrons at Richmond, Wilmington, Charleston, Savannah, and Mobile, as well as on the western rivers. Some of these vessels had moments of triumph almost as heady as that of the original *Virginia* on March 8, 1862. The river ironclad CSS *Arkansas* ran through the entire Union Mississippi River fleet in July 1862 and anchored safely under the guns of Vicksburg (see chapter 4); the *Chicora* and the *Palmetto State* sortied from Charleston on January 30, 1863, and temporarily chased off the Union blockading fleet (see chapter 5); and perhaps most audacious of all, the CSS *Albemarle*, built with great effort in a cornfield on the Neuse River in North Carolina, rammed and sank USS *Southfield* in Albemarle Sound on April 19, 1864. The three ironclad rams of the James River Squadron—the *Virginia II*, the *Richmond*, and the *Fredericksburg*—attacked the Union squadron there in June of 1864, but mechanical problems and poor marksmanship made their effort futile. With somewhat greater success, that squadron also participated in the battle for Fort Harrison in the fall of 1864 and the Battle of Trent's Reach that winter. None of these operations, however, proved strategically significant.[51]

Despite the efforts of Mallory, the enthusiasm of the Ladies' Associations, and the bravery and determination of the ships' officers and men, the Confederate ironclad program could not change the trajectory of the war at sea. Though Mallory's instinct to rely on cutting-edge iron-armored warships rather than Maury's swarm of small gunboats, or even conventional steam frigates, was undoubtedly correct, the South simply lacked the wherewithal to make their challenge effective. In the end, the South had to revert to the strategy that the naval board had recommended back in February of 1861 and which was confirmed by Robert E. Lee that November: a reliance on forts aided by small gunboat squadrons to defend the coast. Even this limited goal proved unachievable because of the dominance and the technological superiority of the Union navy. The advent of steam power and heavy guns had changed the dynamic between ships and forts. For a hundred years and more it had been assumed that, as the *New York Tribune* declared on the eve of war, "Ships are no match for land batteries." But this hoary piece of naval lore was already out of date. In 1859, the Report of the Committee on Naval Affairs, had noted that "within the last fifteen years the application of steam as a motive power to naval vessels; their improved armament of heavy guns, equally applicable to shot and shell; their increased size and improved models, have revolutionized the character of naval warfare and diminished, in a remarkable manner, the inequality between frigates and forts." Though the South had little option but to place its hope in coastal forts, as one modern scholar has put it, the "coast defenders could only fight delaying actions against overwhelming sea power."[52]

2

The Blockade and Blockade-Runners

LATE ON THE NIGHT OF MAY 10, 1861, four weeks after the first shot of the war was fired at Fort Sumter, the screw steamer USS *Niagara* appeared off the entrance to Charleston Harbor. Officially, the *Niagara* was a *Merrimack*-class frigate, one of the six authorized in 1854, but she had been built along very different lines from her sister ships with a much longer hull and a sharper bow. She was the product of an effort to combine clipper ship styling with steam propulsion, and the result was a very handsome vessel: long and narrow with soaring masts and twin funnels between her foremast and mainmast. She was armed like a sloop with a dozen 11-inch smoothbore Dahlgrens on her weather deck, but her great size marked her unmistakably as a frigate. Altogether, she was the most imposing warship in the U.S. arsenal, and her appearance off Charleston on May 10 marked the beginning of a naval blockade of the South's most prominent Atlantic seaport.

The very next day, the *Niagara* made her first capture. Her captain, William W. McKean, noted that one of the several ships that he had warned not to enter the harbor had edged in toward the shore and was making signals. Closing on the vessel, McKean ordered a shot fired across her bow and sent a boat alongside. She proved to be the merchant steamer *General Parkhill*, and concluding that she was attempting to violate his orders and run into Charleston, McKean put a prize crew on board and sent her off under the command of Midshipman Winfield

Scott Schley to a prize court in New York. It was the first of some fifteen hundred prizes taken during the war in support of Abraham Lincoln's declaration of a blockade of the rebel coast. It was also Midshipman Schley's first independent command, though hardly his last. Thirty-eight years later, as Rear Admiral Schley, he would command a squadron of battleships against the Spanish in the Battle of Santiago off the coast of Cuba.[1]

Lincoln's blockade declaration, announced on April 19, 1861, only five days after Fort Sumter, was virtually the first strategic decision made by his administration. It was also one of the more controversial decisions of the war. Though it began modestly, it grew in size and scope until it involved as many as 500 ships and 100,000 men, a total exceeding the number of ships and men committed to all of America's previous wars combined. Over the ensuing four years, those men and ships captured blockade-runners valued at more than thirty million dollars, but in spite of that, the blockade never completely sealed the South off from the rest of the world, and the Confederacy managed to import enough war materiel through the blockade to sustain its armies. Northern newspapers at the time (and historians since) pointed out the apparent ineffectiveness of the blockade. Not only did daring blockade-runners rush past the watchful Union squadrons with embarrassing regularity, but critics noted that Confederate armies never lost a battle, or apparently even altered their behavior, because of materiel shortages caused by the blockade. To be sure, the Confederacy suffered from shortages—the tales of barefoot soldiers in butternut and gray who survived on meager rations were not entirely mythical. But southern soldiers seldom ran out of bullets or powder, and if they did it was as much the result of weaknesses in internal transportation, especially railroads, as because of the blockade. Stephen R. Wise, who has conducted the most complete study of Confederate blockade-running, concludes that "at no time in the war did the Confederacy lack the proper tools of combat," and William N. Still, Jr., concluded in 1983 that the Union blockade "was not a major factor in the collapse of the Confederacy." Others have noted that the blockade was not only ineffective, it also caused significant legal and logistical problems for the North because it absorbed resources and manpower that might have had a greater impact if they had been applied to the land war.[2]

On the other hand, it is difficult to measure the impact of the blockade simply by counting the number of vessels that managed to sneak through it. Though hundreds of blockade-runners successfully ran through the blockade, far more were deterred from ever trying to run it at all. Moreover, those vessels that did run the blockade were built for speed rather than cargo capacity, and because of the entrepreneurial nature of the blockade-running, they often filled their holds with high-price goods—those with the greatest profit margin—rather than those most needed for the war effort. Then, too, the presence of all those blockading vessels offshore all but eliminated the southern coastwise trade from Fernandina, Florida, to Norfolk, Virginia, which southerners had relied upon for interstate transport. This forced the Confederacy to depend even more heavily on its mismatched, overburdened, and rickety railroad network. Finally, it was not merely the restriction of imports that harmed the Confederate war effort, because the blockade also restricted exports. The South's inability to export its cotton to Europe prevented it from establishing overseas credits that could have been used to buy the goods it needed. To assess the impact of the Union blockade of the Confederacy, therefore, requires more than merely counting the number of ships that ran in—or out—of southern ports.[3]

THOUGH THE STRATEGY of imposing a naval blockade was a traditional option for the stronger sea power in eighteenth- and nineteenth-century warfare, the Union blockade of the South was different from anything that had ever been attempted previously. Historically, the purpose of a naval blockade was to keep the enemy's warships off the high seas and thereby secure safe passage for one's own commerce. During the American Revolution and the War of 1812, the Royal Navy attempted an intermittent blockade of the American coastline with the object of suppressing American privateers as well as bottling up its tiny national Navy. In the more than two decades (1793–1815) that Britain blockaded Republican and Napoleonic France, its goal had been to keep the French Navy, especially its powerful ships of the line, confined to its harbors. Horatio Nelson blockaded the French battle fleet at Toulon for nearly two years before chasing it back and forth across the Atlantic to its doom at Trafalgar. All that time, seaports where the French had no significant naval forces were seldom blockaded at all.[4]

In contrast to this, the object of the Union blockade was not to bottle up the Confederate blue water navy since it barely existed except in name, or even to confine the handful of rebel privateers that soon disappeared from the sea anyway. Rather, its purpose was to seal off the entire southern coast to trade. In Lincoln's words, it would "prevent entrance and exit of vessels" from all the ports in all of the seceded States. This was a hugely ambitious goal. Once Virginia and North Carolina seceded and Lincoln added them to his blockade declaration, the national government assumed responsibility for shutting down a coastline that ran from Alexandria, Virginia, to Brownsville, Texas, a distance of more than 3,500 miles, and which, by one count, had 189 harbors, inlets, and navigable river mouths that could be used by commercial shipping. No navy in history had ever attempted to assert such complete control over so vast a coastline.[5]

Because of that, Lincoln's declaration initially provoked ridicule in the South and skepticism abroad due to the obvious disparity between the assigned mission and the resources available. According to the international laws of war, a naval blockade was not legally binding on neutrals unless the blockading power stationed "a competent force" off every harbor that was under blockade. In other words, unless a squadron of warships was physically present to guard the entrance to each of those 189 harbors and inlets, the merchant ships of neutral powers were free to continue to trade there no matter what proclamations Lincoln might issue. Clearly, the first step in making Lincoln's pronouncement a reality was to dramatically expand the size of the navy to five, ten, or even twenty times its prewar strength, and this would have to be done at the same time that the Union was attempting to raise an army of unprecedented size.

Even if all that could be accomplished, there was still a legal problem, for Lincoln's pronouncement of a blockade could easily be considered a *de facto* recognition of the Confederate government. Throughout the war, Lincoln insisted that the Confederacy had no legal standing as a sovereign entity; those who had taken up arms against the government, he declared, were merely rebels. Lincoln's Secretary of State, William Henry Seward, warned Britain that any recognition of the Confederacy as a belligerent by receiving its ambassadors, or even making a public reference to it as a country, would be considered an unfriendly act. As far as the Lincoln administration was concerned, there was no such thing as the Confederate States of America. But the blockade declaration seemed to contradict this policy. How could Lincoln's government proclaim a blockade of a country that did not legally exist?[6]

Seward proposed that because the rebellious citizens at southern ports could not be counted on to collect the duties on imports, the United States should declare those ports closed to trade, and Navy warships could be stationed off southern harbors with orders to collect the appropriate duties and redirect the ships to other ports. To a group of foreign ministers, he explained that it would not be a real "blockade," for the U.S. warships would be placed offshore merely "to collect duties and enforce penalties for the infraction of United States Custom laws." The European ministers, however, rejected this clumsy gambit, and in any case, the excuse of collecting tariffs would not allow U.S. warships to stop or pursue any vessel except those that were immediately inbound to a particular port. In the end, Lincoln and Seward had to accept the name "blockade" despite the implied recognition of the Confederacy as a belligerent.[7]

Whatever the long-term consequences of these legal complications, the more immediate problem was making the blockade "effective." Welles dispatched the few warships that were available, like the *Niagara*, to patrol the waters off the South's principal seaports; he ordered home the vessels on distant station patrol; and he embarked on a crash program to acquire new ships. Of course building warships from the keel up was both expensive and time consuming. In addition naval appropriations required Congressional action, and at the outset of the conflict, Congress was not in session and not scheduled to meet until July 4. Given the national emergency, however, Welles was unwilling to wait, and on his own authority he let contracts for the construction of two dozen new screw steamers to be delivered, according to the contract, within three months, which gave them their nickname as 90-day gunboats. Welles calculated (correctly, as it proved) that Congress would approve the contracts once it convened, but his willingness to go out on a limb suggests something about the sense of emergency surrounding the mobilization. Eventually, the United States built twenty-three of these 90-day gunboats, the first of which was christened the *Unadilla*. At 158 feet, these *Unadilla*-class ships were 30 feet shorter than the

Mohican class and nearly 100 feet shorter than the *Hartfords*. They drew only 10 feet of water, however, and were therefore well suited to working along the southern coast.[8]

Readying the ships in ordinary, bringing home those from overseas, and adding twenty-three 90-day gunboats to the fleet gave the U.S. Navy a total of more than one hundred warships, most of them steamers. But this was still only a fraction of what would be needed. Most of the rest came from converting merchant steamers into wartime use. This was both faster and cheaper than building new warships from scratch, and though converted merchant steamers would pack a smaller offensive punch than purpose-built warships, their main job, after all, was not to contest the seas with warships of other countries, but to deter mostly unarmed blockade-runners.

Welles appointed his own brother-in-law George D. Morgan to oversee the acquisition of appropriate vessels for conversion. There was some squawking about this in Congress—Morgan took a commission of 2.5 percent for each purchase—but in the end his efficiency quieted most of the critics, and Morgan purchased a total of 89 warships at an average cost to the government of $40,000 each. They were then sent into one or another Navy Yard to be refitted for war use. Their decks were strengthened in order to support the heavy guns, magazines were constructed under the waterline, the crews quarters were expanded, and often in just a few weeks, the ship received a new complement of officers and crew, and off it went to join the blockading force. In one extreme example, the *Monticello* was converted from a luxury passenger ship into a warship at the Brooklyn Navy Yard in a mere twenty-four hours. As a result of this activity, by December, the Union Navy boasted a total of 264 warships, and the blockade that had been no more than a notion in April was well on the way to becoming a reality.[9]

The Confederacy could not match this kind of mobilization even if command of the sea had been part of its long-term strategy, which it was not. As noted in the previous chapter, Stephen Mallory recognized from the outset that the South lacked both the shipyards and the machine works to match the Union mobilization. In addition to Mallory's commitment to ironclad warships, therefore, the South also pinned its hopes on coastal fortifications, assisted by gunboats, to protect its harbors and river mouths. Combined with the more mature forts (like Sumter) seized from national forces after secession, the South hoped that a series of earthworks, small gunboat flotillas, and local militia forces could protect southern ports from the Yankee blockaders. As for war on the high seas, some southerners cherished a notion that England would not stand for being cut off from the South's agricultural resources, especially cotton, and use the Royal Navy to raise the blockade. Barring that, they hoped that southern commerce raiders would so savage northern shipping that the North would call off its hopeless quest to suppress the Confederacy (see Chapter 3). Indeed, Jefferson Davis' declaration that he would begin to issue letters of marque to private ship owners to authorize them to prey on Union commerce was one of the principal justifications for Lincoln's announcement of the blockade in the first place. On the whole, however, the South saw no way that it could either halt or even significantly interfere with efforts by the North to establish a blockade. The bigger question was: could the Union make its blockade effective enough to have a significant impact on the southern war effort?[10]

HAVING PROCURED THE SHIPS—or at least having made a start in that direction—the Union still had to decide how to organize the blockade. Sending ships willy-nilly down the coast to anchor off one or another port simply would not do; some overall concept of blockade strategy had to be developed and adopted. In the American Revolution, the Royal Navy had conducted what was known as a cabinet blockade, patrolling singly or in small squadrons up and down the Atlantic coast. If the British spotted a strange sail, they pursued and investigated. During the wars with France, the British established permanent battle squadrons off every harbor where French warships rested at anchor. In order to shut down trade completely, however, the Union would not only need to establish squadrons off every harbor along the rebel coast, but also, and more importantly, maintain them there for as long as the war lasted. Clearly, some organization had to be imposed on the growing armada, and to accomplish that, the Union authorized what became known as the Blockade Board or Strategy Board.[11]

The board was headed by Navy Captain Samuel Francis Du Pont, who soon emerged as the first Union naval hero of the war. Du Pont was a kind of American aristocrat. His father and uncle were not only wealthy (his uncle founded what became the du Pont Chemical Company), but also politically connected. Those connections won young Frank Du Pont an appointment as a midshipman at the age of 11. Though teenage midshipmen were not unusual in the nineteenth-century navy, 11 was a rather tender age to become a naval officer even then. Consequently, when the Civil War broke out, even though Du Pont was only 58 years old, he had nearly half a century of naval experience. During that half century, he had become a leading champion of naval reform. In the 1850s he had headed a board whose purpose was to cut through the dead wood within the officer corps and replace a promotion system based entirely on seniority with one based on merit. Alas, the entrenched interests of many senior officers ensured that the reform was, at best, incomplete. With the onset of war, however, most of the impediments to reform were swept away, and Du Pont was excited by the prospect that his decades of hard work were at last to reach fruition. He eagerly accepted the invitation to join a board of officers meeting at the Smithsonian Institution to plan the blockade strategy.[12]

The report of that board recommended the establishment of separate squadrons for the Gulf of Mexico and Atlantic coasts. Eventually these were subdivided into the East and West Gulf Squadrons and the North and South Atlantic Squadrons. Acknowledging the transformative effect of the new technology, the board also asserted that only steam ships could function efficiently on blockade duty. Sailing ships, for all their seakeeping capability, could not maneuver safely close inshore, hold their positions in all tides and all weather, or pursue steam-powered blockade-runners. Though a few sailing vessels did serve on the blockade (the yacht *America*, original winner of the America's Cup was one noteworthy exception), all but a handful of the blockading vessels were steam ships. But this imposed another difficulty, for those ships would have to be kept supplied with both provisions and especially fuel. Since the Union lacked any coaling stations between Hampton Roads, Virginia, and Key West, Florida, a key recommendation of Du Pont's Strategy Board was to seize and hold several such bases along the South Atlantic coast as a necessary precondition to maintaining an effective blockade. Initially, Du Pont's Board recommended Bull's Bay, South Carolina, and Fernandina, Florida, but after

Samuel Francis Du Pont was the Union's first naval hero of the war. He presided over the Strategy Board, took command of the largest of the blockading squadrons, and won the North's first victory at Port Royal, South Carolina. Subsequently, however, he earned the disapproval, even the animosity, of his civilian masters. (Courtesy of the Naval Historical Center)

further consideration, the initial site was shifted to Port Royal, South Carolina.[13]

Port Royal became the navy's first target for three reasons. First was its location almost exactly halfway between Charleston and Savannah, which would provide the blockading squadrons at both those cities a convenient base of supply and repair. Second was Port Royal's physical geography. Not only was it an enormous roadstead, large enough to accommodate the entire Union navy, but in addition the swampy marshes that separated the offshore islands from the mainland would protect the occupying Union forces from a rebel counterattack. Finally, Port Royal and the Broad River estuary constituted a watery wedge into the interior of South Carolina that offered a means by which Union forces could penetrate into the interior and break the north-south Charleston & Savannah Railroad at Coosawhatchee.

Du Pont's plan of attack was straightforward. His fleet of eight wooden steamers led by the *Merrimack*-class screw frigate *Wabash* and the older sidewheeler *Susquehanna* would escort a flotilla of army transports crammed with troops and supplies down to the South Carolina coast. The soldiers, as far as Du Pont was concerned, were merely baggage, useful for occupying the site after the navy had suppressed the southern forts. Very quickly, Du Pont developed a disdain for the soldiers' inability to accommodate themselves to living aboard ship for nearly a month in the confined spaces of their crowded transports. Most became seasick almost at once and remained that way for the next three weeks. To his wife, Sophie, Du Pont smugly confided that "Soldiers and marines are the most helpless people I ever saw."[14]

Du Pont was a worrier by nature. He agonized almost every day that something would go wrong. There was so much to do and the government seemed to be completely scatterbrained, displaying lots of energy but little direction. "Oh, the confusion here everywhere," he wrote to Sophie from Washington. "I hope Providence will not desert us." As the expedition was inevitably delayed by all the various things that can delay large-scale expeditions, Du Pont feared that the rebels would use the time to make the target stronger. "The defenses are increasing all along the southern coast," he wrote in September, "I hear of their having two hundred guns there." In fact, the rebels had only 43 guns at Port Royal, but Du Pont's imagination multiplied the difficulties.[15]

All of Du Pont's concerns paled before his fear of professional failure. He had witnessed how General Irvin McDowell had been victimized by unrealistic expectations at Bull Run in July, and wondered if the same fate awaited him at Port Royal. "I feel oppressed by the amount of expectations," he confessed to Sophie. And to his brother he wrote that the expedition had raised "undue expectations—so that the points originally intended will seem insignificant." Eventually, this last characteristic became so dominant in Du Pont's mind that his fear of failure became an undercurrent in his correspondence.[16]

Du Pont's fleet rendezvoused with the army transports and supply vessels at Hampton Roads in October 1861. It was the largest collection of U.S. naval power ever assembled and consisted of just about every type of ship afloat: screw steamers, paddle steamers, sailing frigates, troop transports, coal ships, two New York ferry boats, and, in the words of one officer, "vessels without shape [never] before known to the maritime world." Du Pont thought it looked like "a city on the waters."[17]

This mongrel armada got under way on October 28, and now Du Pont added one more worry to his list: the weather. The previous July he had warned that the expedition should take place no later than August, "for in September," he wrote, "the West Indian hurricanes may come and make it a second Armada." Du Pont knew that the great Spanish Armada of 1588 had come to grief less because of the efforts of the English defenders under Francis Drake and Lord Howard of Effingham than because the forces of nature. "God blew," the English victory medal read, "and they were scattered."[18]

For once, Du Pont was right to worry, for a similar fate awaited his fleet. The ships safely weathered Cape Hatteras off North Carolina—the so-called graveyard of ships—but at about noon on November 1, just as the fleet entered South Carolina waters, the barometer dropped dramatically and a gale blew up into a hurricane that threatened to drive the whole force onto shore. Du Pont ordered the fleet to heave to and anchor. Du Pont's own cabin on the *Wabash* was inundated with water, and most of his personal stores, including his clothes, were soaked with seawater. He was grateful, however, that his personal papers and his Bible were unharmed. "During the night," he recorded, it was the old story—fetching away of furniture, rolling of glasses and bottles about the sideboards, rolling off sofas . . . blowing great guns above with torrents of rain."[19]

Du Pont was not particularly worried for the safety of the *Wabash*; she was a large enough ship to weather the storm, even though, as one officer wrote, she "wallowed and rolled like a pig." Du Pont's concern was for the smaller ships in his command. "If this great leviathan could be made to twist and roll, and writhe as she did," he wrote, "what must those tiny vessels in comparison be doing?" Perhaps by now he was beginning to feel some compassion for those soldiers locked up below deck on the transports.[20]

When it finally began to clear the next morning, Du Pont looked about him and saw mostly empty seas. Only half a dozen of the 75 vessels were within sight; the rest of the invasion fleet was simply

RESCUE OF MAJOR REYNOLDS'S BATTALION OF MARINES FROM THE FOUNDERING STEAMER "GOVERNOR," BY THE U. S. FRIGATE "SABINE" NOVEMBER 2d, 1861, OFF CAPE HATTERAS, N. C.

Atlantic storms nearly wrecked Du Pont's invasion fleet before it arrived off the South Carolina coast. Here survivors from the sinking transport *Governor* are rescued by USS *Sabine* off the South Carolina coast on November 2, 1861. (Courtesy of the Naval Historical Center)

gone. In despair, he wrote in his journal, "This morning the fleet was nowhere. . . . The fine ordered fleet, the result of so much thought, labor, and expense, has been scattered by the winds of heaven." He did not think the ships were lost, only dispersed. Each captain had sealed orders designating the fleet rendezvous, and hopefully they would all get there eventually, but it would destroy the element of surprise.[21]

Du Pont and the *Wabash* arrived off Port Royal Sound on November 4 with about eight other ships, and over the next week or so the rest of the fleet gradually straggled in. The small gunboat *Isaac Smith* had been forced to throw its guns over the side to stay afloat, and two of the transports had been blown literally across the Atlantic fetching up on the Azores before they could set a course for Port Royal. Eventually, however, all of the warships and most of the transports made it safely to the rendezvous. Now it was time to put the fleet to the test. It would be the first trial of steam-powered warships armed with heavy rifled guns against shore fortifications.

INSIDE PORT ROYAL, the Confederates pinned their hopes on the two forts that guarded the headlands at the entrance to the sound: Fort Walker

on Hilton Head Island guarded the southern headland, and Fort Beauregard on St. Helena Island guarded the northern headland. Walker was
the stronger of the two—an earthwork fort mounting 23 guns. Though
the Confederates had less than half the number of guns that Du Pont
had in his warships, the conventional wisdom was that guns ashore were
superior to guns afloat. Gunners in forts had a stable firing platform,
better protection, and unlimited ammunition. Then, too, while forts
could be damaged, they could not sink. The long history of warfare
before 1861 had proved time and again that when ships fought forts, the
forts had an overwhelming advantage. As noted in the previous chapter,
however, the technological revolution of the mid-nineteenth century
had changed that calculation. Steam power allowed the ships to remain
in motion during the attack making them more difficult targets; the
big rifled guns firing explosive shells gave ships greater fire power than
they had possessed in any previous war; and finally, at Port Royal the
rebel forts were log-and-earth fortifications built at sea level rather than
masonry structures built on high ground.

The Confederates also had a small naval flotilla in Port Royal,
but here as elsewhere, it was a weak and eclectic collection of small
steamers, mostly armed tugs. They were under the command of Flag
Officer Josiah Tattnall, who four months later would become the
last commanding officer of the *Virginia*. Tattnall was a career U.S.
Navy officer, the son of a former governor and senator from Georgia,
who had resigned his commission when Georgia seceded. He was an
aggressive officer best known for having ordered his squadron into
battle in Chinese waters two years before to aid a British squadron
that was under fire from the Taku Forts at the mouth of the Pei Ho
River. When asked why he had done so, he had famously replied that
"blood is thicker than water," implying an Anglo-American, or at least
a western, kinship against non-European foreigners. True to his pugnacious instinct, when Tattnall observed several of Du Pont's ships taking
soundings off the Port Royal bar, he assumed the offensive, ordering his
seven small steamers to the attack. Their 32-pound smoothbores were
no match for the rifled guns on the Union ships, however, and Tattnall's
little flotilla retired after a brief and unequal exchange of fire.

At 9:00 a.m. on November 7, Du Pont's *Wabash* led a column of
nine Union ships into the sound. They proceeded in the time-honored

line-ahead formation passing up the middle of the channel between the two forts, then turning to port one by one to pass Fort Walker at a range of 800 yards. The rebels fired first. A shell screamed over the heads of the crouching sailors on the *Wabash* and splashed harmlessly beyond them. "Not that time, my dear," one of the gunners on the *Wabash* muttered aloud. Finally, when the *Wabash* was directly opposite the fort, she fired a concentrated broadside with her 8-, 9-, and 10-inch Dahlgren guns. Directly behind her, the *Susquehanna* followed suit. As the ships of the Union squadron passed the fort, firing as their guns bore, Confederate gunners in Fort Walker fired as fast as they could at the moving targets. When Tattnall and his small Confederate flotilla again attempted to sortie, Union gunboats chased them back into shallow water.[22]

After all nine Union warships had passed the fort, each unleashing a full broadside, Du Pont turned the *Wabash* to port again completing an elliptical circle, and the column of ships ran back into the bay to make another pass, this time at 600 yards. Du Pont had decided to concentrate on Fort Walker, ignoring the smaller Fort Beauregard across the sound, in the conviction that the smaller fort could not hold out alone if Walker capitulated. From the closer range, the fire of the Union warships was devastating. Shells struck the fort at the rate of one every second. The navigator on the *Wabash* wrote that "the air over the fort was filled with clouds of sand, splinters, and fragments of gun carriages and timbers." As if this was not bad enough for the defenders of Fort Walker, their commander, Brigadier General Thomas Drayton, saw that a tenth warship now joined the Union squadron for the third pass. It was the side-wheel steamer USS *Pocahontas* commanded, as fate would have it, by Drayton's own brother, Percival Drayton.[23]

After the third pass, the Federal gunners had disabled many of the fort's guns and the defenders were down to only 500 pounds of powder. Accepting the inevitable, General Drayton gave orders to evacuate. Once it was evident that the enemy had fled, Du Pont sent a landing party ashore, and Navy Captain John Rodgers raised the American flag over the ramparts of Fort Walker at 2:20 that afternoon.[24]

The Federal victory at Port Royal had several important consequences. Psychologically, the news was extremely welcome in the North, which was still burdened by the incubus of the defeat at Bull

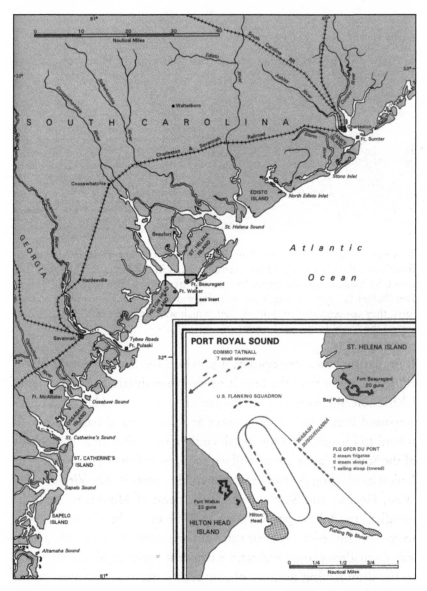

THE UNION ATTACK ON PORT ROYAL SOUND, NOVEMBER 7, 1861. Map by Bill Clipson, reprinted with permission from *The Naval Institute Historical Atlas of the U.S. Navy* by Craig L. Symonds, © 1995.

This painting of Du Pont's attack on Port Royal by C. Parsons depicts the action from inside the harbor while army transports wait in the distance. Du Pont's flagship USS *Wabash* is in the center foreground preparing to begin a second pass by Fort Walker (at right). Though this painting shows Du Pont's ships firing on both forts, they concentrated on Fort Walker, which was the larger of the two. (Courtesy of the Naval Historical Center)

Run that summer. Strategically, it provided the South Atlantic Blockading Squadron with the base it needed to maintain the blockades of Charleston and Savannah. For the rest of the war, only Hampton Roads surpassed Port Royal in importance as a Union naval base. Indeed, it is hard to imagine how the North could have maintained its blockade of the South Atlantic coast at all without possession of Port Royal. The Union blockading fleet also relied upon Hampton Roads, Virginia; Key West, Florida; and Ship Island off the coast of Mississippi near the mouth of the Mississippi River as supply bases for the blockaders. Able to re-coal and re-supply their ships at these advanced bases, the blockading squadrons could maintain a constant presence off the entrances to the diminishing number of southern ports that remained in the hands of the rebels.

The battle had an important impact on Confederate strategy, too. One of the witnesses to Du Pont's easy triumph was none other than Robert E. Lee whom Davis had sent there to assess the defenses in South Carolina and report on what could be done to defend the coastline more effectively. Lee's report, in effect, was that nothing could be done; that the Confederacy lacked the ability to protect its own coast against steam-powered Union warships carrying rifled guns of large caliber. Lee pointed out that it would be impossible to move troops up and down the coast as fast as Yankee warships could steam from place to place. "Wherever his fleet can be brought[,] no opposition can be made to his landing," Lee wrote to Samuel Cooper in Richmond. Trying to defend everywhere would use up scarce manpower that was desperately needed elsewhere. Lee's solution was that the South should essentially give up the coastline. Recapitulating the recommendation originally put forward by the committee of five naval officers back in February, Lee suggested that the Confederacy should attempt an effective defense only at a few essential points where geography gave the defenders an advantage. This included New Orleans, the largest city in the Confederacy, plus Wilmington, North Carolina; Charleston, South Carolina; Savannah, Georgia; Fernandina, Florida; Mobile, Alabama; and Galveston, Texas. Though two of those sites—New Orleans and Fernandina—fell into Union hands in the first year of the war, this became, and remained, Confederate policy.[25]

And finally, there was the impact that Du Pont's victory had on Gideon Welles, who became convinced after Port Royal that naval forces could capture key points along the coast unassisted by the army. His belief in this regard took on increased conviction after the *Monitor*'s performance in Hampton Roads the following March. Welles decided that with a few monitors, a Union naval force could steam into any harbor along the southern coast and force the capitulation of forts and cities almost at will. His certainty in this respect would have serious consequences for both Union naval strategy and for the careers of several of his officers during the siege of Charleston (see Chapter 5).

Over time, Union squadrons seized other footholds along the rebel coast. On the very day that the *Monitor* and the *Virginia* fought their historic battle, elements of Du Pont's South Atlantic Blockading Squadron seized Fernandina, St. Augustine, and Jacksonville in Florida. The next day they seized Brunswick, Georgia, and the day after that they pounded Fort Pulaski into submission, which cut off Savannah, Georgia, from the sea. In less than a week, 200 miles of the rebel coast had fallen to Union control. And even as Federal forces seized large chunks of the rebel coast, the blockading squadrons were becoming larger and larger, increasing from one or two warships at each port to whole squadrons. At the important ports, like Charleston, Wilmington, and Mobile, as many as twenty or thirty vessels patrolled offshore.

THE UNION SAILORS who kept the watch, fed the engines, and manned the guns on these blockading vessels from Virginia to Texas found life at sea mostly an endless tedium of routine. The navy tars on blockade duty had little expectation of fighting a rebel warship, though many of them longed for just such an opportunity. Instead, their foes were the swift and elusive, but generally unarmed, blockade-runners. It was an assignment that called for constant vigilance but few opportunities for heroism in the manner of bayonet attacks or cavalry charges. Determined to live up to expectations, the Union sailors nevertheless spent interminable days focused intently on the horizon or peering into harbors hoping to catch a trace of black smoke that might indicate that a potential blockade-runner was getting under way. Alas, day after day— often week after week—passed with no sign of either a blockade-runner offshore or a vessel in port trying to come out, and soon time began to hang heavy on the watchers. In his daily journal, the commander of the blockading squadron off Charleston recorded the plodding pace of the lengthy days of watching and waiting.

- March 13, 1862: "All day had nothing to do as no vessels appeared in sight."
- March 14, 1862: "A very pleasant day and nothing has occurred to destroy its monotony."
- March 17, 1862: "Uninterruptedly all day doing nothing."
- March 31, 1862: "Nothing whatever destroyed the monotony of the day."[26]

On most such days, the familiar routines of shipboard life measured the passage of time: at 6 a.m. orders to turn to and lash up sounded through the ship; the decks were swabbed and sanded; watches changed at 8 a.m. noon, and 4 p.m. dinner was piped; then, late in the day, the sky turned to pink and then to indigo, and finally to full dark as another day ended and night set in.

Night was the most dangerous time, for that was when the blockade-runners were most likely to attempt a run in or out of port. The Union blockading ships were necessarily blacked out, with no lights showing, so as not to be marked by potential violators of the blockade. In the middle of a moonless night, perhaps in a misting rain, a slightly darker shadow amid the blackness might be perceived creeping through the anchored ships of the squadron. Wary of firing into a friend, the officer of the deck might order that the night signal be made asking "friend or foe?" Fumbling in the dark for Coston flares, the signal officer put up the required combination of red or white flares. If the appropriate response was not forthcoming, a rocket might be fired into the dark sky alerting the rest of the squadron. Feet pounded on the ladders and decks as men tumbled up from below to cast loose the big guns and train them out into the darkness seeking the shadowy outline of the blockade-runner, going past now at 10, 12, or even 14 knots. Muzzle flashes lit up the night, temporarily blinding the gunners. Some ships slipped their anchors and set out in pursuit. And then it was over, more often than not with the runner escaped, the men angry about their missed opportunity, and the officers frustrated.

A typical encounter took place off Charleston on June 23, 1862. At three o'clock that morning, in the pitch black of the predawn darkness, the deck watch on the wooden side-wheel steamer USS *Keystone State* spotted the shape of an unidentified steamer coming out of Charleston and making for open water. The watch officer fired a gun, slipped the anchor cable, and set out in pursuit. Thus alerted, the USS *Alabama* and USS *James Adger*, flagship of the squadron, joined the chase, and all three Union warships set out at full speed after the illicit vessel. After three hours and more than 40 miles, the *Alabama* and *James Adger* found themselves falling farther and farther and they gave up the chase to the swifter *Keystone State*, which had a reputation as the fastest ship in the squadron. When the sun rose, the commander of the *Keystone State*, William LeRoy, identified the chase as the *Nashville*, a notorious blockade-runner recently renamed the *Thomas L. Wragg*, and LeRoy ordered the coal heavers to redouble their efforts. To lighten ship and gain speed, he ordered the ship's drinking water pumped over the side and he jettisoned several lengths of anchor chain. Slowly but steadily the *Keystone State* began to gain on her quarry.[27]

On board the fleeing *Nashville*, the officers and crew grew desperate. They threw their entire cargo, cotton valued at more than a million dollars, overboard, and then they began to tear apart the deck cabins, burning the wood to raise more steam, and the *Nashville* pulled ahead again. For more than 300 miles, the two ships raced across the ocean at full speed heading southeast. Finally after an all-day chase, with each ship squeezing every ounce of speed out of its engine, the *Nashville* slipped into a squall just at dusk and disappeared. Eventually she reached Abaco in the British Bahamas. LeRoy, vastly disappointed, returned to resume the interminable blockade of Charleston. Statistically this went into the books as the successful escape of a blockade-runner, though of course the loss of the *Nashville*'s cargo meant that it resulted in no benefit to the Confederacy.[28]

But there was more. When the *James Adger* returned to the blockade squadron off Charleston after its 80-mile roundtrip pursuit of the *Nashville*, her commander, John B. Marchand, learned that during his absence, another notorious blockade-runner, the *Memphis*, had slipped into the harbor past the blockading squadron and was now aground on the beach at Sullivan's Island under the guns of Fort Moultrie. The Confederates were already at work removing its cargo by lighters. It was mortifying to Marchand to report to Du Pont at Port Royal that two ships had successfully violated the blockade. Du Pont, in his turn, was "greatly distressed" and felt the need to apologize to Gideon Welles even as he insisted to the Navy Secretary that "greater vigilance could not be exercised."[29]

There were some moments of relief from this almost schizophrenic combination of endless boredom and frenetic activity. Periodically the blockading vessels had to return to base to re-coal and to obtain drinking water and food. For the men on board the ships of the South Atlantic Blockading Squadron, that meant going to Port Royal where the navy had not only set up floating machine ships and coal deposits, but where the U.S. Army had taken control of the offshore islands. If it was not exactly like having shore leave in a friendly northern city, it was at least a break from shipboard routine. Not everyone got shore leave of course, but even if it only meant a quiet interlude at anchor, it was a pleasant change from blockade duty. Also, at Port Royal, as elsewhere along the coast, many of the Union sailors got their first look at southern slavery.

From the moment the first U.S. Navy vessel appeared off the southern coast, many of the planters who lived on the sea islands of Georgia and South Carolina abandoned their lands and fled inland. Many of their slaves made their way down to the beach and signaled frantically to the Union warships to be rescued. Du Pont reported to Welles that "the negroes . . . came down to the shore with bundles in their hands, as if expecting to be taken off."[30] Most of these refugees, called contrabands in the vernacular of the day, were settled in colonies under the protection of the Union army, and the largest of those was at Port Royal. Alvah Hunter, the ship's boy on the *Nahant*, later recalled that while the ship was at anchor in Port Royal, he was walking on its open deck when an elderly black man eased up in a small dugout canoe and called him over. "Is you-uns goin' to win the wah, for shore?" the man asked. Hunter told him that he certainly believed that the North was going to win. "And will us niggers be free if you-uns win the wah?" Since this was after Lincoln had announced his Emancipation Proclamation, Hunter told him that "all the Negroes in the United States would be free." Hunter recalled that "He looked at my face very earnestly for a minute or two, probably to assure himself that he wasn't being fooled, then he lifted a bit of white cotton cloth which was covering something in the bottom of the canoe and revealed a tin plate bearing a dozen or fifteen nice peaches." They were the first peaches the New Hampshire-born ship's boy had ever seen. The old man gave Hunter a peach, but Hunter offered to buy the whole plate for a quarter. The contraband agreed and Hunter went to get his quarter. When he came back, however, he found that in his absence an officer had bought them for the wardroom proving that for all his apparent gratitude, the contraband was also an entrepreneur. Soon enough after these brief sojourns in port, the ships were back on station at Charleston, Savannah, Wilmington, Mobile, Galveston, or elsewhere, and the tedium of the blockade resumed.[31]

Service on the blockade was not especially dangerous; nor, for that matter, was blockade-running. For all the excitement of those crowded moments when blockade-runners made their dash through the Union fleet either to safe harbor or to one or another northern prize court, the

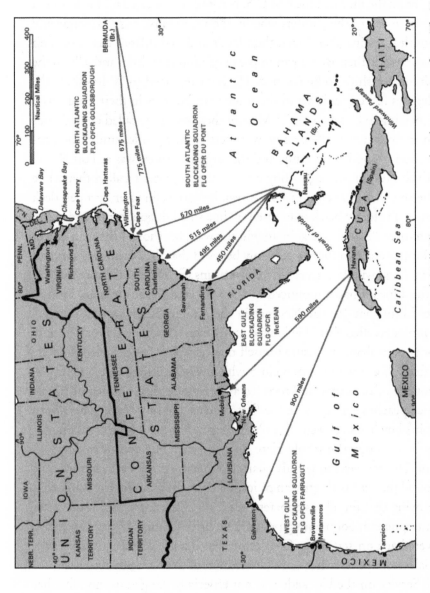

UNION BLOCKADING SQUADRONS AND BLOCKADE-RUNNING ROUTES. Map by Bill Clipson, reprinted with permission from *The Naval Institute Historical Atlas of the U.S. Navy* by Craig L. Symonds, © 1995.

number of casualties was rather small. Assistant Secretary of the Navy Gustavus Fox estimated that mortality in the blockade fleet was no greater than "the normal death rate of civil life."[32] On the other hand, the blockade did represent a major investment of Union assets. The hundreds of ships, thousands of men, and millions of dollars invested in the effort to close down the southern ports ranks as one of the greatest undertakings of the Federal government in its history. Critics, both then and later, suggested that since the blockade cannot be shown to have been decisive in deciding the outcome of the war, it would have been better to commit those assets to the land war. There is, of course, no way to prove such suppositions—or to disprove them, though it seems unlikely that giving George McClellan another seventy to eighty thousand men would have made much of a difference.

FOR THE CONFEDERATES, the blockade-runners were (in the words of Stephen R. Wise) the "lifeline of the Confederacy." Early on, when the blockade was still very porous, opportunistic blockade-runners made tremendous profits, sometimes in excess of 700 percent, for their financial investors such as the British firm of Fraser, Trenholm and Company based in both Liverpool and Charleston. A few southerners argued that blockade-running should be organized and managed as a government undertaking, but such a notion ran contrary to the antigovernment, laissez faire values of southern society, and both Secretary of War James Seddon and Mallory, burdened as they were with fighting a war for survival, decided to leave blockade-running to private entrepreneurs. This was a lost opportunity for the South, for instead of bringing in the kind of materials the Confederacy desperately needed, the profit-driven blockade-runners brought in what was most lucrative.[33]

The general pattern of trade was for legal merchantmen to carry their cargoes from Europe, particularly England, to a neutral port nearer to the United States. St. George, Bermuda; Nassau in the Bahamas; and Havana, Cuba, were the most popular such ports. There the cargoes were transferred into ships especially designed to run the blockade: low, fast, side-wheel or screw steamers with their masts stripped down to reduce their profile and painted a light gray to blend with the sea. Once under way from one of these neutral ports, these ships were subject to capture from the moment they left British or Spanish waters. Every speck on the horizon was a potential foe, and the blockade-runners maneuvered so as to avoid discovery. Their skippers also timed their voyages so that they would arrive 30 to 40 miles off the coast just at dusk in order to make the final run into port at night. Thomas E. Taylor, who served as supercargo (the owner's agent) on the English-built, steel-hulled, blockade-runner *Banshee No. 2*, recorded his feelings as that ship made its first run from Nassau into the blockaded port of Wilmington, North Carolina, in the spring of 1863. "Nothing I have ever experienced can compare with it," Taylor wrote later. "Hunting, pig-sticking, steeple-chasing, big-game shooting, polo—I have done a little of each—all have their thrilling moments, but none can approach 'running a blockade.'"[34]

The *Banshee No. 2* left Nassau for the three-day run to Wilmington in the second week of May 1863, a week after the Confederate victory at Chancellorsville. It was lucky enough to avoid seeing any ships during the transit, but the danger grew as it approached the North Carolina coast, for now it would have to thread its way through "a swarm of blockaders . . . without lights and with a coastline so low and featureless that as a rule the first intimation we had of its nearness was the dim white line of the surf." The captain, Jonathon Steele, gave orders to show no lights at all, not even the tip of a glowing cigar, and to maintain absolute silence. "We steamed on in silence," Taylor remembered, "except for the stroke of the engines and the beat of the paddle-floats, which in the calm of the night seemed distressingly loud."[35]

Suddenly, the pilot grabbed Taylor's arm: "There's one of them," he said pointing. Taylor could see nothing. Then gradually, as he strained to peer through the blackness, he saw "a long black object on our starboard side lying perfectly still." The Yankee blockaders were blacked out, too, and on board them were other men who were peering anxiously into the dark just as Taylor was. Would they see the *Banshee No. 2* creeping in toward the shore?

A moment later the pilot whispered again: "Steamer on the port bow," and there was another one. Then another, dead ahead. "Stop her," Steele whispered urgently to the helmsman. Taylor all but held his breath as the *Banshee No. 2* lay dead in the water with ships of the Yankee blockading squadron all about them until finally the ship ahead of

The Confederate blockade-runner *Banshee No. 2* was typical of the kind of craft that sought to violate the blockade. Low, narrow, and swift, it was both hard to see and difficult to catch. The *Banshee No. 2* made seven successful runs in and out of Wilmington, North Carolina, before being captured (by an armed U.S. Army transport) on her fourth attempt. (Courtesy of the Naval Historical Center)

them slowly moved off. The engines were restarted, and the *Banshee No. 2* crept on toward the shore. The night was coming to an end, and the sky was beginning to show a little gray in anticipation of dawn when Taylor made out "six or seven gunboats." The growing light enabled the lookouts on those gunboats to spot the *Banshee No. 2*, too, and instantly they opened fire. Now the *Banshee No. 2* made a run for it, steaming for New Inlet on the Cape Fear River as shell splashes began to erupt close around it. It was, Taylor, recalled, "an unpleasant sensation," especially considering that much of the *Banshee No. 2* cargo consisted of gunpowder. The Yankee ships were getting closer, and their shots were growing increasingly accurate, when suddenly the big guns from Fort Fisher guarding the entrance to New Inlet boomed out and huge shell splashes erupted just ahead of the pursuing blockade vessels. It was "music to our ears," Taylor recalled. Unwilling to challenge the big guns of the fort, the blockaders "steamed sulkily out of range," and the crew of the *Banshee No. 2* cheered as the blockade-runner rounded the headland and entered the safety of the river.[36]

The *Banshee No. 2* had six more successful runs after this one; her namesake, a similarly designed side-wheel steamer called the *Banshee*, made only four such runs before being spotted well out to sea by the armed army transport *Fulton*. Hulled by the *Fulton*'s second shot, the unarmed *Banshee* rounded to and dropped her flag. The experience of the *Banshee* was typical of Confederate blockade-running through the end of 1863. Despite several successful—and highly profitable—runs, she ended up a prize of the Yankees. Her number of successful runs— four—was the average for a blockade-runner during the war. Even with her eventual loss, and the loss of that last cargo, the initial investment made by her owners still yielded a huge net profit.

Of course every ship that escaped through the blockade, whether running in or out, was fodder for the opposition press in the North and a cause for new editorials about the "imbecility" of the Navy Department in general and Secretary Welles in particular. James Gordon Bennett, publisher of the influential *New York Herald*, was a particularly virulent critic who excoriated the Navy Department regularly. The capture of the *Banshee* by an army transport created a perfect opportunity for him to skewer the Navy Department, and his editorial the next day was a blistering indictment. The *Banshee*, Bennett wrote, "defied any ship in our navy to catch" her, but when "she was at last captured, it will be noticed, [it was] not by one of our naval vessels, but by an army transport." This was simply more evidence, as far as Bennett was concerned, that Welles was "as obstinate as he is ignorant," and he concluded that Welles should be removed at once in favor of some competent person.[37]

Others, though less malicious, were also critical of the fact that the Lincoln administration focused so much of its energies on the blockade instead of protecting Union commerce on the high seas. The New York Chamber of Commerce petitioned Lincoln to take warships off the blockade in order to escort convoys to Europe, South America, and the Cape of Good Hope. Welles was unwilling to do it. Though it cost him some political support in New York, Lincoln stood by his Secretary. For his part, Bennett concluded that Lincoln was "a great deal more kind than just" and continued to berate both the blockade and the administration.[38]

WHATEVER THE PERCEPTION in New York City, in much of the Confederacy the impact of the blockade on the southern economy was becoming increasingly evident by the end of 1863. Though a lot of those difficulties were the product of a collapsing internal transportation system, many in the South began to resent the fact that, as one contemporary put it, blockade-running "was fast degenerating into an illicit and unpatriotic traffic." With unconscious irony, Confederate planters complained that the fabulous profits made by blockade-runners were enriching a small class of moneyed men while making little, if any, contribution to the war effort. The Richmond *Enquirer* decried the "unbecoming vanity" demonstrated by the elaborate wardrobes of the richest merchants, unsuitable for a nation struggling for its survival. The way to curtail this "disgraceful extravagance," it asserted, was for the government to regulate the blockade-running traffic. It declared unequivocally that "The State governments and the Confederate government should monopolize the entire blockade business."[39]

A few states had already moved in that direction. As early as January of 1863, Governor Zebulon Vance of North Carolina initiated a state-managed program of blockade-running designed to bring in clothing and supplies for that state's soldiers, but he got little cooperation from Secretary of War Seddon, who worried that better-supplied soldiers from the Tarheel State might trigger jealousy and resentment from other states. Seddon reminded Vance that it was the survival of the whole Confederacy, not merely that of North Carolina, that was at stake, and he suggested that Vance should "recognize the primacy of the Richmond government," a suggestion that was more likely to inflame than suppress Vance's concern as it ran counter to Vance's state rights philosophy. In time of war, however—and particularly in wars of survival—ideology often gives way to necessity, Here was more evidence, along with universal conscription and the circulation of paper money, that it was difficult, perhaps impossible, to fight a total war with a limited government.[40]

Despite the concern that it constituted breaking faith with the country's ideological pole star, the increasingly desperate condition of the rebel armies and the weakening Confederate economy led to a popular clamor for the Richmond government to take over the regulation of trade altogether. As J. Thomas Scharf, the semi-official historian of the Confederate navy, put it, "The regulation of the blockade business, rather than its suppression, was demanded both by the sentiment of the people and by the necessity of the army." In addition, the dramatic decline in the amount of government-owned cotton that made it overseas to underwrite Confederate promissory notes threatened Confederate credit in Europe. In February of 1864, therefore, Jefferson Davis pressed the Confederate Congress to pass a law that required all out-bound blockade-runners to reserve half of their cargo space for government-owned cotton. A month later, he urged on Congress another law forbidding the importation of the kind of high-value luxury goods that had yielded such high profits in the first two years of the war. It was a long list that included ale, beer, rum, brandy, billiard tables, furniture, carpeting, tapestries, carriages, lace, jewelry, dolls or toys, glass, marble, fur, hats, capes, paintings, statuary, wallpaper, bricks, roofing slates, perfumes, playing cards, and velvet, as well as any kind of wine, including champagne, claret, Madeira, port, and sherry. Of course, there was considerable grousing about these new regulations, not only from the companies that stood to lose future profits, but from state rights conscious governors like Vance and Joe Brown of Georgia who believed that Richmond was becoming altogether too intrusive into the lives of southern citizens.[41]

A case study that illuminates the tension between the government in Richmond and the state governments over these issues concerns the small-Glasgow-built-iron-hulled blockade-runner *Little Ada*. Governor Brown chartered the *Little Ada* on behalf of the state to carry Georgia cotton to European markets, and when Richmond insisted that half its cargo space be reserved for cotton belonging to the central government, Brown refused. Jefferson Davis retaliated by refusing to grant clearance for the vessel, even ordering artillery batteries erected near its anchorage with orders to open fire on *Little Ada* if it attempted to leave its wharf without clearance. This turned out to have ironic benefit when a U.S. Navy cutting-out expedition attempted to capture the ship, only to be driven off by the batteries that had been erected to keep the ship from leaving.[42]

A month after this farcical standoff, in April 1864, the Confederate government took the ultimate step. Rather than attempt to regulate the merchants, it embarked on a program to run its own government-owned blockade-runners. It bought an initial eight steamers and soon purchased six more. The government in Richmond lacked the money to buy the ships outright, however, and therefore "paid" for them with more Cotton Certificates, essentially promissory notes that were redeemable if and when sufficient cotton could be exported. Fraser, Trenholm and Company acted as the agent for the initial sale and also operated the ships on behalf of the government. Confederate navy officers on furlough rather than profit-driven entrepreneurs commanded the ships. The increasingly dominant role that Fraser, Trenholm and Company was playing in the economic life of the Confederacy was formalized in July when George A. Trenholm, the senior partner in the Charleston office, replaced Christopher Memminger as Confederate Secretary of the Treasury. Trenholm's primary goal was to increase the importation of military supplies, and to do this he stipulated not only what could be brought in by blockade-runners, but what could be taken out. In effect, by the middle of 1864, blockade-running had become nationalized.[43]

Those who had been engaged in blockage running complained at this turn of events and predicted that the absence of financial incentives would cripple the business. Instead the new rules resulted in increased efficiency and a surge in both exports and imports. Despite the continued growth of the Union blockading squadrons and the loss of several important ports, including Mobile, Alabama, in August, there were as many successful blockade-runners in January of 1865 as there had been a year earlier under the old system. The historian Raimondo Luraghi has concluded that "blockage running was at its best, indeed, reached its apex, in 1864." The Confederate government's credit abroad improved, and Confederate bonds actually rose in value.[44]

IT WAS TOO LITTLE, TOO LATE. With the loss of so many of its ports, and the breakdown of its internal railroad system, along with the shrinking size of the territory from which supplies—even food—could be drawn, the Confederacy tottered onward toward its doom. But how much of that final denouement, if any, was due to the direct or indirect effects of the blockade? Most historians who have addressed this issue have done so by appealing to statistics. Such an effort, however, is as likely to breed skepticism about the value of statistics as it is to resolve the question, since the numbers can be used to make very different, indeed diametrically opposite, points. Back in 1931, the southern historian Frank Owsley estimated that ships successfully violated the blockade some eight thousand times. But in compiling that number, Owsley included every skiff and rowboat that moved from town to town along the coast. A better calculation is the one made in 1988 by Stephen R. Wise, who concluded that in addition to the smaller and less efficient sailing ships that sought to run the blockade early in the war, a total of about 300 different steam-powered vessels were responsible for most of the blockade-running after 1862. Those 300 steamers made an average of four successful trips (two round trips) per vessel. That works out to about 1,300 attempts, of which more than 1,000 were successful. In other words, statistics prove that steam-powered blockade-runners made it through the blockade 77 percent of the time. On the other hand, of those 300 steamers, Union warships eventually captured 136 of them, and another 85 were destroyed—run into the shore by pursuing vessels or lost at sea—for a total of 221 vessels. Thus statistics also prove that more than 73 percent of all steam-powered ships that tried to run the blockade were destroyed or captured. In other words, both of the following statements are true: three quarters of all attempts to run the blockade were successful, and three quarters of all ships that tried it were destroyed or captured.[45]

A better way to measure the impact of the blockade is to calculate how much the Confederacy was able to import during the war to sustain its economy and its war effort, and here the numbers are more revealing. On the whole, it is clear that the Confederacy did manage to import a sufficient number of rifles and cannon, an adequate amount of powder and lead, and other essential materials of war, to sustain its armies. Stephen Wise writes that "the South imported at least 400,000 rifles, or more than 60 percent of the nation's modern arms," that "About 3 million pounds of lead came through the blockade," and that "over 2,250,000 pounds of saltpeter, or two thirds of the vital ingredient for powder, came from overseas." Without doubt, these imports were crucial to the Confederate war effort. Wise is undoubtedly correct in concluding that "without blockade-running the nation's military would have been without proper supplies of arms, bullets, and powder."[46]

When rebel armies did suffer shortages, they were more often than not the result of weaknesses in its internal transportation network. This becomes particularly evident in consideration of the fact that even when they had a sufficient amount of guns and bullets, Confederate armies often found themselves suffering from a dearth of food. During the bitter winter of 1864–65, while Grant's much-larger Union army besieged Lee's army in Richmond and Petersburg, ill-clad rebel soldiers starved in the trenches "while foodstuffs rotted in the lower South." Clearly this was not a product of the naval blockade. Raimondo Luraghi notes correctly that "The most deadly cause of the dearth that starved soldiers on the front line was not the blockade but the collapse of the Southern railroad system." On the other hand, this collapse was itself attributable, at least in part, to the Union naval blockade that virtually shut down the coastwise trade and compelled the South to redirect cargoes that might otherwise have been carried on coastal shipping onto its weak and already overburdened railroad system. And, of course, the blockade also severely restricted the importation of locomotive engines, iron rails, and machine parts that could not be produced domestically.[47]

Moreover, the fact that rebel armies managed to sustain themselves despite the blockade does not mean that its effects were not felt elsewhere in the Confederacy. Coffee and tea became luxury goods so prized that one Atlanta jeweler (perhaps in jest) set coffee beans into pins instead of diamonds. The shortage of these and other goods contributed to hoarding, speculation, and inflation, and thereby affected civilian morale. Two economic historians have recently concluded that "The adverse effects of the Union blockade on the amount and kinds of supplies getting to the Confederacy over the war years were debilitating for both citizens and the war effort."[48]

Moreover, in assessing the impact of the blockade, it is necessary to consider not only its impact on imports, but also on exports. Gustavus Fox adopted the language of the King James Bible to proclaim that the rebellion was sustained "not by what entereth into their ports but by what proceedeth out."[49] Both before and during the war, the southern economy was almost entirely dependent on its production of cash crops for export, especially cotton. The export of cotton was essential to Confederate economic health since it created the overseas credits that were necessary to purchase imports. At first, southerners overestimated the importance of "King Cotton" to England. They assumed that the mill owners of England were so dependent on the South's "white gold," they would do anything to get it. Consequently the Confederacy halted all cotton exports in 1861 expecting that the British would enter the war on their behalf to obtain access to it. Once it became clear that this scenario was unlikely to bear fruit, the embargo was lifted, but by that time the Union blockade had become more effective and a golden opportunity to establish foreign credits abroad had been lost.

Measuring how much the blockade affected cotton exports is relatively simple. In the last year of peace, between September 1860 and August 1861, the cotton states exported a total of 2,854,543 bales of cotton. By contrast, during the first full year of war, the South exported a total of only 55,000 bales, less than 2 percent of the peacetime total. Over the next two years, as Union forces occupied more and more of the southern coast, cotton exports fell further. Even after the nationalization of the blockade-running industry early in 1864, the export numbers remained anemic. That year, the two remaining Atlantic ports of Charleston and Wilmington exported a total of 25,403 bales of cotton, half of what had been exported in 1862, and less than one percent of the pre-war total. During the four years of war, a total of no more than 350,000 bales of the South's "white gold" made it out through the blockade, about a ninth of what had been exported in a single year before the war. To be sure, the price of cotton went up as the exports declined. The price per bale jumped four fold between 1861 and 1862 (from $50 per bale to $200), but even at these new, higher, prices, the net revenue from the South's dominant economic commodity dropped from more than $133 million in 1860 to less than $12 million in 1862, a decline of more than 90 percent. Moreover, if the price of cotton rose, so did the price of the goods the South sought to acquire overseas—marine engines, railroad machinery, rifled cannon, and modern breech-loading rifles. Stephen Wise concludes that the South never managed "to accumulate enough funds in Liverpool to finance their Europe operations." And the economic historian David Surdam estimates that "The shortfall in Southern revenues from exporting raw cotton rivaled, if not exceeded, the Federal government's [total] expenditures on its navy during the war." Given that, a simple cost-effective analysis suggests that the Union blockade was worth the effort.[50]

The blockade never did become completely effective. Even with dozens of warships patrolling off Wilmington, blockade-runners still managed to find a way to get in and out. The last blockade-runner out of Wilmington was the *Hansa*, a Scottish-built side-wheel steamer that ran out of the Cape Fear River on the night of January 3, 1865, at a time when there were nearly a hundred Union warships in the area preparing for a grand assault on Fort Fisher. Twelve days later, Fort Fisher itself fell, and only then did blockade-running out of Wilmington stop entirely.[51]

At Wilmington, as elsewhere, the only way to ensure the complete closure of a southern port was by physical occupation. Back in the spring of 1862, the capture of the South's largest port city, New Orleans, Louisiana, plus the occupation of some 200 miles of South Atlantic coast from Port Royal to Jacksonville, had begun the process. After that, only four major ports remained open: Galveston, Mobile, Charleston, and Wilmington. Union forces captured Galveston in 1863, though the Confederates got it back soon afterward and it remained open to blockade-runners until the very end. Charleston, too, held on despite repeated efforts by Union forces to seize it (see Chapter 5), though blockade-running dropped off dramatically after Union forces took control of Morris Island and reduced Fort Sumter to rubble. In the six months between August 1863 and March 1864, not a single steam blockade-runner successfully got into or out of Charleston Harbor. The trade revived slightly in the last six months of 1864 until William T. Sherman's army cut off Charleston from the west during his march northward in the winter of 1864–65. After that, the Confederates abandoned the city, blowing up the three ironclad warships they had built there with such effort and sacrifice. Mobile was closed by Farragut's bold dash into Mobile Bay in August 1864, and, as noted above, Fort Fisher, the citadel that guarded the entrance to the Cape Fear River and Wilmington, North Carolina, fell in January of 1865.[52]

Despite all this, blockade-runners continued to make it through the cordon of Union ships until quite literally the last days of the war. The very last of them was the side-wheel steamer *Lark*, which escaped out of Galveston on May 24, 1865, six weeks *after* Lee surrendered at Appomattox, and two days before the surrender of Edmund Kirby Smith's army in Texas that finally ended hostilities. By then, the logistic base on which the Confederacy had to depend had disappeared entirely. The fall of Vicksburg in July of 1863 had cut off the trans-Mississippi West, slicing the Confederacy not quite in half; Sherman's March to Atlanta and from there to the sea had cut what remained in half again; and

Sherman's northward march through the Carolinas reduced it further until by the time Wilmington fell, only relatively small portions of North Carolina and Virginia remained to support Lee's dwindling army.

Despite the apparently porous character of the Union blockade, the cumulative effect of the reduction in the South's cotton exports, the loss of its coastline, and eventually the occupation of its major seaports weakened the Confederate economy, impacted civilian morale, and effectively undermined the Confederate government and its war effort. As historian William H. Roberts has put it, if the blockade was "never airtight," it "was constricting enough that the South was constantly gasping for economic breath." That slow asphyxiation, combined with the reduction in the size of the logistic base from which the Confederacy could draw support, so isolated Lee's indomitable army in Virginia that in the end it had no choice but to surrender. Almost certainly the North could have won the Civil War without the blockade, but almost as certainly, the blockade made the war shorter, and in doing so it probably saved many thousands of lives.[53]

3

The War on Commerce

The Hunters and the Hunted

NOT ALL OF THE SHIPS that ran out through the Union blockade did so to trade—some were bound on a more destructive mission. Three weeks before the first Battle of Bull Run in Virginia, the Confederate warship *Sumter*, a small (473-ton) five-gun steamer that had been converted to military purposes from the merchant ship *Habana*, was lying quietly at the head of passes below New Orleans where the Mississippi River extends its delicate fingers out into the Gulf of Mexico. It was trapped there by the USS *Brooklyn*, a *Hartford*-class screw steamer, which had been guarding the Pass a L'Outre into the Gulf since April. On June 30, however, the *Brooklyn* left its station to pursue a strange sail to the east, and the *Sumter*'s captain, Raphael Semmes, decided to make a run for it. When the *Brooklyn*'s captain, Charles H. Poor, saw the telltale black smoke from the *Sumter*'s stack, he at once abandoned the chase and headed back toward the Pass a L'Outre to cut off the *Sumter*'s escape. Watching from the *Sumter*'s quarterdeck, and making a quick calculation of the converging course of the two ships, Semmes thought his chances were slim, but he was determined to break out of the river where he had been confined since June 3. When the *Sumter* crossed the bar at the river's mouth and headed into the Gulf of Mexico, the *Brooklyn* was only 3 miles away and closing fast.

The *Brooklyn* was reputed to be a fast ship; rumor had it that she could maintain a speed of 13, knots under both sail and steam, and she had been known to make 14, On the *Sumter*, Semmes ordered an officer to heave the log, and he returned to report that they were making only 9.5 knots. At that rate, the *Brooklyn*, with its twenty guns, would be on the five-gun *Sumter* in a matter of minutes. The *Sumter*'s rig allowed her to run a little closer to the wind than the *Brooklyn*, and Semmes bore up to gain the maximum relative benefit. Still the *Brooklyn* continued to close, and Semmes could see the officers on her quarterdeck watching him—just as he was watching them—through their telescopes. Reluctantly, he ordered the *Sumter*'s paymaster to bring the ship's papers up on deck in case he had to throw them overboard before surrendering. But as the *Sumter* headed further up into the wind, the square-rigged *Brooklyn* was forced to furl her sails and continue the chase under steam power alone. And now the *Sumter*'s engines, cranky after all that waiting in the river, got into rhythm, and slowly but perceptibly the *Sumter* began to pull away. Late that afternoon, after several hours of fruitless pursuit, the *Brooklyn* finally gave up the chase.[1]

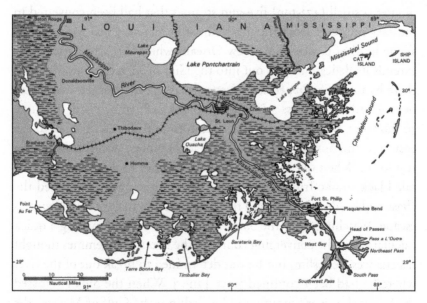

NEW ORLEANS AND THE MISSISSIPPI DELTA, SPRING 1862. Map by Bill Clipson, reprinted with permission from *The Naval Institute Historical Atlas of the U.S. Navy* by Craig L. Symonds, © 1995.

Three days later, the *Sumter* took her first prize, the 700-ton, Maine-built bark *Golden Rocket*, carrying ballast en route to Cuba to pick up a cargo of sugar. The *Sumter* ranged up alongside, fired a gun across the bark's bow forcing her to heave to, and sent a boat over to inspect her papers. Satisfied of her nationality, Semmes ordered the boarding party to help itself to whatever items might prove useful, take off the crew, and then set fire to her. Flames raced quickly up the rigging of the *Golden Rocket* and set her sails ablaze. One of those sails, fully aflame, detached itself from the mast and went winging away shedding sparks and pieces of burning canvas. It was a magnificent sight, Semmes thought, as the fire, "roaring like the fires of a hundred furnaces," engulfed the ship. The former captain of the *Golden Rocket* stood stoically alongside Semmes at the *Sumter*'s rail and watched as the masts of his ship fell one by one, and the bark finally slipped beneath the sea.[2]

IF BLOCKADE was the traditional strategy of dominant naval powers, commerce raiding was the traditional response of weaker ones. Because the French had pioneered this form of maritime economic warfare, it was often referred to by its French name as *guerre de course*, or literally war on commerce. It bore some resemblance to guerilla warfare at sea. Instead of sending out fleets or squadrons to battle other warships, nations employing *guerre de course*, relied upon small, fast, lightly armed vessels whose goal was to avoid contact with enemy warships altogether and instead target the slow, unarmed merchant ships of their foe, either capturing them (and thus earning prize money) or destroying them. The idea was to weaken the opponent's economy. Historically, the United States had found this to be a particularly effective tactic in its two wars with Britain since, as an island power, Britain was fully dependent on maritime trade for its economic survival. In the twentieth century, the Germans would use submarines to conduct *guerre de course* warfare in both World Wars, and the United States did much the same thing against Japanese shipping in the Pacific between 1943 and 1945.

In the nineteenth century, there were two ways to conduct *guerre de course* warfare. One was by using small commissioned warships such as the *Sumter* that were part of the national navy. The other was to rely on what were known as privateers—privately owned ships that were licensed to attack enemy vessels. This, too, had been pioneered by the French. To become a privateer, a citizen first had to get a certificate from the government, what was called a "letter of marque." It was, quite literally, a license to steal, for it authorized the person named to "subdue, seize and take any armed or unarmed vessel" of the enemy. All expenses of fitting out a privateering ship and supplying it, as well as feeding and paying its crew fell to the ship's owner, and in exchange, the owner got to keep any prizes taken—both ship and cargo—which were delivered to a prize court and sold at auction. Often, the owners of privateers avoided the expense of paying a captain and crew by making them junior partners in the enterprise. A typical arrangement allowed the ship's owner (who was sometimes, but not always, its captain) to take half the proceeds from any prize in order to compensate him for the expense of fitting out the ship in the first place. The officers split a quarter share, and the crew split the remaining fourth. Though a sailor's share was tiny compared with that of the owner or captain, a lucky cruise might still make him a wealthy man. Sailors were therefore willing to forego a salary for the chance to strike it rich. This scheme also created a powerful incentive for the officers and crew since every prize they took was money in their pocket. Finally, privateers were attractive to sailors because the discipline on board was generally more lax, and since privateers were not expected to fight battles with enemy warships, there was less danger of being killed.[3]

There was a downside, however. The sponsoring nation had virtually no control over how these privately owned ships were deployed and used; they were, after all, free agents, not instruments of the government. There was a downside for the participants, too, for it was possible to come home empty-handed from a cruise without either salary or prize money. And finally, though they fully intended to avoid enemy warships altogether, privateering could still be dangerous, and not merely because of the inherent danger of the sea itself. The merchant ships that the privateers hunted might be slow and helpless, but privateers were themselves helpless before any legitimate warship. Few privateers carried more than a few guns—many carried only one—and even a converted merchant ship was more than a match for them. If a privateer encountered a hostile warship at sea, its only hope was in flight.

Raphael Semmes was the most successful of all Confederate commerce raiders. In command first of the small *Sumter* and later the more efficient *Alabama*, he ravaged Union shipping on three oceans and provoked terror in the hearts of Union shippers. (Courtesy of the Naval Historical Center)

Despite these disadvantages, the Confederacy had nothing to lose by adopting this traditionally American form of naval war, and on April 17, 1861, five days after the first shot was fired at Fort Sumter, Jefferson Davis invited "all those who may desire, by service in private armed vessels on the high seas, to aid this government in resisting so wanton and wicked an aggression" to apply for a letter of marque. His announcement horrified northern shippers and was very likely a factor in Lincoln's decision to announce a blockade of the South two days later. Though the Declaration of Paris of 1856 had officially abolished privateering among civilized nations, the United States had declined to sign the protocol because it had relied so heavily on privateering in its wars against Britain. Now the shoe was on the other foot, and Secretary Seward approached the British Minister, Lord Lyons, to ask if the

United States could change its mind and adhere to the agreement after all. Lyons found the request "rather amusing," and replied that while the United States was certainly welcome to accept the Declaration of Paris, its terms could not be applied *ex post facto* to the current war. Seeing that there was nothing to be gained by it, Seward let the matter drop.[4]

Lincoln and Seward next adopted the position that while privateering might still be legal for nations that had not signed the Declaration of Paris, they insisted that the Confederacy was not a real government and therefore letters of marque issued in its name were invalid. Just as Britain had referred to American privateers during the Revolution as "pirates," so now did Lincoln declare that persons operating as privateers on behalf of the Confederacy would "be held amenable to the laws of the United States for the prevention and punishment of piracy." Very likely, Lincoln hoped that his draconian declaration would act as a deterrent and prevent privateers from setting to sea, but that proved to be a vain hope.[5]

The initial sortie of Confederate privateers was delayed because Jefferson Davis, in a punctilious display of Constitutional scruple, waited until the Confederate Congress could ratify his declaration before he actually issued any letters of marque. Congress met on April 29, and on May 6 it affirmed that "The President of the Confederate States is hereby authorized to use the whole land and naval forces of the Confederate States to meet the war thus commenced, and to issue to private vessels commissions or letters of marque. . . ." Within days, armed ships manned with southerners bearing letters of marque were at sea searching for prey.[6]

The first rebel privateer—its letter of marque dated May 18, 1861—was the *Savannah*, a schooner-rigged former Charleston Harbor pilot boat that displaced only 54 tons and carried a single pivot gun. She went to sea on June 3, 1861, and made her first capture that same day, taking the brig *Joseph* out of Rockland, Maine, carrying a cargo of West Indian sugar bound for Philadelphia. The *Savannah*'s captain, T. Harrison Baker, put a prize crew on board the *Joseph* and sent her into Georgetown, South Carolina, where a Confederate prize court adjudged her a lawful prize. Eventually both the ship and her cargo were sold at auction and the money put into an account for the officers and crew of the *Savannah*.

It would be some time before they could get it, however, for the same day that it captured the *Joseph*, the *Savannah* was herself captured by the sailing brig USS *Perry*. The *Savannah* attempted to flee—her only real hope—but the *Perry* quickly closed the range, fired a shot across her bow, and the *Savannah* dropped her sails in token of surrender. The *Perry's* captain took the *Savannah's* officers and crew on board, clapped them in irons, and sent them to New York. A few weeks later, the USS *Albatross* recaptured a prize that had been taken by another rebel privateer, the *Jeff Davis*. The officers and men of the *Savannah* and the prize crew from the *Albatross* were put on trial in Philadelphia and New York for piracy, a crime for which the only prescribed punishment was death by hanging. Jefferson Davis wrote to Lincoln to protest, claiming that the men were entitled to be treated as prisoners of war, and warning that for every privateersman hanged in the North, he would execute one Union prisoner of war. In the end, that threat proved effective, for despite a guilty verdict in one of the trials, all of the privateersmen were transferred from the Judiciary to the War Department, and eventually they were quietly exchanged.[7]

The early success of a handful of privateers operating out of Charleston and New Orleans caused a near panic among merchants in New York and provoked the first in a series of increases in marine insurance rates that would continue throughout the war and eventually threaten the whole industry. But for all the panic that it provoked, Confederate privateering soon played itself out. There were two reasons for this: The first was that privateers found it increasingly difficult to send their prizes into port where they could be condemned and sold. On June 1, two days before the ill-fated *Savannah* made its first and only capture, the British government announced that as part of its policy of strict neutrality, it would not allow prizes of either belligerent to be sent into its ports for condemnation. Other European powers soon followed suit, which meant that Confederate privateers could not send their prizes into Nassau, Bermuda, or Havana, and instead had to send them into Confederate ports. Alas, the waxing strength of the Union blockade along the Atlantic coast meant that sending prizes into Confederate ports was very risky. The prizes, after all, tended to be broad-beamed, sail-driven tubs with no turn of speed. Manned by a prize crew of only four or five men, they were helpless against the faster, well-manned blockaders and were frequently recaptured. Of course the privateers could burn their prizes like Semmes burned the *Golden Rocket*, but the whole point of privateering was the prospect of profit. Absent that, there was no reason to take the risk of going to sea at all.

The other reason privateering soon faded away was that the owners of privateers discovered that there was more money to be made, and fewer risks to be had, by blockade-running than by privateering. As a result, Confederate privateers quickly gave up the notion of getting rich by raiding Union shipping and reconfigured themselves as blockade-runners.[8]

THAT WAS NOT THE END of the Confederacy's *guerre de course* strategy; it simply meant that the war against Union commerce would have to be conducted by government warships rather than by independent entrepreneurs. Convinced that "The capitalists of the North could only be reached through the destruction of Atlantic commerce," the South set out to establish and maintain a strategy of commerce raiding by Confederate warships. Raphael Semmes in the *Sumter* set the pattern for this strategy. No privateer, Semmes was a commissioned officer in the Confederate Navy, but his mission was similar: to capture or destroy as many Union merchant ships as he could. In the six months after escaping into the Gulf of Mexico in June of 1861, Semmes and the *Sumter* seized a total of eighteen U.S. merchant ships, eight of them off Cuba, several more off Brazil, and still others as the *Sumter* worked her destructive way across the Atlantic. Semmes would have preferred to put prize crews on board and send them in for adjudication so that his crew would benefit from the prize money. But as with the privateers, finding a port where prizes could be condemned proved extremely difficult. Then, too, sending men off with the prizes depleted the crew of the *Sumter* and meant that Semmes would either have to find replacements for them or sail short-handed. In the end he found it was safer and easier simply to burn them. In his postwar *Memoir*, Semmes felt the need to justify his profligate behavior. He blamed the British for closing their ports to his prizes and thereby forcing him to destroy the ships at sea. "I made every effort to avoid the necessity of destroying my prizes," he wrote, "I only resorted to this practice, when it became evident that there was nothing else to be done."[9]

In January, 1862, six months after escaping from the Mississippi River, Semmes and the *Sumter* dropped anchor in Cadiz, Spain, where his presence caused some embarrassment for the Spanish government. The laws of neutrality forbade warships of a belligerent power from using foreign ports as bases. They could effect only those repairs necessary to the survival of the ship, and buy only as much coal as would enable them to return to their home port. Pressured by Union diplomats, the Spanish ordered Semmes to leave Cadiz within 24 hours. Semmes protested this "unfriendly order," and insisted that if he were forced to go to sea at once, lives would be put at risk, including those of the forty-three prisoners he had on board. The Spanish unbent enough to allow him to land his prisoners and make minor repairs, but after that, they insisted that he must leave within six hours. Having only enough coal on board for a few hours steaming, Semmes set a course for British Gibraltar, the only port he could make easily. There, he hoped for a friendlier reception.[10]

En route to Gibraltar, the *Sumter* chased down and boarded two more American ships inside the Straits. One, carrying a neutral cargo, he released after requiring the ship's captain to sign a "ransom bond" that pledged the owners to make a payment to the Confederacy equal to the value of the ship and its cargo once the war was over. Of course such a bond would have effect only if the Confederacy won the war, and even then full payment was problematical. Still, it was all Semmes felt he could do without alienating the neutral powers. The other ship, carrying an American cargo, he burned, doing so near enough to Gibraltar that the smoke was visible from atop the rock. Despite bringing the naval war to their doorstep—or perhaps because he had done so—Semmes and the *Sumter* received a cordial welcome from British authorities at Gibraltar who declared they would gladly supply him with coal, so long as he did not use the harbor as a base.[11]

Semmes was gratified by this reception, but he was also out of cash. In order to pay for the coal, he had to wait until he received a letter of credit from Fraser, Trenholm and Company in London. By the time it arrived on February 3, 1862, the British mood had shifted. Pressured by ever-active Union officials, the British now declared that Semmes could not buy coal there after all. Worse, three Union warships had arrived in the Straits to keep the *Sumter* confined in the harbor. Unable to obtain fuel, and skeptical of his chances of escaping, Semmes decided to pay off his crew, abandon the *Sumter* where it lay, and live to fight another day. The *Sumter* had already proven how much damage one small raider could do against the far-flung American merchant marine and more than justified the investment the Confederates had made in her. Semmes took passage in a British passenger ship for Southampton to await a new assignment.[12]

BY THEN, Stephen Mallory had already moved to acquire more, bigger, and better-armed ships for commerce raiding. To orchestrate this effort, he relied on a Georgia-born, 38-year-old former U.S. naval officer named James Dunwoody Bulloch, who among other claims to fame was the uncle of the then four-year-old future president Theodore Roosevelt. Despite his relative youth, Bulloch had a receding hairline for which he compensated by sporting spectacular mutton chop whiskers. He was an active and vigorous man whose first choice of duty was command at sea, but when he reported to Richmond, Mallory declared at once that he wanted him to go to England. Bulloch did not hesitate; he announced that he was ready to leave as soon as Mallory told him what he was to do there. Taking passage on a steamer from Montreal, Bulloch arrived in Liverpool in June of 1861, the same week the *Sumter* was commissioned in New Orleans.

To fulfill his mission of obtaining warships specially designed for commerce raiding, Bulloch had to walk a fine line, for building warships in neutral Britain was a violation not only of Britain's proclamation of neutrality, but also its Foreign Enlistment Act which set very specific limits on what British subjects could do in dealing with foreign governments. Bulloch was aided greatly in his effort by Charles K. Priolieu, the managing partner of Fraser, Trenholm and Company in Liverpool, the same company that played a key role in blockade-running. A South Carolina native, Priolieu personally guaranteed Bulloch's letter of credit, effectively bankrolling the effort. Because of that, the first ship built expressly for Confederate commerce raiding was under construction at the Liverpool shipyard of William C. Miller and Sons even before Bulloch received any funds from Richmond to pay for it.[13]

After the war, Bulloch insisted that "The contract was made with me as a private person, nothing whatsoever being said about the ultimate

James Dunwoody Bulloch was the mastermind behind the Confederate ship acquisition program in England. Though he would have preferred command afloat, he suppressed his own ambitions to fulfill the mission assigned him by Secretary of the Navy Mallory. (Courtesy of the Naval Historical Center)

destination of the ship, or the object for which she was intended." But the true purpose of the ship was an open secret. It was constructed from a set of plans that Miller & Sons had on the shelf for a Royal Navy gunboat, and even Bulloch acknowledged that the builders had to have guessed the ship's real owner and her intended use, but with a wink and a nudge, they kept quiet about it and participated in the hoax by calling the vessel the *Oreto* and putting it out that she was being built for the Italian government, though the Italian Minister denied any knowledge of her. Despite that, Union officials—the U.S. Minister, Charles Francis Adams, and the American consul at Liverpool, Thomas H. Dudley—met only frustration in their efforts to convince the British government to step in and halt the project. Bulloch's solicitors argued that "the mere building of a ship within her Majesty's dominions" was not, by itself, a violation of British law, and that "the offence is not the building but the equipping." In effect, so long as the ship in question did not have guns on board her, she could not be classified as a warship. Though the sides of the *Oreto* were pierced for sixteen guns and she had platforms fore and aft for pivot guns, because she had no actual guns on board, British officials overlooked her obvious purpose and left her unmolested.[14]

The *Oreto* was a bark-rigged, wooden-hulled steam ship. (Bulloch could have ordered an iron-hulled ship, but he wanted a vessel that did not require a major shipyard to make repairs.) Though she had two 300-horsepower engines, she also carried an oversize suite of sails and a retractable brass propeller that allowed her to sail more efficiently. These characteristics were essential for a ship that would have no home base of operations. Dependent in part on supply ships that would meet her at predetermined locations, she would necessarily have to conserve her fuel and rely mostly on sail power to move from place to place. Bulloch knew that (in his words) "A vessel without good sailing qualities . . . would have been practically useless to a Confederate cruiser." She was ready for sea by early January 1862, the same month that the *Sumter* dropped anchor in Cadiz, though she remained in port until March when Bulloch returned from a blockade-running trip to Savannah. Unwilling to wait for the arrival of a prospective captain, Bulloch ordered her to sea on March 22 under the command of a British captain and with a British crew.[15]

A month later, the *Oreto* arrived at Nassau. There she met a cargo vessel carrying her guns and ammunition, and a week later, Confederate Navy lieutenant John N. Maffit arrived at Nassau on a blockade-runner. At an isolated key in the Bahamas, Maffitt took formal command, changing the ship's name from *Oreto* to CSS *Florida*, in honor of Mallory's home state. Maffit had hoped that most of the *Oreto*'s English crewmen would agree to sign on with the Confederate Navy, but only thirteen of them did so. This was a serious setback because the *Oreto*—now *Florida*—required a crew of 140. Working long hours in the August heat, the ship's tiny crew struggled mightily to transfer the heavy guns brought out from Nassau onto the *Florida*, but even though she was now armed, the *Florida* still could not fight, or even raid Union commerce, without a crew. Worse, yellow fever soon broke out on board, and it was evident that Maffitt would have to find a friendly port where he could lay up, recruit a crew, and allow his ill sailors to recover. Maffitt first put in at Cardenas, Cuba, but concerned that Federal warships might attack him at that semi-remote port, he sailed for Havana where he thought Spanish officials were more likely to interpret the neutrality laws in his favor. Unable to obtain a crew there, Maffitt determined to take his ship into the nearest Confederate port, which was Mobile, Alabama.[16]

At five in the afternoon on September 4, 1862, U.S. Navy Commander George Preble, the senior officer on the blockading squadron off Mobile, spotted a strange sail approaching from the southeast. It was flying the British Union Jack, but that meant little since flying false colors was a common *ruse de guerre*. It seemed unlikely that this was a blockade-runner since it was still broad daylight and this vessel was making no effort to disguise its approach. Moreover, it had the appearance of a warship rather than a merchantman. When the vessel failed to respond to his signals, Preble closed on her in his flagship, *Oneida*, and hailed her deck. He got no reply, and the ship continued to steam on passively toward the entrance to the bay. Preble next fired a warning shot across her bow, but this did not elicit a response either. Concerned that this might be a Royal Navy warship, and unwilling to provoke an international incident, Preble fired two more warning shots before he finally fired for effect, his shells smashing into the hull and rigging of the vessel. That, at least, provoked a response from the still-unidentified vessel as the British flag fluttered down. But the ship neither stopped nor fired back; it simply continued on toward the entrance to Mobile Bay.[17]

On board the *Florida*, Maffit could not fire back, not only because he lacked enough men to steam and fight at the same time, but also because he did not have any rammers or spongers on board. He therefore simply held his course and hoped that he could make it safely into Mobile Bay before he was sunk by Union warships. The *Florida*'s rigging was badly cut up, and at least two 11-inch shells hulled her. One "passed clean through her just above the waterline," another came to rest in the captain's cabin, but did not explode. Once the *Florida* reached the protection of Fort Morgan on the eastern headland at the entrance to Mobile Bay, the Union ships hauled off. Preble was forced to report to the squadron commander, David G. Farragut, that the quarry "by his superior speed and unparalleled audacity managed to escape."[18]

The Confederate commerce raider *Florida* (formerly *Oreto*) depicted here in the harbor at St. George, Bermuda, was the first of the South's foreign-built commerce raiders. Though constructing Confederate warships in British ports was a clear violation of law, British officials winked at it until late in 1864. (Courtesy of the Naval Historical Center)

Farragut replied that he was "much pained" to hear that a rebel warship had run into Mobile right through the Union blockade in broad daylight, but "incensed" would have been more accurate. He reported the incident to Secretary Welles, bemoaning Preble's failure to fire into her at once when she first failed to respond to his hail. Welles took the complaint to Lincoln, whose normal patience had been strained recently by his dealings with George McClellan and who decided to make an example of Preble. By order of the president, Preble's name was struck from the rolls of the Navy and he was banished from the service. Even Farragut was shocked by this draconian punishment, and he responded that while Preble no doubt "deserved some censure," his hesitation to fire into a ship that he believed might be a British warship was perhaps understandable. Others in the Navy were shocked as well. Preble bore one of the most honored names in the service; his grandfather Edward Preble had been the hero of the Barbary Wars back in the first decade of the century and the role model for a whole generation of officers. Moreover, this Preble's service had been exemplary up to now.

Even Gideon Welles suggested that Preble's case deserved a second look. In response to this reaction, Lincoln restored Preble to his former rank five months later in February 1863.[19]

By then, the *Florida* was back at sea, having run out through the blockade in the dark of a rainy night as easily as she had run in. Now with a full crew, and all the necessary equipment, she began a campaign of maritime destruction. Mallory's orders were open-ended, instructing Maffitt to do Union trade "the greatest injury in the shortest time," which Maffitt proceeded to do. He took his first prize on January 19, 1863, stopping a sailing brig off the coast of Cuba by firing a shot across her bow. She turned out to be the *Estelle* of New York bound from the West Indies to Boston with a cargo of sugar. Maffitt took her officers and crew—eight men—on board and set her afire. The next day, Maffitt put into Havana to re-coal. He got a warmer welcome from Spanish authorities there than Semmes had at Cadiz. In general, the further a port was from the political pressure of European capitals, the more welcoming the representatives of European governments were to Confederate visitors. Consequently, Maffitt was "enthusiastically welcomed" in Havana, though he was less pleased after putting back to sea the next day when he found that the coal he had purchased there was "worthless" and had to be thrown overboard.[20]

That same afternoon, the *Florida* took two more prizes: a Maine-built brig with another cargo of sugar and a Philadelphia brig with a mixed cargo bound for Cardenas, Cuba. Maffitt burned them both, though he was embarrassed when the latter vessel, still afire, drifted into the harbor at Cardenas, which may have moderated the enthusiasm of his welcome when he put in there soon afterward. After a week of fruitless cruising, Maffitt took the *Florida* into the British port of Nassau in the Bahamas. Once again he received an enthusiastic welcome from a putatively neutral power, and though the coal he purchased there proved to be of good quality, he was chagrinned when twenty-six of the *Florida*'s crew deserted. Tasting sour grapes, Maffitt noted in his journal that only two of those sailors were of much use anyway, and he managed to recruit six new crewmen before leaving.[21]

The *Florida* had its way with every merchantman it encountered, but on February 1, the lookout espied an armed side-wheel steamer that Maffitt pegged as a Yankee warship. Though the *Florida* was heavily armed—indeed, more heavily armed than most Union warships—Maffitt's mission was not to fight, but to pillage. He therefore turned away from this stranger, which began at once to pursue him. For most of two days the vessels raced across the ocean, the *Florida* at first seeming to have the faster turn of speed, then losing ground as the stranger came up to within 3 miles. Finally with all sails set, and the engines working at full capacity, the *Florida* pulled away and left the Yankee warship over the horizon. This episode underscored the dual role of Confederate commerce raiders as both hunters and hunted.[22]

On February 12, the *Florida* encountered the clipper ship *Jacob Bell* returning to New York from China with a cargo of 1,380 boxes of tea and 10,000 boxes of firecrackers, the total valued at more than $2 million. Here was a prize worth keeping. The *Jacob Bell* also carried 41 passengers, including two ladies. Instead of burning her, therefore, Maffit put a prize crew on board with orders to keep in company. That proved difficult, however, and the two ships became separated in the night. Moreover, having the *Jacob Bell* in company inhibited the *Florida's* freedom of movement. Maffitt reluctantly decided that he would have to burn the ship after all. He brought the *Jacob Bell's* passengers on board the *Florida* and set fire to her. There is no notation in Maffitt's journal about the resulting spectacle of setting fire to a ship laden with 10,000 boxes of firecrackers.[23]

Over the next seven months, the *Florida* caught and burned eighteen more ships before steaming into the harbor at Brest, France, for a refit. She stayed there for six months. Among other things, the propeller shaft was so out of line that the resulting vibration threatened to shake the ship to pieces. Maffitt, too, was out of sorts, and after making his way overland from Brest to Paris to report his arrival to the Confederate Minister (Ambassador), John Slidell, he declared himself too ill to continue in command. Lieutenant Commanding Charles M. Morris relieved him in January 1864.[24]

BY THAT TIME there were several more Confederate raiders at sea, none of them more important or consequential than CSS *Alabama*, the vessel that, more than any other, embodied the Confederate commerce raiding strategy. Like *Florida*, *Alabama* was built in Liverpool under a veil of secrecy and was initially designated simply as "Number 290."

Though contemporaries conjured up a number of theories, most of them sinister, about why it bore this designation, the simple explanation was that it was the 290th hull to be laid down in the Laird shipyard at Birkenhead across the Mersey River from Liverpool. Bulloch struck a deal for her construction with the Laird Company soon after he arranged for the construction of the *Oreto/Florida*, but the work had been delayed because the Lairds wanted cash in hand before starting. Even after the work began, there were additional delays due to the Lairds' determination to use only the best quality materials with oak ribs and copper fasteners.[25]

The ship was worth the wait. The *Alabama* was one of the finest, if not the finest, ship of her class. Nearly as long as a Union *Hartford*-class sloop, she was 12 feet narrower, which gave her rakish lines and significantly less displacement. Bark rigged with twin 300-horsepower engines, she was designed to make 12 knots under steam, but she was also a graceful sailor since in fifteen minutes she could detach her propeller and raise it into a well that was built into her hull. This allowed her to use her coal sparingly and remain at sea for long periods. Moreover, her distiller allowed her to produce drinking water from seawater. Since food and other supplies could be obtained from her captures, she could remain at sea independent of the shore for months at a stretch. Bulloch called her in every respect "a first class ship," and during his blockade-running trip back to the Confederacy, he formally requested the command for himself. Mallory gave Bulloch a commission as a commander in the C.S. Navy and promised that he would have her.[26]

But Mallory soon had second thoughts. Because Bulloch had made all the contacts with British builders, and successfully fended off inquiries into the ships that became the *Florida* and *Alabama*, Mallory decided that he was irreplaceable in the role of warship procurer. The Navy Secretary therefore told a disappointed Bulloch that he should stay where he was. "Your services in England are so important at this time," Mallory wrote, "that I trust you will cheerfully support [suppress?] any disappointment you may experience in not getting to sea." To take command of the *Alabama*, Mallory ordered Raphael Semmes, late of the *Sumter*, to go to Liverpool. Though Bulloch was hugely disappointed, he accepted Mallory's decision and recommitted himself to preparing the *Alabama* for sea. Despite his disappointment, Bulloch very likely made a greater contribution to the Confederate war effort as an agent in England than did Semmes or any other Confederate Navy official in or out of uniform.[27]

Meanwhile, U.S. diplomats were working hard to expose the 290 as a Confederate warship, and eventually their work bore fruit. On July 21, the U.S. Consul Thomas H. Dudley finally found someone who would swear in an affidavit that the 290 was a Confederate warship. Dudley passed the document on to Charles Francis Adams in London who presented it to the British Foreign Office. That same day, Adams also ordered the USS *Tuscarora* to stand by to intercept the 290 if it attempted to go to sea. On July 28, 1862, the British Attorney General, William Atherton, agreed that the construction of the 290 (now officially named the *Enrica*) was a violation of the Foreign Enlistment Act and that it should not be allowed to sail. He passed this decision on to Lord Russell, the British Foreign Minister, the next morning: July 29.

Too late. Tipped off that British authorities were about to intervene— perhaps by Russell himself—Bulloch took the *Enrica* to sea that morning on what was officially advertised as a trial run. She never returned. After making several runs off Liverpool to test the engines, Bulloch announced to the guests and dignitaries on board that he wished to keep the ship out overnight as an additional trial of her sea-keeping capabilities and that they should go ashore in a tender. He entrusted the ship to an English skipper, Matthew J. Butcher, giving him instructions to anchor at Moelfra Bay on the Welch coast, and Bulloch went ashore on the tender with the dignitaries.[28]

The next day Bulloch brought out a crew of 45 or so men that he had recruited on the Liverpool docks, accompanied by a nearly equal number of women. He did not want to bring the women, who were (in Bulloch's words) "of that class who generally affect a tender solicitude for Jack when he is outward bound," but the need for haste compelled him to do so because the women would not let the men go until "they could first get a month's pay in advance." There was no time for negotiations—Bulloch feared not only that British authorities might intervene, but he had also learned of the approach of the *Tusca-rora*—and so he took the women as well as the men out to Moelfra Bay. Once on board the *Enrica*, he served them all a meal—as well as a generous tot of grog—and only then did he invite the men to enlist for a cruise "to Havana" promising them a month's pay in advance. All but a few agreed, most immediately turning their month's pay over to their hovering consorts. The women then cheerfully went back aboard the tug and cast off. Bulloch went ashore, too, leaving *Enrica* in charge of Butcher, with secret orders to proceed, not for Havana, but the Bay of Praya on the island of Terciéra in the Portuguese Azores. There he would rendezvous with the sailing ship *Agrippina* out of London, which carried the guns and gun carriages that would turn the *Enrica* into a warship.[29]

Thus it was that when Semmes arrived in Liverpool pursuant to Mallory's order to go there and take command of the *Alabama*, he found that "the bird had flown." Bulloch took him on board the blockade-runner *Bahama*, and together they made their way to the Azores to meet the *Enrica* and the *Agrippina*. There, on August 30, 1862, Semmes read his orders, the British flag was struck, the Confederate flag unfurled, the ship's little band struck up "Dixie," and the *Enrica* became CSS *Alabama*. As yet, however, the *Alabama* had no crew. The men who had sailed her from Liverpool had signed on for a commercial cruise to Havana, not to serve as Confederate sailors. Like Maffitt, Semmes hoped to talk them into enlisting. He promised them adventure and mentioned the noble cause they would be serving, but he got a better reaction when he promised to pay them double wages ("hear, hear") and prize money. Eighty of the ninety men on board signed on. With a handful of officers from the southern states and an international crew composed of "English, Dutch, Irish, French, Italian, and Spanish sailors," the *Alabama* was at last ready for sea. At just about the time that *Florida* put into Brest for a refit, CSS *Alabama* embarked on her own career of destruction.[30]

SEMMES BEGAN HIS CRUISE by scouring the waters around the Azores for American whaling ships, and on September 4, the *Alabama* took her first prize, the whaler *Ocmulgee*, caught hove to with a whale alongside which its crew was harvesting. Semmes took off the crew, helped himself to "some beef and port and small stores," and burned the *Ocmulgee* along with her catch. In quick order, Semmes captured and burned four more whaling ships in as many days, removing whatever stores he needed, and after paroling their crews, allowed them to row for shore in their own boats. In this manner, he worked his way through the American whaling fleet until the end of the month when, having burned ten prizes, he set sail for the waters off New England where his target was the ships carrying grain from New York to Europe.[31]

By the end of October, 1862, Semmes had accumulated more prisoners than he could easily accommodate. He decided to consign them all to one of his prizes and release it as a cartel. Before he turned it loose, however, he entrusted a message to its skipper. Annoyed by the repeated references in captured New York newspapers to the *Alabama* as a "pirate," and by allusions to himself as a tyrannical and inhumane plunderer, Semmes asked the captain of the *Baron de Castine* to give his "special thanks " to the president of the New York Chamber of Commerce "for the resolutions it has passed condemning the *Alabama*."[32]

Semmes' taunting message fed a growing sense of near panic within New York's maritime community. Marine insurance rates had already shot up from the traditional 1.25 percent of the cargo's value to 4 percent, and soon they would reach 6 percent. Those who risked sending their cargoes to sea without insurance paid an even stiffer penalty if their ship was caught and burned by the "English pirate." Rumors spread in New York that Semmes was planning to attack the city. In fact, Semmes did toy with the idea of steaming into New York Harbor at night, burning whatever shipping he found at anchor, throwing a few shells into lower Manhattan, and running out again before dawn. It didn't happen because Semmes knew that to pull off such a raid, he would need full coal bunkers to outrun any pursuers, and he had not had a chance to re-coal since leaving the Azores. Instead, therefore, Semmes turned the *Alabama* south toward the West Indies.[33]

There, Semmes lay in wait for the biggest prize of all: the semi-annual gold shipment from California via Panama on one of the huge Aspinwall steamers. On December 7, 1862, in the Windward Passage east of Cuba, his lookouts espied the enormous but unarmed Aspinwall steamer *Ariel*. To Semmes' great disappointment, however, the *Ariel* was southward bound from New York, not northward bound from Panama. Semmes stopped her anyway and held her for two days while he pondered what to do with her. In addition to having 500 passengers on board, there were 140 U.S. Marines on their way to the garrison at

San Francisco. Semmes could not take so many prisoners on board the *Alabama*, and obviously he could not set fire to the ship and burn them alive, so in the end he reluctantly released the *Ariel* after taking what supplies he found useful and requiring her skipper to sign a $260,000 ransom bond. The audacity of Semmes in stopping such a huge vessel at sea triggered additional criticism of the Navy Department for not responding more effectively—or at all—to the rebel threat.[34]

Indeed, Gideon Welles came under enormous pressure to do something about the *Alabama*. The *New York Herald*, in particular, became a regular and vicious critic. Its acid-tongued editor, James Gordon Bennett, was positively shrill in declaring that "in the name of the people, we demand from the head of our government some sign of concern in this matter—some show of sympathy for the undeserved obloquy to which we are now subjected through the neglect, the carelessness, the incompetency, the utter imbecility of the Navy Department." The New York Chamber of Commerce petitioned the government to inaugurate convoys from New York to England, Brazil, and the Cape of Good Hope. Britain had employed merchant convoys during its ways with France, and they would prove critical during the World Wars of the twentieth century in response to commerce raiding by German submarines, but in 1862 Welles resisted the idea. As he saw it, committing warships to convoy duty would weaken the blockade, which both he and Lincoln saw as the Navy's primary mission. Even Semmes was surprised by Welles' priorities, noting archly that "The enemy was too busy blockading the Southern coasts to pay much attention to his commerce."[35]

Welles did, however, send warships out to look for the rebel raiders, though searching for one ship over the broad ocean was like looking for the proverbial needle in a haystack, or, as the *Boston Post* put it, "like ten cats looking for a weasel in a hundred acre lot." Welles sent the USS *Kearsarge* under John Winslow to Europe to look for the *Florida*, and he sent a five-ship "flying squadron" under Charles Wilkes to the West Indies to look for Semmes and the *Alabama*. Other ships followed until a total of eighteen U.S. Navy warships were abroad searching for the rebel "pirates." Despite the long odds, the USS *San Jacinto* found the *Alabama* at anchor in French Martinique in the West Indies in November 1862. Semmes had gone there to rendezvous with *Agrippina*

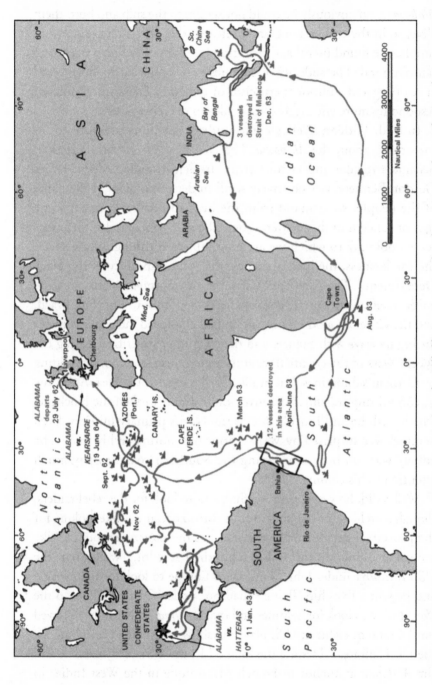

THE CRUISE OF THE CSS *ALABAMA*, JULY 1862–JUNE 1864. Map by Bill Clipson, reprinted with permission from *The Naval Institute Historical Atlas of the U.S. Navy* by Craig L. Symonds, © 1995.

in order to re-coal and re-supply. Fortunately for Semmes, he had just sent the slow-sailing *Agrippina* off to another rendezvous point at the remote island of Blanquilla off Venezuela before the *San Jacinto* arrived.[36]

Unwilling to violate French neutrality by charging into the harbor with guns blazing, the *San Jacinto's* commander, Captain William Ronckendorff, kept his ship outside the harbor intending to pounce on the *Alabama* when she departed. Semmes later professed to be more amused than alarmed by the presence of this powerful Union warship outside the harbor, for he was confident that once it was dark he could slip out undetected. And so it proved. That very night, a proverbial "dark and rainy night," the *Alabama* got up steam and, completely blacked out, ran through the southern passage out into the open sea. An incredulous Ronckendorff hovered for several more days off Martinique, perplexed at how Semmes could have eluded him.[37]

Despite his string of successes, Semmes sought an opportunity to strike at the Union war machine, not just its unarmed merchant vessels. Learning from captured northern newspapers of a Union thrust at Galveston, he planned to steam in amongst the U.S. Army transports there and shell them. What a coup it would be for a Confederate navy warship to defeat a Yankee army! But as he approached Galveston on January 11, 1863, instead of a host of army transports, he found a squadron of Union warships. One of them evidently spotted him, for it began to move in his direction. Semmes steamed away as if trying to escape, though he was actually trying to lure it away from its consorts.

On board the USS *Hatteras*, Captain Homer Blake began to suspect that he was being drawn off deliberately, and when the ship he was pursuing hove to and waited for him, he deduced at once that it was the *Alabama*. He nevertheless closed to within hailing distance and asked her identity. Semmes ordered an officer with a British accent to reply that it was "Her Britannic Majesty's Ship Vixen." Blake, either still uncertain or playing out the game to the end, replied that he was going to send a boat. Before that could be done, the same voice called out "We are the Confederate steamer Alabama!" and simultaneous with the last syllable, came a full broadside. The fight was short and one-sided. The *Hatteras* was a converted passenger steamer with a top speed of only 8 knots. It carried seven guns, the largest of which was a 32-pounder. The

Alabama carried only eight guns, but they included a 68-pounder and a 100-pounder along with its broadside of 32-pounders. Blake thought briefly about trying to close and board the *Alabama*, but well-aimed shots from the Confederate vessel smashed the walking beam on the *Hatteras*, pierced her engine cylinder, and started two fires. The Union ship could neither move nor maneuver, and already it was taking on water. Blake saw no option but to surrender, and he fired a gun to leeward to signal his capitulation. After removing the Union crew of 118 men, Semmes watched as the mortally wounded *Hatteras* went down. It was the first time in history that a steam warship of any nationality sunk another steam warship in battle, and it was the *Alabama*'s only victory over a Union warship in its two-year career.[38]

After a re-coaling stop in Jamaica where he paroled his prisoners, Semmes headed south for the Brazilian headlands, a traditional landfall for much trans-Atlantic shipping.

Welles sent Union warships to each of the places where the *Alabama* was reported, but they arrived only to find that the quarry had flown. Perhaps Welles' bitterest disappointment was when he dispatched the huge, coal-eating *Vanderbilt* to the Brazilian headlands, precisely where the *Alabama* was operating, only to have her virtually hijacked en route by one of his own officers. Acting Rear Admiral Charles Wilkes had never been happy with his flagship, the *Wachusett*, which, he said, broke down at least once every four days, and when he encountered the commodious *Vanderbilt* in the harbor at St. Thomas in the Danish Virgin Islands, he simply appropriated her as his new flagship despite her orders to go to Brazil. In his Annual Report for 1863, Welles complained that by taking the *Vanderbilt* for his own use, Wilkes had "wholly defeated the plans of the Department." Wilkes objected to this statement, and his response provoked a bitter quarrel and an eventual court martial that led to Wilkes' suspension from the service.[39]

Long before that, the *Alabama* had left the coast of Brazil and headed east across the South Atlantic Ocean. Semmes wanted to carry the war into the Indian Ocean and the Far East, and he looked forward hopefully to the next phase of the cruise. Though he could not have known it, the *Alabama*'s days of glory were already behind her. The *Alabama* cruised for another year, taking several prizes off the Cape of Good Hope, and a few more in the Straits of Malacca as she carried the

Confederate flag into the South China Sea, but whole weeks went by when she did not encounter a single American merchantman. Moreover, the ship and its crew were showing the wear and tear of a long voyage. The *Alabama*'s copper bottom was literally peeling off, her boilers were in desperate need of cleaning, and much of her gunpowder had gone bad and had to be thrown overboard. The crew was in a sour mood as well. None of them were from the southern states, and they had signed on in the first place because of Semmes' promise of double pay and lots of prize money. Although Semmes promised them that the Confederate government would pay them for the prizes they had burned once the war was over, many began to doubt it, and like sailors everywhere, they wanted their money now. In his private journal, a Yankee prisoner on board the *Alabama* noted the poor morale aboard ship: "Crew much dissatisfied, no prize money, no liberty, and [they] see no prospect of getting any." While the *Alabama* was in Singapore, ten more members of the crew deserted.[40]

That, and the slim pickings in the Far East, convinced Semmes to return to the Atlantic. After stopping at Cape Town to re-coal, Semmes determined "to make the best of my way to England or France for the purpose of docking, and thoroughly overhauling and repairing my ship." The *Alabama* dropped anchor in Cherbourg on June 11, 1864. It turned out to be an unfortunate choice, for the *Alabama* needed a dry dock, and the only dry dock facilities in Cherbourg were reserved for the French Navy. The nearest commercial dry dock was across the Bay of the Seine at Le Havre, but on June 14, the USS *Kearsarge* steamed into the harbor at Cherbourg, confirmed the presence of the *Alabama*, and went back out to wait for her off the breakwater.[41]

SEMMES' DECISION to abandon his safe refuge in Cherbourg and go out to fight the *Kearsarge* was, and remains, an historical curiosity, if not quite a mystery. To be sure the *Alabama* had handily defeated the *Hatteras* in the Gulf of Mexico two years before, but the *Hatteras* had been a converted passenger steamer, and the *Kearsarge* was a purpose-built *Mohican*-class sloop of war with a battery that included two 11-inch Dahlgren smoothbores, bigger than anything on board the *Alabama*. Moreover, the *Alabama* was no longer the vessel it had once been. Semmes himself wrote that his ship was "like the wearied fox hound limping back after a long chase, foot sore, and longing for quiet and repose." Much of its powder had gone bad, and only one in every three of the shell fuses was reliable. Semmes knew this, but declared that he would take "the chances of one in three."[42]

Semmes' decision may have been a product of his own exhaustion, for he, too, was worn down, both physically and emotionally. Newspapers he had captured in the last month had shown him how desperate the South's military circumstances had become. Though his initial plan in coming to Cherbourg had been to give the *Alabama* a lengthy refit, when the *Kearsarge* arrived, Semmes determined on a different course. To his first lieutenant, John McIntosh Kell, he confessed that he was "tired of running," and that he planned to go out and fight the *Kearsarge*. There is a hint of fatalism in what Kell wrote in his own post-war memoir about that conversation with Semmes: "Our cause was weakening daily, and our ship was so disabled it really seemed to us our work was almost done! We might end her career gloriously by being victorious in battle, and defeat against an equal foe we would never have allowed ourselves to anticipate."[43]

Whatever his motive, Semmes delivered a challenge via the U.S. Consul in Cherbourg requesting that the *Kearsarge* remain off the port since he intended to go out and fight her. He put on a bold face for his mostly English crew of adventurers in announcing his plans to them. Despite their sagging morale, they rose to meet his enthusiasm, and Semmes later wrote, "My crew seemed not only willing, but anxious for the combat." On June 19, 1864, as the *Alabama* steamed out to sea, Semmes mounted a gun carriage to address them. He praised their service over the past two years and asked if that record would now be sullied by defeat? "Never! Never!" they cried. "The eyes of all Europe are at this moment on you," Semmes called out in his quarterdeck voice. "The flag that floats over you is that of a young Republic that bids defiance to her enemies, whenever and wherever found. Show the world that you know how to uphold it. Go to your quarters."[44]

Outside Cherbourg, the captain of the *Kearsarge*, John A. Winslow, waited impatiently for the *Alabama* to come out. Winslow was a North Carolina native, but he had accepted a warrant as a midshipman at the age of 16 and since then he had become not only a Union nationalist but an abolitionist. He had gained command

The CSS *Alabama* duels with USS *Kearsarge* off the coast of Cherbourg, France, on June 19, 1864, in this contemporary engraving. (Courtesy of the Naval Historical Center)

of the *Kearsarge* the year before and had spent most of his time since looking for one or another of the rebel raiders, first the *Florida* and then the *Alabama*. He was not about to lose this chance. He had received Semmes' challenge on June 15, but several days passed without any sign of the rebel cruiser, and Winslow began to wonder if the challenge were part of an elaborate ruse. Then at about 10:20 on Sunday morning, June 19, lookouts on the *Kearsarge* reported that the *Alabama* was coming out of port accompanied by a French warship and a private yacht flying the British ensign. To make sure that the fight took place well beyond the marine league required by the neutrality laws, Winslow headed out to sea at a leisurely pace, with the *Alabama* following. The French warship stopped at the 3-mile limit, satisfied that it had enforced the neutrality of French waters; the yacht continued on, but at a respectful distance. Once Winslow was satisfied that he was well out in international waters, he turned and steamed toward the *Alabama*. Semmes fired first, getting off several shots before the *Kearsarge* replied. At 11:00 the firing became general, and the two ships steamed in a circle around a central point, each firing as fast as possible.[45]

Winslow had prepared for the fight by hanging spare anchor chain over the sides of his ship and covering the chain with a false hull of 1-inch planking painted black so that it seemed merely a part of the hull. Semmes later complained that this was cheating and insisted that it was like a man going out to a duel while secretly wearing a chain mail shirt under his jacket. In the 19th century there were many who agreed with him, though in the 21st century, when American soldiers go to war wearing body armor, it may seem only commonsensical that a commander would do all that he could to protect his ship and secure victory.

Over the next hour, the *Kearsarge* took several hits though none of them were critical in part because of her chain mail protection. One shell from the *Alabama*'s 100-pound rifle lodged in the sternpost of the *Kearsarge*, but apparently it had one of the two-in-three fuses that failed to function for the shell did not explode. Had it done so, it might very well have sent the *Kearsarge* to the bottom.* Meanwhile several shells from the *Kearsarge*'s 11-inch Dahlgren guns hulled the *Alabama*, which began taking on water at an alarming rate. After an hour, Semmes ordered Kell to go below and find out how long the ship could remain afloat. Kell's reply when he returned was "perhaps ten minutes." The ship was settling quickly, and there was no hope of trying to make it back to port. Continuing the fight would condemn his crew of 149 men to near-certain death. "Cease firing," Semmes ordered, "shorten sail, and haul down the colors."[46]

On the *Kearsarge*, the absence of a flag on the *Alabama* was ambiguous amongst the smoke and clamor of battle, and the *Kearsarge* fired several more shots (Semmes claimed it was five) before stopping. To erase all doubt, Semmes sent an officer in a boat over to the *Kearsarge* to announce his surrender and to request Winslow's aid in saving the crew of the rapidly sinking *Alabama*. Only two of the boats on the *Kearsarge* were undamaged, and Winslow ordered them into the water to pick

---

*Semmes later boasted that the unexploded shell in the sternpost of the *Kearsarge* "was the only trophy they ever got of the Alabama." He noted, "This shell . . . was carefully cut out, along with some of the timber, and sent to the Navy Department in Washington, to be exhibited to admiring Yankees" (Semmes, *Service Afloat*, 762). That shell is still on display to "admiring Yankees" at the Navy Museum in the Washington Navy Yard.

up survivors, though not fast enough to satisfy Semmes who charged later that Winslow was not earnest in his effort. The undamaged dingy from the *Alabama*, which had brought the news of the surrender to Winslow, also went back to find survivors. On board the sinking *Alabama*, Semmes ordered "every man to save himself," and urged them to grab a spar or an oar as a life preserver and to paddle away from the sinking ship quickly to avoid being caught in the vortex. Semmes himself stripped down to trousers and vest, threw his sword into the sea, and jumped over the side.[47]

The sea between the two ships was now "a mass of living heads" as men struggled to stay afloat. The English yacht *Deerhound* that had come out to watch the fight also lowered boats and joined the effort to save the drowning men. Winslow was at first grateful until it was reported to him that after picking up twenty-seven crewmen and fifteen officers, including both Semmes and Kell, the *Deerhound* was making for the English coast crowded with men that Winslow considered his prisoners. Even the officer who had come on board the *Kearsarge* to announce the surrender of the *Alabama* found his way onto the *Deerhound*, which made port in Southampton that same afternoon. Winslow considered the escape of men who had surrendered to be as dishonorable as Semmes believed it was to hang anchor chain over the sides of the *Kearsarge*.[48]

The escape of the "pirate" Semmes did not diminish the impact of the news of the destruction of the *Alabama* when it reached the northern states in early July during Grant's siege of Petersburg. Welles was pleased to be able to report to the Cabinet that the English pirate ship had at last been run to ground. The New York Chamber of Commerce voted Winslow and his men a $25,000 cash prize, a huge sum in 1864 dollars, and Winslow received the formal thanks of Congress and a promotion to commodore.

OF COURSE THERE WAS STILL THE *FLORIDA*. On the day the *Alabama* went down, the *Florida* was anchored in St. George Bay, Bermuda. Two days before, it had captured and burned the brig *C. W. Clarke* with a cargo of lumber out of Boston. Manpower and supply problems on board *Florida* were becoming acute. Her new commander, Charles Morris, found the English at Bermuda accommodating enough, but he was disgusted that the Portuguese refused to let him have any coal at all, or even fresh water, when he put in at Funchal. Morris complained to Mallory that "The American vessels get whatever they wish," but that Confederate raiders were peremptorily told to leave. With the war now clearly shifting in the favor of the Union, European nations did not want to end up on the wrong side.[49]

From Bermuda, Morris took the *Florida* toward the Delaware Capes capturing seven prizes in as many days, bonding one and burning six. One of those prizes was the U.S. mail steamer *Electric Spark* bound from Philadelphia to New York. It had a crew of thirty-nine as well as forty-two passengers. Morris did not have room for eighty-one prisoners on board the *Florida*, but reluctant to let the *Electric Spark* go free, he chased down an English schooner that he had stopped earlier, and negotiated a deal whereby Morris bought the schooner's entire cargo of fruit for $720 in gold, then threw the fruit overboard to make room for the eighty-one prisoners. Morris then scuttled the mail steamer.[50]

Fearing to overstay his time off the Delaware Capes, Morris headed for Teneriffe in the Portuguese Azores where this time he was allowed to buy coal, but only after officials informed him that he would have to leave within 24 hours. From there he worked his way back across the Atlantic to Bahia (now Salvador) on the coast of Brazil. As he steamed into the harbor on October 4, 1864, he noted that one of the ships anchored there was the USS *Wachusett*, a relatively new (1861) bark-rigged screw sloop under the command of Napoleon Collins.

Collins was an aggressive officer who had previously been reprimanded for having seized a blockade-runner within British waters. From the moment he saw the *Florida* come into port, he resolved to take her regardless of the fact that both ships were in a neutral harbor. He sent a boat over to confirm her identity, and when it returned, he ordered steam up and cleared for action. He did not strike at once, however. He waited until the middle of the night two days later when half of the *Florida*'s crew, including her captain, was ashore on liberty. At three o'clock in the morning on October 7, 1864, Collins ordered the *Wachusett* to slip her cable and steered her directly into the *Florida* at full speed fully expecting to send her to the bottom. Though the raider was badly damaged by the collision, she remained afloat. The senior officer on the *Florida*, Lieutenant Thomas K. Porter, came on board the *Wachusett* to protest this flagrant violation of the laws of the sea, but Collins was the picture of sangfroid. He knew it was against the law, he said, but the law be damned. Seeing that the *Florida* had not sunk after all, he ran a cable to her and towed her out to sea while Brazilian authorities ashore fired on him. The Brazilians even sent a gunboat in pursuit, but even while towing the *Florida*, the *Wachusett* easily outdistanced it.[51]

Eventually, Collins brought the *Florida* into Hampton Roads where it was moored among the ships of the Union Navy. Naturally the Brazilian government protested, and though the northern press cheered Collins for ridding the seas of the "pirate" *Florida*, his behavior had been too flagrant not to convene a court martial. Collins pleaded guilty to the charges, but offered, as mitigation, that his action had been "for the public good." The members of the court may well have agreed, but they could hardly ignore the facts. On April 7, 1865, as Robert E. Lee's army moved toward Appomattox, the court found Collins guilty and sentenced him to be suspended from the service.

There were two postscripts to this tale. The first involved the *Florida* itself. Still leaking from her initial collision with the *Wachusett*, she collided with the army transport ship *Alliance* in the crowded roadstead. The *Florida* began taking on water, and on November 28, 1864, she settled to the bottom. Consequently, though the United States officially apologized to Brazil for Collins' flagrant violation of her neutrality, it could not comply with the request to return the ship. These circumstances led to speculation that the *Florida* had been sabotaged, sunk deliberately so that the United States would not have to return her to Brazil and perhaps eventually to the Confederates. An investigation conducted at the time found no evidence to support this and concluded that it was simply "one of the common accidents which occur in a crowded roadstead."[52]

The second postscript concerned Collins. Lincoln's assassination a week after Collins' court martial meant that the verdict was never confirmed, and the *Wachusett*'s erstwhile commander remained in a kind of professional limbo. Finally on September 17, 1866, nearly two years after the event, and eighteen months after the war ended, Gideon Welles notified Collins that "the sentence of the court is not approved," and he restored Collins to duty.[53]

THERE WERE OTHER REBEL RAIDERS on the high seas. The most successful of them was CSS *Tallahassee*, an English-built, iron-hulled
former blockade-runner that was converted into a commerce raider in
July 1864, and which, under the command of John Taylor Wood (a
grandson of Zachary Taylor and nephew of Jefferson Davis), captured
some thirty-three Union ships in ten days off the New England coast.
Renamed the *Olustee* that fall, and given new officers, she captured six
more ships in November before returning safely to Wilmington and
resuming her career as a blockade-runner. Other, less spectacular raiders
like CSS *Georgia* (nine prizes) and CSS *Chickamauga* (five prizes) added
to the total. Finally, there was the CSS *Shenandoah*, whose remarkable
story rightfully belongs to a later chapter. Altogether during the war,
eight Confederate commerce raiders captured and destroyed some 284
Union merchant ships valued at more than $25 million. Most of them
were sailing ships, and a third of them (97) were taken by either the
Alabama or *Florida*.[54]

In assessing the impact of these rebel raiders, as in assessing the
impact of the blockade, numbers alone cannot tell the full story.
William Dalzell, whose 1940 history, *The Flight from the Flag*, remains
a classic, argued that the ripple effect of those 284 lost ships went well
beyond the immediate impact of sunken ships and lost cargoes. The
success of the *Florida* and *Alabama* in particular led to a significant
jump in maritime insurance rates, which reduced the profit margin
even for ships that never encountered a rebel raider. Moreover, the rebel
raiders engendered such fear within the American maritime community
that many merchants abandoned American-flag ships altogether and
shipped their goods in foreign bottoms. Facing a dearth of customers,
American shippers either sold out or reregistered their ships in foreign
countries. Whereas in 1858 only thirty-three American-built vessels
registered as British ships, in 1863, a total of 348 did so. Thus while the
raiders sank or burned some 150,000 tons of Union shipping, they were
also instrumental in provoking the transfer of another 800,000 tons
to foreign registry. In all, nearly a million tons of merchant ships—
half of the U.S. merchant marine—ceased to fly the American flag.
In the fall of 1863, a reporter for the *New York Herald* noted that of
the 176 ships then in New York Harbor, only nineteen of them flew
the American flag. The others flew the flags of England (93), Bremen

(20), France (10), Denmark (6), Hanover (6), Hamburg (6), Prussia (4), Belgium (3), Norway (3), Austria (3), Holland (2), and Sweden (1). Indeed, American-flag shipping dropped nearly as spectacularly during the war as southern cotton exports. While the blockade reduced southern cotton exports from 2.8 million bales in 1860 to 55,000 in 1862, rebel commerce raiders effectively reduced Union shipping from 2.2 million tons in 1860 to less than 500,000 by 1865. Considering that the South invested considerably less in building and equipping its handful of raiders than the North did in establishing and maintaining the blockade, the southern decision to adopt a strategy of *guerre de course* seems more than validated.[55]

On the other hand, the impact of the raiders on the economy of the North was not nearly as devastating as the impact of the blockade was to the economy of the South. The hundreds of American-owned ships that adopted foreign registry to avoid being targeted by the rebel raiders were not lost, merely re-flagged. During Britain's wars with France earlier in the nineteenth century, much of her trade shifted to American-flag vessels to prevent their capture by French privateers. American commerce in this period had thrived as a result, but so, too, had the British economy. Now the situation was reversed, and during the Civil War much of America's trade shifted to British-flag vessels. In both cases, the home economy continued to prosper. An editorial in the *New York Sun* in March of 1865, only weeks before Appomattox, noted that "There never was a time in the history of New York when business prosperity was more general, when the demand for goods was greater, and payments more prompt, than within the last two or three years. Manufacturers have been crowded with orders, dealers have had an abundance of customers, and every branch of legitimate trade has flourished." Despite the best efforts of John Maffitt, Raphael Semmes, Charles Morris, John Taylor Wood, and others, American goods still found their way to markets in Europe, South America, and the Far East even if it was often in ships flying the flags of other countries. The "flight from the flag" was harmful, to be sure, but not catastrophic.[56]

There is one more postscript to the story of the Confederate raiders. Once the war was over, the victorious Union states claimed that Britain should be held responsible for the role it had played in building and funding the rebel raiders. At the very least, many argued, the British should pay for the damage wrought by the ships they had built along the banks of the Mersey. Charles Sumner, chair of the U.S. Senate Foreign Relations Committee, went further than that. He asserted that Britain should pay not only for the direct damage done by the rebel raiders, but also for the entire cost of the war after the Battle of Gettysburg—several billion dollars in all—on the grounds that British support for the Confederacy had prolonged the war and encouraged southerners to hold out to the very end. The international court that adjudicated the dispute in 1872 rejected this last claim, but it did rule that Britain should pay for the damage done by the *Florida* and *Alabama*. In the Treaty of Washington (1871) the British agreed to pay the United States the sum of $15 million.[57]

4

"Unvexed to the Sea"

The River War

AT MIDDAY ON AUGUST 20, 1861, an odd-looking vessel steamed northward up the Mississippi River between Missouri and Illinois some 20 miles upriver from Cairo, Illinois, where the Ohio flowed into the Mississippi. The steamer had two very tall smoke stacks that rose precariously above a wooden superstructure that looked for all the world like a floating barn or, as some said, a gigantic wooden shoe box. It was the USS *Tyler*, which had been converted into a warship from the merchant steamer *A. O. Tyler* at Cincinnati, and her barn-like appearance was the result of her "armor" of 5-inch thick timbers that completely covered both her superstructure and paddle wheels. That wooden sheathing, though useless against artillery, was designed to protect her from small arms fire and made her, in the parlance of the day, a timberclad. For all her ungainly appearance, the *Tyler* was powerfully armed with one 32-pounder in the bow and six 8-inch guns in broadside on her 180-foot deck.

In command of the *Tyler* was 49-year-old John Rodgers, who had been a Navy man virtually all his life. The son of another John Rodgers who had been the senior U.S. Navy officer during the War of 1812, this John Rodgers had become a midshipman at the age of 16, and when the Civil War began he was a commander with thirty-three years of service.

A month after Fort Sumter, Gideon Welles ordered Rodgers to Cincinnati to assist the army in creating a squadron of river gunboats for the western campaign. Since the inland rivers were the responsibility of the army and not the navy, Rodgers was to take his orders from the local army commander and, somewhat understandably, Rodgers viewed his assignment as a kind of exile. Nevertheless, when he arrived in Cincinnati, he got to work at once, purchasing three wooden steamboats and transforming them into men of war by reinforcing their decks to hold the heavy guns, dropping the boilers into the lower hull, rerouting the steam pipes, and sheathing them with thick planks of wood. One of the three was the merchant steamer *A. O. Tyler*, now called simply the *Tyler*. Rodgers worried that some would assume the vessel was named for former president John Tyler who had sided with the Confederacy, and he proposed re-naming it the *Taylor* after Zachary Taylor, but no one else seemed to think it mattered, and the original name stuck. Now the *Tyler* breasted the sluggish Mississippi current as she headed upriver toward the tiny town of Commerce, Missouri.[1]

Rodgers was bound toward Commerce not because the little town had particular strategic significance, but because he had learned that a force of rebel cavalry, which the panicked residents overestimated at

The "timberclad" USS *Tyler*'s boxy appearance gave rise to her several nicknames as a floating barn or a wooden shoebox, but as one of the first armed vessels on the western rivers, she had a great impact on several early battles, including Shiloh. (Courtesy of the Naval Historical Center)

about a thousand, had occupied the town and was looting it of supplies. Worse, the rebels had unlimbered some guns along the bank and were interfering with river traffic. Rodgers was "determined to dislodge them." Though it was the first confrontation between a river gunboat and forces along the shore, the results were anticlimactic. As soon as the *Tyler* steamed into sight, the rebels limbered up their guns and fled, taking with them a long wagon train that Rodgers estimated to include as many as fifty wagons filled mostly with corn from the town's mill. Landing at Commerce's small dock, Rodgers went ashore and saw that the rebels had "committed a great deal of wanton destruction" during their brief occupation, including, he reported melodramatically, "tearing up women and children's clothes." It was just the beginning of the vicious fratricidal war that would course through Missouri for much of the next four years.[2]

The rebels had left the town, but they had not gone far. The next day, a group of them appeared on a small rise near the river and began to fire on the *Tyler* with small arms. Rodgers ordered his gunners to send "a couple of well directed shells" toward the hilltop where they exploded with gratifying effect, causing the cavalrymen to mount hastily and disappear. Rodgers could not stay at Commerce indefinitely, however, and he suspected that when he left, the rebels would reoccupy the town. He therefore offered safe passage to those residents of Commerce who had not already fled, and took them downriver. "I return to Cairo with reluctance," he informed Welles in his report, for Commerce was a Union town and its residents deserved protection.[3]

This early encounter on the upper reaches of the Mississippi River suggested much about the nature of the war in the western theater. Because the rivers were essential to the movement of both troops and supplies, gunboats were necessary to secure and protect the critical lines of communication. Mobile land forces, such as cavalry, might attempt to interdict this traffic, but they were no match for armed gunboats, even the modified wooden steamers and tugs that made up the first armed vessels on the river. Gunboats had an overwhelming advantage of firepower over troops ashore simply because they carried large caliber guns. Because gunboats could move faster and easier than forces on shore, the side that possessed command of the rivers also possessed the initiative. Finally, it showed that gunboats alone could not hold and occupy disputed sites; to do that required both a river force and a land force.

The war in the West was inextricably tied to the ability of either side to control the traffic on the rivers. Though the Confederacy made a serious effort to construct a riverine force of its own, the Union enjoyed many of the same industrial and resource advantages on the rivers that it did on the oceans. As a result, the Confederates sought to control the rivers the same way they attempted to defend their Atlantic coast: by building forts along the river banks. The ensuing battle for the control of the Mississippi and its major tributaries was therefore often characterized by a conflict between Union gunboats, often acting on concert with land forces, and Confederate forts.

STRATEGICALLY, this contest on the western rivers was part of the so-called Anaconda Plan suggested by Winfield Scott in the early months of the war. While the naval blockade sought to cut the South off from outside assistance and weaken its economy, a Union occupation of the Mississippi River Valley would divide the Confederacy not quite in half and reduce the area from which its eastern field armies could draw supplies and support. Though this plan was never formally accepted as Union strategy, it nevertheless served as a kind of blueprint for Union efforts. Just as the blockade dominated Union naval efforts on the oceans, the war for control of the western rivers dominated Union naval efforts in the West.

It is important to acknowledge that during Civil War, "the West" referred not to places like Arizona and New Mexico, or even Texas and Arkansas, which constituted the "trans-Mississippi West." Instead, "the West" referred to the expanse of territory between the Appalachian Mountains and the Mississippi River. The Ohio River marked its northern boundary, and the Gulf of Mexico its southern, and it encompassed all or part of six states: Louisiana, Mississippi, Alabama, Tennessee, Kentucky, and Georgia. It may seem odd to think of Georgia as part of the West since it borders the Atlantic Ocean, but strategically much of Georgia—especially Atlanta—was more closely tied to the West than the East. Both at the time and subsequently, this vast western area got less public attention than the epic battles in Virginia, and until recently Civil War literature tended to treat it as a secondary theater, though a good argument can be made that this expansive region was the decisive theater of the war.[4]

Moreover, there were important differences in the way the war was fought in the West. First of all, the western theater was simply much larger. In the East, which contained both of the national capitals, most of the headline-grabbing battles took place in an area bounded by the Allegheny Mountains to the west and the Chesapeake Bay to the east. Gettysburg marked its northern limit and Petersburg its southern. Though it seemed enormous to the soldiers who had to march across it from place to place, it was a relatively small area, roughly the size of Massachusetts. By contrast, the war in the West ebbed and flowed in an area nearly twenty times as large. Given those dimensions, railroads were critical. Confederate General Braxton Bragg moved his army over a thousand miles by rail to outflank a Union army in 1862; James Longstreet took two divisions across four states by rail to reinforce the western Confederate army on the eve of Chickamauga in 1863; and Joseph E. Johnston and William T. Sherman fought an entire campaign over control of the Western & Atlantic Railroad in 1864 in what may have been the decisive campaign of the war.

Even more critical, however, were the rivers. The rivers in the West were essential not only to the movement of armies, but also to the transport of the supplies necessary to sustain those armies. Transport ships could carry more men and goods, and do so more quickly and efficiently than railroads. And while rampaging cavalry might be able to interrupt railroad traffic by tearing up rails and burning bridges, they could not stop the flow of the rivers. Of course transports could be ambushed by parties on shore, such as the battery the rebels had briefly established at Commerce, Missouri, and for that reason, gunboats were necessary to escort the transports and keep the rivers secure.

In addition, the rivers were geographical realities that affected the strategic planning of both sides. In the East, where the main field armies of both sides slugged it out between Richmond and Washington, the rivers ran mostly west to east—that is horizontally as they appear on a map—athwart any potential Union line of advance, making them defensive barriers that worked to the advantage of the South. One Civil War scholar, Daniel Sutherland, has named the Rappahannock-Rapidan River line in Virginia the "dare mark" beyond which Union armies advanced only at their peril. But with the exception of the Ohio River, the principal rivers in the West ran either north-to-south, like the Mississippi, or south-to-north, like the Cumberland and Tennessee Rivers—that is, vertically as they appear on a map. Consequently they served not as barriers to a Union attack, but as avenues along which Union armies, supported by river gunboats, could advance. For these reasons, Union planners began to consider a river gunboat flotilla from almost the first days of the war.[5]

It was not clear, however, whether the War Department or the Navy Department was to be responsible for these gunboats. According to tradition, the authority of the U.S. Navy stopped at the high tide mark. The Union Navy could, and did, maintain squadrons on the tidal rivers along the eastern seaboard, but the brown water flotillas in the western theater were, both by tradition and by law, the responsibility of the army. In spite of that, building and maintaining gunboats was not something the army was eager to do, nor did army officers have the necessary expertise to do it, which is why Welles sent John Rodgers to Cincinnati to help the army obtain and prepare some armed gunboats for the western campaign, and why his orders had specified that river traffic would remain "under the direction and regulation of the Army."[6]

Welles conceived of Rodgers as a kind of advisor to the army. Consequently, when Rodgers purchased three steamers, *Lexington*, *Conestoga*, and, of course, the *Tyler*, for a total of $62,000 and converted them to wartime use, Welles was more alarmed than pleased; he wanted to make sure that the Navy Department did not get stuck with the bill for these vessels. "All purchases of boats," he wired to Rodgers, "must be made by the War Department." Rodgers informed Welles that General McClellan had, in fact, authorized the purchases, but Welles remained suspicious. When a few months later, Rodgers reported to Welles that he had hired pilots, engineers, and masters for the three gunboats, Welles scrawled a terse note at the bottom of the report: "This whole subject belongs to the War Department."[7]

It soon got even more complicated. Even before Rodgers began converting those three river steamers into timberclad gunboats, Welles heard from the Missouri entrepreneur James Buchanan Eads who proposed to build seven ironclad gunboats for service on the western rivers. Eads promised to complete them in sixty-five days—a month faster

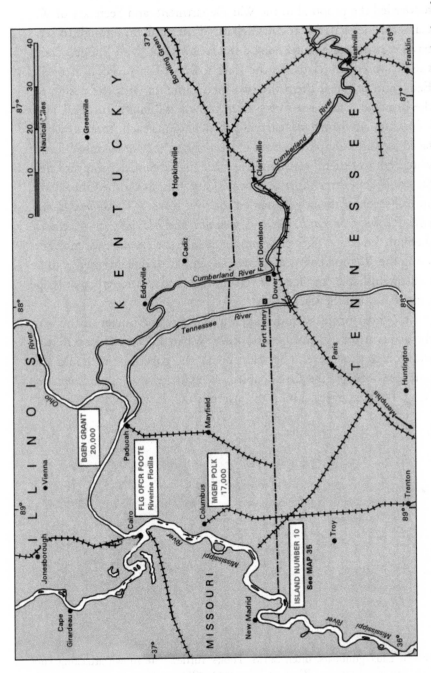

THE WESTERN THEATER: THE RIVER WAR. Map by Bill Clipson, reprinted with permission from *The Naval Institute Historical Atlas of the U.S. Navy* by Craig L. Symonds, © 1995.

than Ericsson built his *Monitor*. Seeing this as an army project, Welles forwarded the proposal to the War Department, and Secretary of War Cameron delegated it to McClellan. Welles unbent enough to send naval constructor Samuel Pook out west to confer with Rodgers about the proposed ironclads. In the river town of Cairo, Pook met with Eads, and between them the two men came up with the design for the ironclad river vessels ever after known as "Pook's Turtles." They were casemate ironclads, carrying thirteen guns each, three of which faced forward. Despite 122 tons of iron armor, they drew only 6 feet of water. Four of them were converted at Eads' Carondelet shipyard near St. Louis, and three more at Mound City, Illinois on the Ohio River, and all seven of them were named for river towns—*Carondelet, Louis-ville, Pittsburg, St. Louis, Cairo, Cincinnati,* and *Mound City*—and were therefore known as City-class gunboats. Like the *Passaic*-class monitors along the Atlantic coast, they were so similar to one another as to be indistinguishable, and for that reason, each had a different color stripe painted around the stack.[8]

Like most projects undertaken quickly at the outset of the war, the acquisition did not go smoothly. When Eads proposed that in addition to these seven City-class boats, the government should also purchase from him the giant double-hulled salvage vessel called *Submarine No. 7,* Rodgers rejected it on the grounds that it was "old and rotten,"

Two of Eads' gunboats, often called "Pook's Turtles," are shown attacking Fort Henry on the Tennessee River on February 6, 1862, in this contemporary sketch by Thomas Nast. (Courtesy of the Naval Historical Center)

though his real objection was that at over 200 feet and a thousand tons, he believed it was simply too large to be efficient. The army's theater commander, John C. Fremont, thought otherwise and bought it, contracting independently with Eads to convert it into USS *Benton*, named in honor of Fremont's father-in-law, Thomas Hart Benton. Fremont subsequently purchased another of Eads' salvage boats, the *New Era*, eventually commanded by William "Dirty Bill" Porter, the brother of David Dixon Porter. It was renamed the *Essex* in honor of the Porters' father who had commanded the frigate *Essex* in the War of 1812.* These two additions gave the Union a total of nine ironclads on the western rivers, plus the three timberclads.[9]

The squabbling about acquisition of the *Benton* and *Essex*, however, had aroused Fremont's pique at Rodgers for interfering (as Fremont saw it) in the army's business. Fremont complained to Welles about Rodgers' uncooperativeness, and to pacify the Pathfinder, Welles replaced Rodgers with Andrew Hull Foote. Welles wrote the order on August 30, 1861, ten days after Rodgers conducted his sortie to Commerce, Missouri. Welles offered Rodgers the option of remaining as Foote's second in command, or coming east to take a post in the salt water navy. Rodgers eagerly opted for the latter, arriving in Annapolis in time to join Du Pont's expedition to Port Royal.[10]

Foote, a Christian warrior who tied shipboard discipline to the Christian ethic, banning "profane language" and mandating a strict observance of the Sabbath, suffered from the same ambiguous command structure that Rodgers had. Welles was willing for the Navy Department to pay the salaries of the *officers* who were assigned to riverine duty, but since the river gunboats were part of the War Department, he insisted that the army should pay the salaries of the crew. Fremont, however, felt no such responsibility, and the result was that the men did not get paid at all. Foote soon reported to Welles that the men and their families were starving for lack of pay. Nor was it clear which service was to provide powder and shot for the guns. These jurisdictional disputes

---

*William D. Porter was the older brother (by five years) of David Dixon Porter and the younger foster brother (by seven years) of David G. Farragut. He earned his nickname "Dirty Bill" by allegedly profiting from his superintendence of supplies for the Navy in the 1850s.

were eventually resolved, but the status of the river gunboats within the Union war structure remained vague.

Foote chafed at this awkward command structure. It was especially annoying when some brigadier general, often a volunteer officer who had been a town mayor or county judge only months before, presumed to give orders to Captain Foote, who, despite more than forty years of professional service, bore a rank that was the statutory equivalent of an army colonel. To resolve that problem, the Union created the rank of Navy Flag Officer, which was equivalent to a major general in the army. That gave Foote more leverage in dealing with the army high command in the West, but it did not fully resolve the question of authority, for there was still no unified command. Even after October of 1862 when the Mississippi Squadron was formally turned over to the navy, there was no existing protocol for the cooperation of soldiers ashore and sailors afloat. The practical result of this awkward command structure was that if the army and navy commanders agreed to cooperate, things got done. If not, success seldom followed.

THE CONFEDERATES, TOO, worked to create a riverine force, but as in the saltwater war, the shortage of marine engines, iron plating, and adequate facilities to convert vessels to wartime use put the South at a tremendous disadvantage. As Jefferson Davis put it after the war, "The efforts which were put forth to resist the operations on the Western Rivers were . . . necessarily very limited. There was a lack of skilled labor, of shipyards, and materials." Though Confederates recognized the crucial role that ironclad warships could play on the western rivers, the material shortfalls meant that they could not produce them in time to assert control of the rivers.[11]

In October of 1861, the Confederate Navy Department contracted to build two ironclad warships at Memphis and two more at New Orleans. John T. Shirley got the contract for the two at Memphis—to be named the *Tennessee* and the *Arkansas*; and E. C. Murray got the contract for the New Orleans ships—to be named the *Louisiana* and the *Mississippi*. They would be large casemate ironclads, nearly 100 feet longer than the Union's City-class ironclads, and collectively they had the potential to give the rebels superiority on the western rivers. Predictably, however, a shortage of both materiel and skilled labor created the inevitable delays. Though Shirley's contract called for him to deliver the ships by Christmas of 1861 (which would have been a month ahead of Pook's Turtles), they were still unready in the spring of 1862. Manpower was one problem. Shirley later complained that although Confederate Army authorities had promised to supply him with the labor force he needed, few men arrived despite his repeated entreaties. Major General Leonidas Polk sent him "six or eight men," but he needed more than a hundred, and as a result, the work lagged.[12]

Polk did make some independent efforts of his own to acquire a river force. The same month that work began on the ironclads at Memphis, Polk purchased the large river steamer *Eastport* on the Tennessee River and sent her to the small town of Cerro Gordo, Tennessee, to be converted into an ironclad. She was a huge ship at 280 feet, with an engine plant that had earned her a reputation as one of the fastest vessels on the river. But here, too, the Confederacy struggled to obtain the necessary materials to make the conversion a reality. It became evident almost at once that it would be impossible to find enough iron to armor all of the *Eastport*'s enormous superstructure, and so Navy Lieutenant Isaac Brown, who supervised the conversion, constructed a double bulkhead of planks 20 to 24 inches apart and stuffed the space in between with cotton, thus making the *Eastport* a "cottonclad." Creative as this was, it was also a kind of metaphor for the materiel problems the Confederacy experienced throughout the war on the western rivers. And even these efforts went for naught because long before any of these ships was ready for service, the Union smashed through the Confederates' defensive fortifications to seize the bases where they were being built.[13]

THE CONFEDERATE THEATER COMMANDER, Albert Sidney Johnston, sought to protect his far-flung command in the West by creating a string of strong defensive positions from the Mississippi to the Cumberland Gap. The western anchor of this defensive line was at Columbus, Kentucky, the highest piece of dry ground on the Mississippi River between Cairo and Vicksburg. Though Kentucky had declared its neutrality, Polk had concluded that the advantage of holding Columbus outweighed the risk of alienating Kentuckians, and he occupied the site in September of 1861. The Confederacy also built fortifications on the Tennessee River (Fort Henry) and the Cumberland River (Fort Donelson), both of them in Tennessee just below the Kentucky State line. Johnston himself established his headquarters at Bowling Green, Kentucky, eighty miles to the east, and another, smaller Confederate force occupied the Cumberland Gap through the Appalachians another 180 miles farther east. From end to end, this lengthy defensive barrier was more than 350 miles long as the crow flies, and its weakness was not only that it left the initiative to the Federals, but also that it would prove difficult for the various elements of the rebel army to support one another.

The advantage of possessing a riverine force became evident in the first confrontation along this defensive line in November of 1861 (at about the same time that Du Pont was attacking Port Royal in far away South Carolina). The Union commander, Ulysses S. Grant, did not have the strength to dislodge Polk's entrenched force at Columbus, but he determined to attack the weaker Confederate contingent across the Mississippi River at Belmont, Missouri. On November 9, he loaded 3,100 soldiers on board several army transports, and escorted by the timberclads *Lexington* and *Tyler*, he moved down the Mississippi to disembark a few miles above Belmont. His men easily overran the rebel camp, but when his green troops stopped to loot the enemy tents, Polk sent reinforcements across the river from Columbus. Threatened now by superior forces, Grant ordered a hasty retreat back to the transports. Things might have ended disastrously had not the *Lexington* and *Tyler* "opened a brisk fire of grape and canister" on the pursuing rebels. Their 8-inch guns "cut up the enemy in a most terrible manner," and gave Grant the time he needed to herd his men back aboard the transports. Grant himself was the last to embark, riding his horse dramatically up the gangplank. The timberclads not only salvaged Grant's first campaign, they ensured that once back aboard the transports, his soldiers were secure from rebel pursuit since the Confederates did not have a comparable riverine force.[14]

Grant's near disaster at Belmont did not deter him from thinking about further offensive operations, and he soon focused his attention on Fort Henry on the eastern bank of the Tennessee River about 80 miles downriver from (that is, north of) Cerro Gordo. Fort Henry was vulnerable because it had been sited on the low ground of the river's

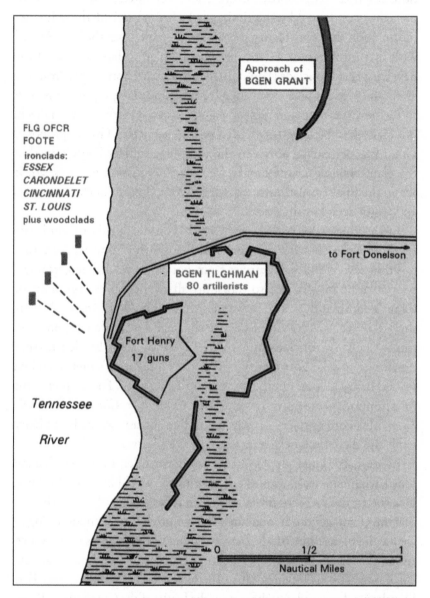

FLG OFCR
FOOTE
ironclads:
ESSEX
CARONDELET
CINCINNATI
ST. LOUIS
plus woodclads

Approach of
BGEN GRANT

to Fort Donelson

BGEN TILGHMAN
80 artillerists

Fort Henry
17 guns

Tennessee

River

0   1/2   1
Nautical Miles

THE UNION ATTACK ON FORT HENRY, FEBRUARY 6, 1862. Map by Bill Clipson, reprinted with permission from *The Naval Institute Historical Atlas of the U.S. Navy* by Craig L. Symonds, © 1995.

flood plain thus forfeiting the one great advantage that shore fortifications still had over gunboats: firing from an elevated position. A reconnaissance conducted by the timberclad *Conestoga* yielded the further information that Fort Henry was also vulnerable from the rear. Armed with that information, Grant developed a plan to have several of the new City-class ironclads (Pook's Turtles) bombard Fort Henry from the river while his soldiers attacked it from behind. He proposed his plan to the new theater commander, Major General Henry Wager Halleck, but Halleck was still getting settled in and he rejected Grant's proposal. Grant was persistent, however, and after Flag Officer Foote joined in the plan, Halleck relented and gave Grant permission to go ahead. It set up the first serious confrontation between Union ironclad gunboats and Confederate fortifications.[15]

In the first week of February, 1862, Foote's flotilla of gunboats escorted thirteen army transports loaded with Union soldiers to a position several miles downriver from Fort Henry. Thirteen steamers proved to be insufficient to transport all twenty-three regiments of Grant's command, so the movement had to made in stages. Nevertheless, by February 5 Grant's entire command was safely ashore, and four of Foote's ironclads plus the three timberclads headed further downriver to take Fort Henry under fire while Grant's men marched toward its back door. On the morning of February 6, Foote ordered his four ironclads—the City-class gunboats *Carondelet*, *Cincinnati*, and *St. Louis*, plus Porter's *Essex*—to advance in line abreast against Fort Henry while the three timberclads stayed back as a reserve.[16]

Inside Fort Henry, the Confederate commander, Brigadier General Lloyd Tilghman, had few illusions that his fort could hold out for long. Heavy rain the previous several days had raised the level of the river so that the Union gunboats could fire directly into the fort without having to elevate their guns. Indeed, the parade ground of the fort was under water. Aware that he could not repel a concentrated and coordinated attack, Tilghman sent his infantry off to the larger, stronger (and dryer) Fort Donelson a dozen miles to the east on the banks of the Cumberland River, and he prepared to hold off the Union gunboats as long as possible with his artillery alone to allow the bulk of his garrison to escape. With only eighty-seven men, barely enough to man the guns, he stood on the ramparts and directed his gunners to open fire on the odd-looking Union ironclads.

Most of the Confederate shells glanced off the armor plating of the river gunboats, though the impact often jarred men off their feet inside the casemate. Foote himself had the wind knocked out of him when a shot smashed into the armored wall of the *Cincinnati* near where he was standing. Nor were the ironclads invulnerable despite their 3 inches of iron armor. This became evident 45 minutes into the fight when a shot from Fort Henry's largest gun, a 10-inch Columbiad, punched through the armor of the *Essex* and penetrated to the boiler. The boiler exploded and the superheated steam killed ten men, scalding a score more including William D. Porter. Though the *Essex* remained afloat, it drifted downriver and out of the fight. Tilghman's men could not duplicate this feat, however, because soon afterward, during a hurried reloading, a priming wire broke off inside the vent of the big Columbiad, effectively spiking it. Tilghman's only rifled gun burst, and soon afterward a 42-pounder also burst killing two men. The other rebel guns were too weak to penetrate the armor of Foote's gunboats, and the fight soon became one-sided. A half hour later, Tilghman ordered the flag lowered and the fighting stopped.[17]

Foote accepted the surrender of the fort on behalf of the Navy, and took some gratification in being able to turn it over to Grant's soldiers when they arrived about an hour later. Foote then ordered his gunboats further upriver (southward) to take possession of the Memphis, Clarksville, and Louisville Railroad bridge over the Tennessee River that connected Bowling Green with Columbus. Once that bridge was in Union hands, Albert Sidney Johnston's army at Bowling Green and Leonidas Polk's force at Columbus were effectively cut off from one another. On February 8, Union soldiers completely dismantled the bridge making the interruption permanent. In effect, by breaking through the Fort Henry barrier on the Tennessee River, Foote had rendered the Confederate positions at both Columbus and Bowling Green untenable. Eventually Johnston and Polk would fall back out of Kentucky, through Tennessee, all the way to Corinth, Mississippi.[18]

Nor was that all. Foote had kept the three Union timberclads in reserve during the fight, but within hours of the Confederate surrender of Fort Henry, they pushed upriver past the railroad bridge. The rebel transports and supply ships fled southward, several ran themselves into the river bank so their crews could escape. By nightfall, the Union

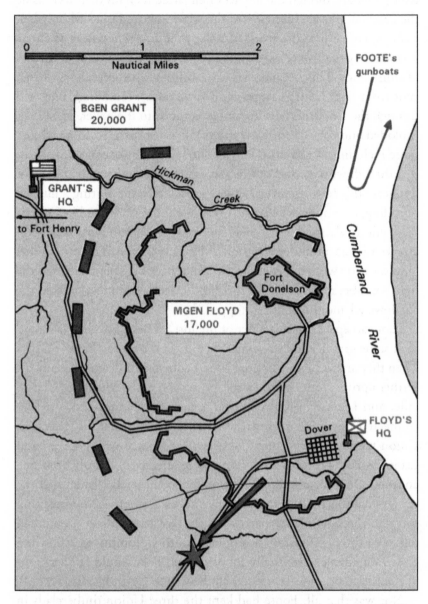

THE UNION ATTACK ON FORT DONELSON, FEBRUARY 12–16, 1862. Map by Bill Clipson, reprinted with permission from *The Naval Institute Historical Atlas of the U.S. Navy* by Craig L. Symonds, © 1995.

timberclads were approaching Cerro Gordo where they found the still-incomplete *Eastport*. It had been hurriedly scuttled, but was still salvageable. Union sailors on the *Tyler* stopped the leaks and began pumping her out. Eventually she was towed north to Cairo where she was completed and became another Union ironclad. Meanwhile, the *Conestoga* and *Lexington* continued up the Tennessee River all the way to Florence, Alabama, where the townspeople pleaded with the senior Union officer, Seth Ledyard Phelps, not to burn their town. Moved by their entreaties, and recalling the number of Unionist sympathizers who had come out to the river bank to cheer the gunboats in their way south, Phelps not only spared the town, he declined to burn the railroad bridge over the Tennessee. That was a mistake. Within weeks, Albert Sidney Johnston's army would use that bridge in its retreat from Nashville to Corinth.[19]

The strategic consequences of the Union victory at Fort Henry were enormous. With a handful of gunboats, the Union had compelled the enemy to evacuate most of two states (Kentucky and Tennessee). Moreover, that easy success suggested that further Union triumphs were imminent. Sidney Johnston himself reported to Richmond that the fall of Fort Henry proved that "the best open earth works are not reliable to meet successfully a vigorous attack of iron clad gunboats."[20]

NOT ONE TO REST ON HIS LAURELS, Grant set his sights next on Fort Donelson on the Cumberland River. But despite his instinct to push on at once, his move was delayed by political and geographic realities. Halleck once again urged caution, suggesting that Grant fortify himself at Fort Henry, promising to send him a supply of picks and shovels for the purpose. A more serious impediment was the fact that while Fort Donelson was only a short 12-mile march eastward for the men of Grant's army, it was more than a hundred miles away for Foote's gunboats which had to steam back down the Tennessee to the Ohio River, up the Ohio to the mouth of the Cumberland, and then up the Cumberland to Fort Donelson. Moreover, Foote had to effect repairs on his banged-up ironclads, especially the badly damaged *Essex*. Consequently, only the *Carondelet* went directly to Donelson; the rest of Foote's flotilla returned to Cairo for repair. Halleck, now suddenly in a hurry, suspected that Foote was dragging his feet, and urged him to move at once even if his vessels were not ready. Grant, too, urged Foote to hurry, though he was more circumspect in his request acknowledging the ambiguous command relationship between the services. Foote notified Grant that he would leave Cairo at once.[21]

Meanwhile, on February 13, the *Carondelet* tested the rebel batteries at Fort Donelson. An early shot from *Carondelet* dismounted one of the rebel guns and killed the officer in charge, but the rebel guns at Donelson were better sited than those at Fort Henry, and a 128-pound iron bolt fired from a 10-inch Columbiad penetrated the armor on the *Carondelet* and wounded several sailors. After that, Captain Henry Walke retired downriver to carry on a desultory long-range artillery duel while he waited for the rest of the squadron. It arrived overnight, and the next morning Grant rode down to the riverbank and went on board the *St. Louis* to talk to Foote. Grant anticipated that Foote's ironclads could do to the batteries at Fort Donelson what they had done at Fort Henry. Foote was less sanguine, suggesting that Walke's experience the day before proved that the circumstances at Fort Donelson were different. Unwilling to disappoint Grant, however, he agreed to mount an immediate attack.[22]

Within hours, four Union ironclads and two timberclads were steaming slowly toward the rebel position. But as Foote had warned, Fort Donelson was no Fort Henry. A sprawling fortified camp near the small town of Dover, Tennessee, it was sited on high, firm ground and protected by two tiers of northward-facing heavy guns that commanded a mile-long stretch of river. This time the rebel guns fired from elevated platforms, and their shot and shell plunged down on the Union gunboats striking them not on the armored walls of their casemates but on their vulnerable overheads. Foote's *St. Louis* was struck fifty-nine times, including one shot that penetrated the armor of the pilothouse, mortally wounded the pilot, and struck Foote in the ankle. Despite his wound, Foote took the wheel from the dying pilot. But the shot had also wrecked the steering gear, and the *St. Louis* became unmanageable. On the *Louisville*, too, a shot cut the tiller ropes, and both vessels drifted downriver out of the fight. That re-energized the rebel gunners ashore who concentrated their fire on the *Carondelet* and *Pittsburg* until they began to take on so much water they were in danger of sinking. One of the *Carondelet*'s big rifled guns burst, and soon afterward Foote called off the fight. This time, guns ashore had repulsed guns afloat.[23]

Of course there was still Grant's army, which was deployed around the perimeter of the extensive rebel fort, and despite their victory over the gunboats, the Confederate commanders at Fort Donelson could not agree on what to do next. Part of the responsibility for the confusion can be laid at the feet of Albert Sidney Johnston. Though Jefferson Davis considered Johnston to be the best soldier in the South, the rebel theater commander made several poor decisions in his first important campaign. The first of them was to remain in Bowling Green and attempt to coordinate the forces of his far-flung command by telegraph. The second was Johnston's allocation of resources. Aware that Grant planned to move against Fort Donelson, he could not decide whether to concentrate his forces at the fort in order to defend it, or abandon the fort in order to build up his field force. In the event, he tried to have it both ways, reinforcing the fort with Simon Buckner's 8,000-man division, but unwilling to put all his eggs in one basket, he rejected the kind of concentration that might have allowed him to defeat Grant in the field. Buckner's men boosted the garrison's strength to 15,000, but in the end all that did was increase the number of prisoners Grant bagged when he eventually took the fort.[24]

Johnston's third mistake, perhaps his worst, was leaving command of the fort in utterly incompetent hands. John Floyd, who was the senior officer present, and Gideon Pillow, his second in command, were arguably the two worst general officers ever to wear Confederate gray. Floyd, a former governor of Virginia, had been James Buchanan's Secretary of War. He had resigned in December 1860 ostensibly because Buchanan refused to evacuate Fort Sumter, but mainly to avoid an impending indictment for mishandling funds. Appointed a Confederate major general despite having no military training or background, Floyd now found himself in command of the lynchpin of Confederate defenses in the West. Pillow at least had some military experience, for he had fought as a militia general in Mexico and against Grant at Belmont. But like Floyd, Pillow proved to be more concerned about avoiding public criticism than achieving military success. Moreover there was a history of animosity between Pillow and the third in command, Simon Buckner.

Even though the fort's water battery had driven off the Union gunboats, Floyd and Pillow decided to try to break out of Fort Donelson to save their garrison, and on February 15, they launched an assault against Grant's right wing south of the fort. The attack achieved initial success and for a moment the road south was open. Having won this small victory, however, Floyd now decided that instead of evacuating the fort, he would stay and try to defeat Grant in a general engagement. It was a mistake. Grant brought up reinforcements and closed the breach, trapping the Confederates inside. At this point, Floyd and Pillow showed their true colors. Deciding that the greatest possible calamity for the South would be the loss of two such important generals as themselves, they orchestrated a pantomime wherein Floyd turned formal command over to Pillow, and Pillow then turned it over to Buckner. After that charade, the two senior officers fled the fort on a small steamer leaving Buckner holding the bag.

Buckner, who knew Grant from the Old Army, sent out Major Nathaniel Cheairs with a flag of truce to suggest "the appointment of commissioners to agree upon terms of capitulation." The first Union officer Cheairs met was Charles F. Smith who had been one of Grant's instructors at West Point, and who was now one of his division commanders. Smith replied gruffly that "I'll make no terms with rebels with arms in their hands—my terms are unconditional and immediate surrender." Nevertheless, Smith passed the message and its bearers on to Grant who responded similarly, writing to Buckner: "Yours of this date proposing Armistice and Appointment of Commissioners to settle terms of Capitulation is just received. No terms except unconditional and immediate surrender can be accepted." Then he added: "I propose to move immediately upon your works." Though Buckner thought the note unchivalrous, he accepted. Grant's victory, and the terms he demanded, made him a hero in the northern papers where his name, U.S. Grant, was universally rendered as "Unconditional Surrender Grant." It was the first step on a road that would lead Grant to Union army command and eventually to the White House.[25]

The capture of Fort Donelson was as strategically significant as the fall of Fort Henry. Not only did it open another major line of advance into the South's heartland, leading directly to the capture of Nashville, but in addition the surrender of an entire Confederate army punctured the aura of invincibility that most southerners, and even some northerners, had embraced after Bull Run the previous July. This time it was the Union army and not the river gunboats that had played the decisive role, but both campaigns had suggested that when army and navy forces worked together, they could achieve decisive results.

Having opened both the Tennessee and Cumberland Rivers, Grant sent his army southward, up the Tennessee River to Pittsburg Landing near a small country church called Shiloh. Foote left the timberclads *Lexington* and *Tyler* on the Tennessee to support him, a decision that paid important dividends when the Union forces around Shiloh Church were attacked there by Sidney Johnston's army on April 6. Driven back to the river's edge by the furious Confederate assault, Grant's men were able to hold on in part because of the support from the two timberclads, which fired their 8-inch shells over the heads of the Union soldiers clinging to the river's edge and into the ranks of the Confederates. Even after the fighting stopped at dusk, the two timberclads kept up the firing all night, lobbing shells into the rebel bivouac, and the next morning, the reinforced Union army counterattacked, reclaiming all the ground it had lost the day before. Though the two-day Battle of Shiloh was a tactical draw, the outcome was a strategic victory for the Union, for Johnston's assault had failed to regain the initiative in the West. Moreover, Johnston himself was one of the mortal casualties of the first day's fighting. The Confederates, now under the command of Major General P.G.T. Beauregard, fell back to Corinth, Mississippi, where they entrenched.[26]

WHILE GRANT ASCENDED THE TENNESSEE RIVER, Foote returned to Cairo with his ironclads to prepare for a descent of the Mississippi. In this effort, he would partner with Major General John Pope. The Confederates had evacuated Columbus after the fall of Fort Henry, and their main defensive position now was at Island No. 10, 60 miles south of Columbus just below the Tennessee-Kentucky state line. This island, so named simply because it was the tenth one in numbered sequence from the confluence of the Ohio and Mississippi Rivers at Cairo, dominated a hairpin turn of the Mississippi River and was supported by fortifications ashore and a small squadron of gunboats under Confederate Navy Commander George N. Hollins.

These defenses created a strategic puzzle for the Union attackers. Pope had twenty thousand men at New Madrid, Missouri, on the western bank of the river, but they could not get across the river to assault the

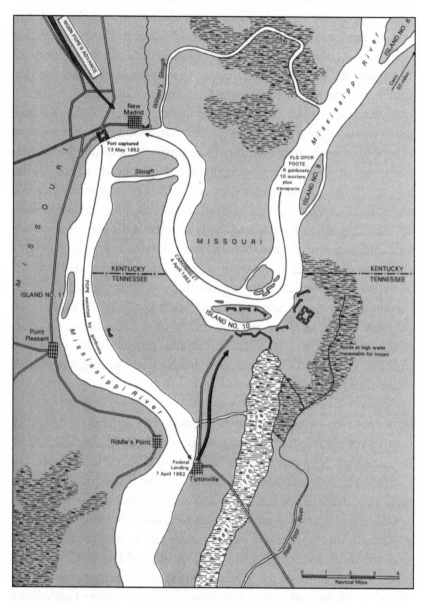

THE UNION ATTACK ON ISLAND NUMBER 10, MARCH 15–APRIL 7, 1862. Map by Bill Clipson, reprinted with permission from *The Naval Institute Historical Atlas of the U.S. Navy* by Craig L. Symonds, © 1995.

rebel fortifications because of Hollins's rebel gunboats and rebel batteries on the opposite shore. If Pope's men crossed the river *above* Island No. 10 where Foote's squadron commanded the river, he would be on the wrong side of a swampy morass known as Reel Foot Lake that blocked his approach to the enemy fortifications. The only way Pope could attack the site was somehow to get his army across the river *below* the fort, and that could be accomplished only if Foote could get his ironclads past the fort to neutralize Hollins's gunboats and escort the army transports across the river. Foote was reluctant to attack the rebel batteries directly not only because of what had happened at Fort Donelson, but because of the southward flow of the Mississippi River: any ships crippled by enemy fire would drift not northward to safety (as on the Tennessee and Cumberland Rivers) but southward into enemy territory.

Though still hobbled by the wounds he had received at Fort Donelson, Foote sought to find the key to this strategic puzzle. He first tried to blast the rebels out of their position by using "bombs": huge mortars on flat-bottomed rafts that could fire their 13-inch shells (bombs) in a high arcing trajectory for up to 3 miles. Though these did considerable damage to the rebel defenses, they did not compel a capitulation. Foote next tried to find a way around Island No. 10 by widening and deepening an old slough that bypassed the rebel fort entirely. In the end, however, the solution proved to be more straightforward. Henry Walke offered to run the *Carondelet* past the rebel fortifications at night to link up with Pope at New Madrid. Choosing the night of April 4 for the attempt, Walke was halfway past the defenses when a clump of soot in the stack caught fire and a flame—like a beacon light—flared out of the top of the stack. The Confederate batteries opened at once, but Walke did not stop to shoot it out with them. His only hope now was in speed—and luck. After several harrowing minutes, he made it safely past the batteries and was soon moored alongside the dock at New Madrid where he was greeted by a jubilant John Pope. Walke's exploit encouraged Foote to send the *Pittsburg* past the batteries the next night. Then on April 7—the day of the Union counterattack at Shiloh—the two ironclads escorted Pope's men across the Mississippi River to the unprotected rear of the rebel defenses at Island No. 10, and Pope won an easy victory capturing the entire Confederate garrison of six thousand men.[27]

More than in any other campaign until Vicksburg, the Union success at Island No. 10 demonstrated what could be accomplished when Union army and navy forces cooperated. Pope's army was four times as strong as the Confederate garrison at Island No. 10, and Foote's flotilla was at least four times stronger than Hollins's little squadron, but neither Union force, acting on its own, could have taken Island No. 10. Together, they made it look easy. In this combined operation, the whole was greater than the sum of its parts.

The Union victory at Island No. 10 opened the upper Mississippi in the same way that victories at Fort Henry and Fort Donelson had opened the Tennessee and Cumberland Rivers. Only Fort Pillow remained between the Union river fleet and Memphis where the Confederates were still trying to complete their two ironclads: the *Arkansas* and the *Tennessee*. Concerned about their safety, Navy Secretary Mallory ordered that the two warships should be sent south at once to prevent their being captured while sitting passively along the wharf as the *Eastport* had been. The *Arkansas* was quickly launched and sent down the Mississippi and then up the Yazoo River where work continued at a makeshift shipyard. The *Tennessee*, however, was a mere frame with partial planking and not yet seaworthy. If Memphis fell, she would have to be burned.[28]

THAT SAME WEEK, a thousand miles to the south as the river winds, Union Flag Officer David Glasgow Farragut was preparing to assault the Confederate forts that guarded the approach to New Orleans from the Gulf of Mexico. From the outset it had been a key element of Lincoln's strategic vision to assault the Confederacy at different places at the same time, which he believed would compel the rebels either to divide their forces, or choose which point to defend. Though Lincoln had been unable to get most of his generals to see it—or at least to act on it—in the Spring of 1862 this concept was at the heart of Union operations in the Mississippi Valley. For his part, Jefferson Davis did not believe that a naval force could get past the river forts below New Orleans, and he therefore left the city relatively unprotected, sending all available troops to Albert Sidney Johnston for his attack on Grant at Shiloh. If Farragut could somehow get past the river forts, New Orleans would be defenseless.

The two big Confederate ironclads being constructed at New Orleans were no more ready for sea than the ones at Memphis, but the Confederates did have another ironclad warship. The CSS *Manassas* was a curious vessel. Originally the icebreaker *Enoch Train*, she had been brought to New Orleans before the war to be used as a tugboat. When the war began, she was purchased by entrepreneurs who planned to use her as a privateer. They completely rebuilt her into a cigar-shaped ironclad ram with a single gun facing forward, and in the fall of 1861, she was the only operational ironclad on the river. (The City-class Union ironclads were not launched until January, 1862.) Not about to let such a useful weapon remain in private hands, Confederate Navy Commander George Hollins seized her, virtually at gunpoint, and sent her downriver to attack the Union squadron at the Head of Passes. There she successfully rammed and sank the USS *Richmond*, which settled to the shallow bottom of the river with most of her hull still above the waterline. The *Richmond* was salvaged, but Union blockading ships subsequently withdrew from the Head of Passes to continue their vigil from the safer waters of the Gulf where the *Manassas* dared not venture.

Farragut assumed command of the Union squadron in February, and his first task was to re-establish a Union presence at the Head of Passes inside the river delta. That proved difficult since the sand bars at the mouth of the river had not been dredged since the war began and had silted up. Getting the screw steamer *Pensacola* and the side-wheeler *Mississippi* over the bar took eleven days, and the 23-foot draft *Merrimack*-class heavy frigate *Colorado* failed to get over at all. Even the 16-foot draft *Brooklyn* struck the bar on her first attempt and had to be towed across. Consequently, not until mid-April did Farragut have most of his fleet assembled at the Head of Passes for an assault on the river forts.[29]

In the meantime, there was a kerfluffle within the Union command about whether Farragut was, in fact, the right man for the job. Concerned when Farragut sent in a request for more shallow-draft steamers, Gustavus Fox began to wonder if the 60-year-old Flag Officer was sufficiently aggressive to carry out his assigned task. Fox wrote privately to David Dixon Porter, who commanded the mortar boats in Farragut's squadron, asking him if the government had made a mistake in appointing Farragut. Porter and Farragut were foster brothers. Porter's natural father, Navy Captain David Porter, had effectively adopted the 9-year-old James Farragut (who subsequently changed his first name to David in gratitude) three years before David Dixon Porter was born. Now, however, Porter saw an opportunity to supersede his older brother and sibling rival. "Men of his age in a seafaring life are not fit for the command of important enterprises," the 48-year-old Porter wrote back to Fox. "What his plans are, I don't know. He talks very much at random at times, and rather underrates the difficulties before him, without fairly comprehending them." This back-channel effort to sabotage Farragut's command failed, mainly because by the time Fox was in receipt of those letters, Farragut had already moved upriver to take the rebel forts under fire.[30]

The forts at Plaquamine Bend were not recent log-and-earth constructions like Forts Henry and Donelson, but masonry fortresses constructed by the Army Corps of Engineers in the 1830s and 40s. The original Union plan, suggested by David Dixon Porter, was to pound them into rubble using bomb vessels—the same type of 13-inch mortars

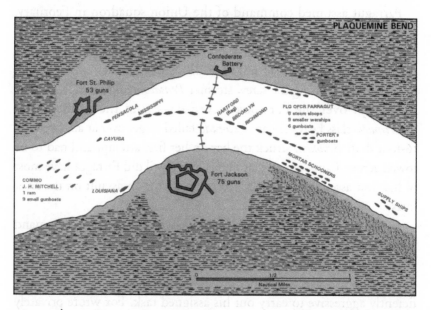

FARRAGUT'S ATTACK ON THE RIVER FORTS BELOW NEW ORLEANS, APRIL 24, 1862. Map by Bill Clipson, reprinted with permission from *The Naval Institute Historical Atlas of the U.S. Navy* by Craig L. Symonds, © 1995.

that Foote had used to try to blast the rebels out of Island No. 10. Porter was convinced that his bomb vessels could destroy the forts in two days and open the river to the wooden steamers. Farragut was skeptical of the "Chowder Pots" (as the sailors called them), but he was willing to give them a try. The bombardment began on April 18, and for five days the mortars rained bombs down on the rebel forts. While they did a great deal of damage, they did not render the forts defenseless. Finally on April 23, Farragut decided that he had given them a sufficient trial, and he resolved to run his warships past the forts at night. The result was one of the most dramatic set piece battles of the naval war.[31]

Farragut got his ships under way at two o'clock in the morning on April 24, 1862. The Confederates had placed a boom composed of eight dismasted schooners connected by heavy chains across the river, and bold Union volunteers had cut a gap in that barrier the day before. Now, in the darkest part of the night, the first of Farragut's ships, the *Cayuga*, passed safely through this gap. Spotting the darker shadow moving on the inky river, the gunners in the rebel forts opened fire and orange stabs of flame lit up the darkness. Gunners afloat and ashore fired as fast as they could load as the rest of Farragut's ships made their way one by one through the gap in the river barrier. The Confederates added to the smoke and confusion of the battle by sending fire rafts downriver into the midst of the Union fleet. Maneuvering to avoid one of these, the *Hartford* went aground under the guns of Fort St. Philip. Soon the flagship was on fire "halfway to her tops," and her crew fought the fire and the enemy at the same time. In the midst of this, Farragut's signal officer dropped 20-pound shells onto the raft, and when they exploded, it broke up the raft, which swirled away downriver. The crew of the *Hartford* got the flames under control, and soon she freed herself from the shallow water to continue upriver.[32]

Farragut had calculated from the beginning that the most serious threat to his squadron was not the two forts, but the Confederate naval squadron. On paper it looked quite imposing: a dozen ships, including three ironclads. In reality it was a hodgepodge of unfinished, or partially finished, ships divided into three different commands. The ironclad *Louisiana* had both her armor and her guns on board, but no steering mechanism; the *Mississippi* was a mere skeleton and could not participate in the fight at all. Moreover, the rebel fleet lacked unified command. Initially, George Hollins had commanded it, but that officer was now a thousand miles upriver helping (unsuccessfully) to defend Island No. 10. Commander John K. Mitchell of the Confederate Navy had authority over the ironclads *Manassas* and *Louisiana*, plus the gunboat *McRae*, but eight other small gunboats belonged either to the Louisiana State Navy or the Confederate Army. Most of the Confederate vessels were small one-gun rams, and easy meat for Farragut's big ships. It was the two ironclads that worried him, and rightly so.

The *Manassas* attacked first, coming downriver under the command of Lieutenant Alexander F. Warley. Gamely, Warley attempted to ram the big USS *Pensacola*. Missing her, Warley headed next for the USS *Mississippi*, striking her a glancing blow and doing serious but not fatal damage. Undiscouraged, Warley then aimed his ironclad at the *Brooklyn*, firing its forward gun just before the collision. The shot plunged into the *Brooklyn* and lodged in the sandbags that the *Brooklyn*'s crew had placed around the steam drum. The collision itself was indecisive since the *Manassas* had lost much of her momentum from earlier damage, and her weak engines could not generate enough speed. Consequently, the impact was a "feeble bump" though it managed to stave in 5 feet of hull. It was not fatal, however, since Captain Thomas T. Craven, like all the Union captains, had placed anchor chains over the sides of his ship to act as a kind of chain mail, as John Winslow would subsequently do on the *Kearsarge* in its battle against CSS *Alabama* two years later off Cherbourg. By now the *Manassas* had been all but wrecked from hurling herself into enemy ships, and Warley was forced to run her ashore where his crew escaped into the swamp. A boat crew from the *Mississippi* went aboard the abandoned craft and set her on fire.[33]

The only other serious threat to Farragut's squadron was the *Louisiana*. At 264 feet, and mounting sixteen guns including two 7-inch Brooke rifles, she was a formidable warship. Her problem was that though her engines were functional, the propellers needed to steer her had not been installed. As a result, she was essentially a floating battery that had to be towed from place to place. When Farragut's wooden ships came upriver past the forts, the *Louisiana* was moored against the northern (eastern) bank above Fort St. Philip. Her guns, especially those Brooke rifles, did some damage to Farragut's *Hartford* as it passed, but because she could not maneuver she could use only six of her sixteen guns, and once the Federal warships had run the gauntlet, there was no way for her to continue the fight. Like the forts, she was rendered impotent as soon as the Federal warships passed upriver where she could not follow. When, several days later, the forts eventually surrendered to Porter, the crew of the *Louisiana* set their ship afire and set her adrift. She blew up off Fort Jackson in a spectacular explosion.[34]

By dawn, fourteen U.S. Navy warships were safely in the Mississippi River above the rebel forts. Three more Union ships had turned back and were with Porter's mortar squadron below the forts. Only one, the *Varuna*, had sunk after being rammed by two of the rebel gunboats, though she had managed to sink both of her attackers in the process. The Union fleet had suffered 36 killed and 135 wounded, but now there was nothing between it and the South's largest city. Farragut left two of his ships behind to ensure the isolation of the forts, and proceeded with the other twelve upriver to New Orleans. Anchoring off Jackson Square in the heart of the city, Farragut sent Captain Theodorus Bailey ashore with a demand for its surrender. Though the citizens howled and shook their fists, there was nothing they could do, and Bailey raised the American flag over the custom house.[35]

In advance of Farragut's arrival, the Confederates had attempted to tow the still-unfinished *Mississippi* upriver to save her, but her great size, and the weak engines of the tugs, made it impossible. To prevent her from falling into the hands of the Yankees, she was set on fire and cut loose. Soon after the fall of the city, Farragut noted that the *Mississippi* "came floating by us all in flames and passed down the river." The Yankees had arrived before the Confederates could complete the ironclad warships that might have enabled them to put up an effective resistance.[36]

The loss of New Orleans was a blow to the South even more severe than the loss of its forts on the upper reaches of the river. In 1944 Charles Dufour published a book in which he argued that the night Farragut passed the river forts and compelled the surrender of New Orleans was "the night the war was lost." That may be a stretch, but without doubt it was a devastating blow to southern hopes, for it gave the Union control over the outlet for the entire Mississippi Valley.[37]

LESS THAN A MONTH after the fall of New Orleans, the action resumed on the upper Mississippi. Because Halleck had sent Pope's army off to join Grant at Shiloh for a tedious advance toward Corinth, Foote's orders were to cease offensive operations on the Mississippi and simply keep an eye on the eight vessels of the Confederate River Defense Fleet.* That fleet, composed mostly of lightly armed rams and commanded by the former steamboat captain James Montgomery, protected Fort Pillow and the city of Memphis where Confederate naval authorities were still struggling to get the *Tennessee* ready for battle. With no prospect of immediate action, and suffering horribly from the wound he had received at Fort Donelson, Foote asked to be relieved, and to take his place, Welles sent 55-year old Captain Charles Henry Davis. Davis became an Acting Flag Officer and arrived on May 9. He did not have to wait long for his baptism of fire.

The very next morning, the City-class ironclad *Cincinnati* set out on a routine reconnaissance of Fort Pillow when from around Plum Point Bend there appeared a rebel ram, then another, and another, until six of them could be seen heading north at full speed and apparently intent on a confrontation. The *Cincinnati* quickly beat to quarters and opened fire with her 32-pounders. Before the rest of the Union squadron could get downriver to assist her, she was struck by no fewer than three different rams. The CSS *General Bragg* smashed into her starboard quarter; the CSS *Sterling Price* struck her in the stern, smashing her sternpost; and the CSS *Sumter* struck the *Cincinnati* in the stern quarter. The ironclad began taking on water, and her wounded captain, Roger Stembel, ordered her toward the river bank where she settled on the muddy bottom. The USS *Mound City*, coming up to assist, was then struck by the CSS *Van Dorn*, a blow which spun the *Mound City* all the way around and opened a 4-foot hole in her hull. Her captain, too, ran his ship ashore to avoid sinking. With the rest of the Union squadron coming up, Montgomery decided not to press his luck and withdrew. Though both Union ironclads were salvaged and eventually

---

*Initially there had been fourteen of these, but the Confederates sent six of them south to assist in the defense of New Orleans. This suggests that Lincoln's notion of attacking two places at once in order to force the Confederates to divide their assets worked as planned.

repaired, the Battle of Plum Point Bend (May 10, 1862) was a humiliating Union defeat. The timber and cotton-clad rams of the Confederate River Defense Fleet had sunk two ironclads without losing a single ship.[38]

A week later, Davis's command was reinforced by a ram fleet of its own. The brainchild of the entrepreneur and bridge builder Charles W. Ellet, Jr., this fleet was administratively separate from Davis's gunboat flotilla. Ellet had proposed to Gideon Welles the creation of a fleet of unarmed rams for use on the western rivers. Welles sent him over to the War Department where Secretary Stanton thought it a splendid idea and gave Ellet a commission as an army colonel with the authority to purchase and modify a number of river steamers as rams. Charles Henry Davis was skeptical of both Colonel Ellet and his rams, and not quite sure how they would fit into his flotilla. The two Union river forces did not even share signal codes.[39]

Meanwhile, events at Corinth were having a profound effect on the river war. Halleck had concentrated the Union armies of Pope, Grant, and Buell at the railroad junction of Corinth, Mississippi, for an attack on Beauregard, and that officer decided that the place could no longer be held. His evacuation of Corinth uncovered Memphis, and so on June 4, 1862, the Confederates at Fort Pillow set fire to their own fort and abandoned it. The next day, the Union gunboats got under way to drop downriver and take possession. That led to the decisive Battle of Memphis (June 5, 1862).[40]

Though the Confederate army had already evacuated Fort Pillow, when the Union flotilla came downriver, Montgomery's rams came out to challenge them. Davis was not sure whether the Confederates had come out to fight or to surrender until the rebels opened fire with their long guns. While Davis was still trying to decide what to do about it, Ellet decided to take the bull by the horns. From his flagship *Queen of the West*, he called over to his brother who commanded the ram *Monarch*: "Follow me. Now is our chance." And with that he charged through the Union flotilla and headed downriver at full speed. Though Ellet clearly expected the rest of his rams to follow, they lagged behind so that only two unarmed rams charged down into the midst of the Confederate fleet. The Confederates were as startled by this as Davis was. One of the rebel rams, the *Lovell*, turned away from the charging

Queen of the West, and Ellet drove his ram full into her side, nearly cutting her in two. While the *Queen* was still entangled with the *Lovell*, she was herself struck by the rebel ram *General Beauregard*. Then it became a melee. The USS *Monarch* struck the CSS *General Price*, which headed for the shore to avoid sinking and collided with the grounded *Queen*. The *Monarch* then rammed the CSS *Beauregard*. By now Davis' gunboats had joined the fray, and other rebel rams were hit by shell-fire. By the time it was over, two Confederate rams had been sunk and four more had been captured. The rest fled. Though Ellet himself was mortally wounded in the fight, his rams had spearheaded the victory. The defeat was a shock to the residents of Memphis who hurriedly evacuated whatever military supplies were left in Memphis. Just as Confederate navy authorities in New Orleans had been forced to burn the *Mississippi*, so now they set fire to the still-uncompleted *Tennessee* at Memphis. The Union victory gave the Federals command of the Mississippi all the way south to Vicksburg.[41]

OF THE FOUR BIG IRONCLADS planned by southern authorities for river defense, three of them had been destroyed by their masters to prevent them from falling into the hands of the Yankees. Only the *Arkansas* was left, sent south from Memphis and up the Yazoo River. In May, the Confederate Navy Department ordered Lieutenant Isaac N. Brown there to take command of her. Brown found her in a half-finished state—"a mere hull, without armor," in his words—and in order to make her both seaworthy and battle ready, he found himself in a race with time. The level of the river fell dramatically in midsummer, and soon it would be too low to float the ship. Brown commandeered two hundred army soldiers who worked throughout June and into July to finish, armor, arm, and equip the ship, and finally Brown had a serviceable ironclad. It was a powerful vessel with two 8-inch Columbiads in the bow, two rifled 32-pounders in the stern, and three more on each broadside including two 6.4-inch Brooke rifles, though its armor of railroad rails was suspect.[42]

By then, Farragut had taken his ocean-going warships from New Orleans up to Vicksburg where they met Charles Henry Davis' flotilla above the city. For a brief moment, Union gunboats controlled the Mississippi River all the way from Cairo to New Orleans. But the moment did not last. Farragut could not stay there because the level of the river was dropping. Moreover, he could not maintain communication southward so long as the Confederates held Vicksburg, and he could not seize the city because—as David Dixon Porter pointed out—gunboats could not climb up hills 200 feet high. Finally, though Farragut had run past the Vicksburg batteries for his rendezvous with Davis, the Confederates were strengthening those batteries, and soon they would be too powerful for wooden ships to hazard.

The rebel commander at Vicksburg, Major General Earl Van Dorn, feared that the Union combined fleets were preparing to attack, and he called upon Lieutenant Brown to bring the *Arkansas* to the city to aid in its defense. Brown dutifully got the *Arkansas* under way and carefully navigated her down the shallow waters of the Yazoo River to the Mississippi on July 15. There he encountered three Union ships that Charles Henry Davis had sent upriver to look for her. They were the City-class ironclad *Carondelet*, the timberclad *Tyler*, and the unarmed ram *Queen of the West*. Upon sighting the apparently fully operational *Arkansas*, the three Union ships turned and fled downriver with the rebel ironclad close behind. During a running battle, a shell from the *Arkansas* took out the *Carondelet*'s steering gear, and the Union ironclad drifted ashore and aground. The other two Union ships continued downriver with the *Arkansas* in hot pursuit. Soon all three ships closed on the crowded stretch of river above Vicksburg where Farragut's and Davis's fleets were anchored. Brown was not surprised to see them, but it was nevertheless daunting to encounter "a forest of masts and smoke-stacks—ships, rams, iron-clads, and other gun-boats on the left side, and ordinary river steamers and bomb vessels along the right." The *Arkansas* ran right through this gauntlet, firing in both directions and receiving in turn "the broadsides of the whole fleet" before she arrived safely at the wharf at Vicksburg where she was greeted "with enthusiastic cheers."[43]

Farragut was mortified that one rebel ironclad had run through his entire fleet, and that same night he led his squadron downriver past Vicksburg hoping to sink the *Arkansas* en route. A 160-pound bolt from one of his ships did strike the *Arkansas*' armor and penetrate to the engine room, but the rebel ironclad remained afloat. Over the next several days, Davis tried to destroy the *Arkansas* by lobbing 13-inch "bombs" at her from his mortar rafts, but despite many near

The CSS *Arkansas* was one of four big ironclads planned by the rebels for the defense of the Mississippi River, but the only one to become completely operational. In the action depicted here, she ran through the entire Union river fleet on July 15, 1862, to moor under the guns at Vicksburg. This engraving is based on a sketch by J. O. Davidson. (Courtesy of the Naval Historical Center)

misses, none found its mark. Then on July 22, Davis sent three ships, including William Porter's *Essex*, to attack the *Arkansas* by ramming her. Porter's balky *Essex* made a run at the rebel ironclad, but missed her and instead ran up on the river bank. After ten desperate minutes, the *Essex* managed to free herself and, unable to return upriver against the current, she continued downriver to join Farragut. The *Queen of the West* did manage to ram the *Arkansas*, but with insufficient force to do serious damage. After that, Farragut headed back to Baton Rouge, and Davis took his flotilla upriver to Helena, Arkansas.[44]

What ultimately led to the demise of the *Arkansas* was Van Dorn's decision to order her downriver to Baton Rouge to assist Major General John C. Breckinridge in an attack on that city. The *Arkansas* was barely seaworthy, but she gamely headed downriver where she once again encountered the *Essex* 5 miles above the city. This time, before the two ships could engage, the engines of the *Arkansas* failed and she drifted ashore. Like all three of her three sister ships, she was set afire and destroyed by her crew to prevent her from falling into the hands of the Yankees.*

BY THE FALL OF 1862, Vicksburg had become the buckle on the strap that held the two halves of the Confederacy together. What made Vicksburg a daunting objective was its geography. The city sat on a high bluff some 170 feet above the river's flood plain, and powerful guns atop that bluff commanded a hairpin turn in the river. Since gunboats alone could not take the city, it would require another joint or combined operation.

By the time the Union set out to seize the city, the river gunboats were no longer under the aegis of the army. Accepting the reality that gunboats commanded by navy officers were part of the navy, the army's Gunboat Flotilla became the navy's Mississippi Squadron on October 1, 1862.* It also got a new commander. Thanks in large part to the support of his friend Gustavus Fox, David Dixon Porter was promoted in one step from Commander to Acting Rear Admiral, and he took over the Mississippi Squadron on October 15. Porter's army counterpart in the campaign for Vicksburg was Ulysses S. Grant, the conqueror of Forts Henry and Donelson and the victor of Shiloh. Despite Porter's suspicion of West Pointers, he, Grant, and William T. Sherman made up a compatible command team that demonstrated how effective joint operations could be when the commanders cooperated.

This Union command team first tried to approach Vicksburg from the north and east. In December of 1862, Grant moved his army overland through central Mississippi to attack the city from the east while Sherman and Porter threaded their way up the Yazoo River to assail the bluffs north of the city. These efforts were undone when Confederate cavalry raids disrupted Grant's supply lines, and Sherman's assault on

---

*Characteristically, Porter asserted (incorrectly) that it was the attack of the *Essex* and not the failure of the *Arkansas* engines that led to her demise. Porter objected when Welles' subsequent general order did not adhere to this view, and Porter demanded that Welles "at once" correct his order. Welles replied that Porter's demand was "discourteous" and one "to which no answer can be returned." See ORN, 19:122–23.

*One exception to this reorganization was the ram fleet that had played such a conspicuous role in the Battle of Memphis. While the ram fleet became subject to navy orders, it remained administratively under the War Department.

ADMIRAL PORTER'S FLEET RUNNING THE REBEL BLOCKADE OF THE MISSISSIPPI AT VICKSBURG, APRIL 16TH 1863.

This Currier & Ives print captures the drama of David Dixon Porter's run past the Vicksburg batteries on April 16, 1863. (Courtesy of the Naval Historical Center)

Chickasaw Bluffs was repulsed. After several unproductive and frustrating attempts to approach Vicksburg from the north, one of which resulted in the loss of the City-class ironclad *Cairo* to a Confederate torpedo (mine), Grant finally decided that his best option was to strike at the city from downriver.

Farragut's fleet could no longer help in this effort because the Confederates had fortified Port Hudson, Louisiana, 240 miles downriver from Vicksburg, which kept the deep-draft ships of Farragut's command below that point. To escort his army across the river, therefore, Grant asked Porter to run a portion of his squadron past the Vicksburg batteries at night, as Walke had done at Island No. 10 the year before. Though the Mississippi Squadron was no longer under army command, Porter readily agreed, and on April 16, he led ten ironclads and three army transports past the city. The Confederates lit bonfires on both sides of the river to illuminate the Yankee ships as they ran past. Porter noted, "The fire from the forts was heavy and rapid, but was replied to with such spirit that the aim of the enemy was not so good as usual."

One of the transports was sunk, but the rest of the vessels made it with only minor damage.[45]

Meanwhile, Grant marched his men southward in a circuitous route through the marshy delta on the western side of the river, to meet Porter at Hard Times Landing some 45 miles below Vicksburg. Porter's fleet then escorted Grant's army across the river, and after another month of hard marching and hard fighting, and a siege that lasted forty-seven days, Vicksburg fell to Union arms on July 4, 1863, the day after the failure of the grand Confederate charge at Gettysburg in far away Pennsylvania.

As at Island No. 10, neither Grant's army nor Porter's gunboats could have captured Vicksburg unassisted. Together, they made a team that, in hindsight, made the outcome seem inevitable. When Lincoln heard about the fall of Vicksburg and the surrender of an entire Confederate army, he was ecstatic. He threw his arms around Gideon Welles, who brought him the news, and declared "I cannot in words tell you my joy over this result. It is great, Mr. Welles. It is great." A month later he was more poetic about the meaning of the campaign, writing in a public letter that "the Father of Waters again goes unvexed to the sea."[46]

SEVERAL FACTORS had made this Union success possible. First, the Union was able not only to produce more ironclad warships than the Confederacy for service on the western rivers, but also to do so quickly. The construction of James Eads' ironclads (Pook's turtles) in just over two months meant that the Union had ironclad gunboats on the western rivers by January of 1862—two months ahead of either the *Monitor* or the *Virginia*—which enabled the Union to break through the Confederate river defenses before the South had any of its major ironclads ready for service. Since the South had to depend almost entirely on forts for its defense of the Mississippi and its tributaries, it was compelled to accept a passive defense at Fort Henry, Fort Donelson, Fort Pillow, New Orleans, and even Vicksburg. When the rebels did seize the initiative, as in the ramming of the USS *Richmond* by CSS *Manassas* in October of 1861, the daring attack of the Confederate Defense Fleet at Plum Point Bend in May of 1862, and in the dash of the *Arkansas* through the entire Union fleet above Vicksburg in July of 1862, they gave a good account of themselves. But in the West, as along the Atlantic coast, the

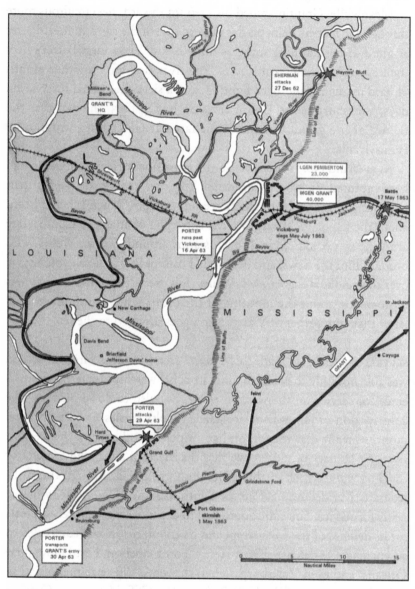

THE VICKSBURG CAMPAIGN, APRIL 16–JULY 4, 1863. Map by Bill Clipson, reprinted with permission from *The Naval Institute Historical Atlas of the U.S. Navy* by Craig L. Symonds, © 1995.

Union's overwhelming industrial superiority, and the loss of most of the Confederacy's planned ironclads before they were even serviceable, undercut their efforts to hold on to the rivers.

Finally, the ability of Union army and navy commanders to overcome interservice rivalry and cooperate in the achievement of specific objectives was crucial to eventual Union success. Despite the lack of any protocol for joint operations, and despite a culture of jealous independence, it was not so much the Union army or navy that triumphed, it was their ability to work together that ensured victory. The fall of Vicksburg did not end the war in the West, but it completely changed its character. It was, as Lincoln recognized, a vital turning point in the conflict.

5

Civil War Navies and the Siege of Charleston

EARLY IN THE PRE-DAWN DARKNESS of May 13, 1862, a lookout on board the USS *Onward*, part of the blockading squadron off Charleston, spied a small side-wheel steamer coming out of the harbor. At once he reported it to the officer of the watch, Lieutenant J. F. Nickels, who ordered the *Onward* to beat to quarters. Sailors rushed to cast loose the guns and train them on the approaching steamer, but the guns remained silent as the steamer made no effort to escape and flew a large white flag. The lookouts who had been watching the harbor for months recognized her as the dispatch boat *Planter*, which the Confederates used to carry messages among the several forts around the harbor. On this night, however, the *Planter* steamed boldly into the midst of the blockading vessels. The explanation for her peculiar behavior became evident when she came alongside the *Onward* and Lieutenant Nickels saw that she was "wholly manned by negroes" who were under the supervision of a black pilot named Robert Smalls. With the rebel officers ashore, Smalls had quietly gotten up steam and, donning the captain's cloak and hat, had piloted the *Planter* past Fort Sumter, making all the necessary recognition signals, and brought his family and a handful of friends out of slavery to the Union fleet.[1]

Smalls' exploit was not only a satisfactory poke in the eye to Confederate authorities in Charleston, Smalls himself proved to be an invaluable source of military intelligence. Taken to Port Royal, Smalls met with Samuel F. Du Pont, the commander of the Union's South Atlantic Blockading Squadron, and told him that the Confederates were pulling back their defenses around Charleston—specifically that they had abandoned the small fort on Cole's Island that guarded the entrance to the Stono River a dozen miles south of Charleston. A subsequent reconnaissance of the Stono by Commander John B. Marchand proved that Smalls was correct, and equally important, that the Stono River offered undefended deep-water access to James Island and a backdoor approach to Fort Johnson, which protected Charleston's southern flank. Marchand saw that Union occupation of Fort Johnson would facilitate the bombardment of Fort Sumter, and that in turn would allow Du Pont's deep-water warships to enter the harbor. "Fort Johnson is the key of Charleston," he wrote Du Pont. "An army movement towards that place across Stono River . . . will accomplish its reduction."[2]

Two weeks later, the army transport *Flora* brought the first elements of a Union division up the Stono River to James Island. It was the first move of a prolonged Union operation against Charleston that would last three years and stands to this day as the longest siege in American military history. Before it was over, the Union effort to take Charleston involved over forty thousand men and sixty warships, and despite that, Charleston remained defiantly unconquered until it was finally cut off from the interior by William T. Sherman's northward march in 1865. This lengthy campaign for Charleston illuminated the strengths and weaknesses of the commanders on both sides, and in particular the inherent difficulties of conducting joint or combined operations in the Civil War era.[3]

CHARLESTON WAS IMPORTANT not only because it was the second most active blockade-running port on the Atlantic seaboard after Wilmington, North Carolina, but also because it was a symbol of southern rebellion. South Carolina was the state with the highest percentage of slaves in its population (58 percent), and its representatives had been the most tenacious and defiant in support of slavery in the decades before the war. It was the home of John C. Calhoun, who had promulgated the doctrine of states' rights and spearheaded resistance to the national government during the Nullification crisis in 1831–32. It was the first state to secede from the Union in December of 1860, and Charleston Harbor was where the first shots of the war had been fired the following April. Many northerners blamed South Carolina, and Charleston in particular, for both causing and starting the war. As the *New York Tribune* declared in June of 1862, "If there is any city deserving of holocaustic infamy, it is Charleston." For the blockaders, the rebel flag flying from the ramparts of Fort Sumter was an implied challenge and a continual affront. Gustavus Fox spoke for many when he wrote to Du Pont that "the fall of Charleston is the Fall of Satan's kingdom."[4]

Early on during the siege of Charleston, however, the campaign also became a political football in the rivalry between the Union army and navy. Worried about the bad publicity the navy was getting due to ships running the blockade and the rampage of Confederate raiders, Welles and Fox wanted Du Pont to make the capture of Charleston "purely naval" in order to win public credit and support. In the same letter to Du Pont in which he referred to Charleston as "Satan's kingdom," Fox declared that "I feel my duties are two fold: first, to beat our southern friends; second, to beat the army." With that in mind, Welles and Fox convinced Lincoln that with a few ironclads, Du Pont "could go right into the harbor, with little or no risk, and destroy the Forts, batteries, and the Town itself."[5]

Du Pont was skeptical of this vision. Though he had led the squadron that seized Port Royal in November of 1861 (see Chapter 2), the circumstances at Charleston were very different. To dash into the harbor, even with ironclads, meant getting past not only Fort Sumter and the other batteries which the rebels had constructed around the harbor, but also the line of obstructions and torpedoes that the Confederates had strung across the harbor entrance from Fort Sumter to Sullivan's Island. He could not send in small boats to clear those obstructions because the boats would be under fire from the guns of Fort Sumter. The strategic geography of Charleston Harbor, Du Pont believed, required that the army first occupy one or more of the surrounding islands on which it could erect batteries facing Fort Sumter. Once those batteries had silenced the guns in the fort, the navy could then disable the mines, which would allow his ships to enter the harbor and demand the surrender of the city. At Savannah, 90 miles south of Charleston, batteries erected by the army compelled Fort Pulaski to surrender in April, and Du Pont believed that a similar approach would open the way for the navy at Charleston. That is why he was energized by the idea of an army advance up the Stono River. In a true joint operation, the army would clear the way for the navy. Of course, this was not at all what Welles had in mind, and in the end this disagreement would both undermine the Union campaign for Charleston and shorten Du Pont's tenure of command.

It did not help that the Union army's campaign on James Island was itself marred by miscommunication and bungling. Before Union soldiers on the Stono River could seize Fort Johnson, they first had to overcome a long line of field works that ran diagonally across James Island from Wappoo Cut, where the Stono shoaled to a depth that would not accommodate the Union gunboats, to Newtown Cut where solid land gave way to marsh. This defensive line was anchored on its northern end by a battery dubbed Fort Pemberton in honor of the rebel commander, John C. Pemberton, and on its southern end by Battery Lamar, named for its commander, Colonel Thomas G. Lamar. Behind Battery Lamar, the Confederates had erected a tall observation tower that allowed them to keep an eye on the Yankee enclave along the Stono River, and the Yankees consequently referred to it as the Tower Battery.[6]

The Union army theater commander for South Carolina, Georgia, and Florida was Major General David Hunter, a political general better known for his abolitionist views than his skill in the field. Indeed, only days before the Union secured its foothold on the Stono River, Hunter had shaken things up in Washington by issuing a proclamation that all the slaves in his three-state command area were "forever free." This was well in advance of administration policy at the time, and Lincoln was forced to repudiate it. For all his eagerness to change the war's objective, however, the 60-year-old Hunter was rather lethargic in prosecuting the war itself. Once he had two divisions, about 6,500 men, ashore on James Island, he left them there in charge of 49-year-old Brigadier General Henry W. Benham, and returned to Hilton Head for several days to be with his wife.[7]

Benham was as mercurial as Hunter was lethargic, and, aware of that, Hunter specifically ordered him to "make no attempt to advance on Charleston or to attack Ft. Johnson" while he was gone, though he did tell him to "provide for a secure encampment." That was all the opening Benham needed. Because the rebel guns at Battery Lamar could reach portions of the Federal camp, Benham decided that to

DU PONT'S ATTACK ON CHARLESTON, SOUTH CAROLINA, APRIL 7, 1863. Map by Bill Clipson, reprinted with permission from *The Naval Institute Historical Atlas of the U.S. Navy* by Craig L. Symonds, © 1995.

"secure" his encampment, he had to neutralize that battery.[8] Forbidden to attack Fort Johnson itself, he decided instead to seize Battery Lamar near the small village of Secessionville.*

It would have been better both for Benham and the cause he served if he had simply ignored his orders and attacked Fort Johnson itself, for Battery Lamar—small as it was—was a kind of Thermopylae. Built on a narrow stretch of solid ground only 125 yards wide between two impassable swamps, it funneled the Union attack squarely into the rebel guns. Moreover, the narrow front compelled Benham to feed his regiments into the fight piecemeal. As a result, the Battle of Secessionville (June 16, 1862) was a Union disaster. After two and half hours of vicious combat, the Union troops were repelled with nothing to show for their effort besides 700 casualties. (Confederate defenders suffered about 200 casualties.) Hunter placed Benham under arrest, but far worse for Union prospects in the campaign, he used the repulse as an excuse to evacuate James Island altogether, reloading his men onto transports and taking them all back to Port Royal and Hilton Head. There would be no Union assault on Fort Johnson, no combined operation on James Island. In that act, Hunter very likely gave up what one authority calls "the North's last best chance to capture the city of Charleston."[9]

WITH THE COLLAPSE of the effort to take Charleston by the back door, Union planners returned to the idea of storming the front porch. In Washington, Welles and Fox saw the withdrawal of the army from James Island as an opportunity for the navy to assert itself. Even before Hunter evacuated James Island, Fox was asking Du Pont "If we give you the Galena and Monitor, don't you think we can go squarely at it by the Channel and make it [the attack on Charleston] purely navy?" No, as a matter of fact, he didn't. Indeed, Du Pont was absorbing quite a different lesson based on what happened that same month 500 miles to the north on the James River in Virginia where the Galena and the Monitor tried unsuccessfully to fight their way past Drewry's Bluff. To his wife, Du Pont wrote that "It was a very ill-advised and incorrect

---

*Secessionville had been named long before the war for the antisocial proclivities of its residents, and not for the secession of 1860–61.

operation to expose those gunboats [at Drewry's Bluff] before the Army could take the fort in the rear." Now Welles and Fox were urging him to do much the same thing at Charleston where the enemy fortifications were vastly stronger than those on the James.[10]

Despite Du Pont's skepticism, Welles and Fox continued to push for a direct assault by navy ironclads as the only viable alternative to a long and costly siege. If the *Galena* and the *Monitor* were insufficient, they would supply Du Pont with some of the new *Passaic*-class monitors. Over the next six months, the Navy Department sent Du Pont one monitor after another, almost as fast as they could be built, and by January of 1863, Du Pont had seven of them, plus the giant iron-hulled frigate *New Ironsides* and an experimental armored warship called the *Keokuk* which had two non-revolving towers.

Du Pont was happy enough to have the reinforcement, but he remained skeptical that even with nine ironclads he could smash his way past the forts and the obstructions into the inner harbor. The reality was that for all their apparent invulnerability, monitors carried only two guns each, and their rate of fire was painfully slow. The massive 15-inch guns on the *Passaic*-class monitors could fire only once every seven to ten minutes. To demonstrate this point, and to test the capability of his monitors against shore fortifications, Du Pont ordered John Worden, who had commanded the original *Monitor* in the Battle of Hampton Roads, to attack Fort McAllister on Ogeechee Sound south of Charleston with three *Passaic*-class monitors. On the morning of January 27, 1863, Worden's monitors pounded the earthwork fort for nearly four hours until they ran out of ammunition. Afterward, Worden reported to Du Pont that the shelling had no perceptible effect on the enemy. Another attack four days later produced similar results. Though McAllister was both smaller and weaker than Sumter, three Union monitors firing large-caliber shot and shell for four hours could not batter it down. How, then, could they be expected to overwhelm Sumter? Moreover, as if to illustrate that monitors were not entirely invulnerable, the *Montauk* was badly damaged by an underwater torpedo (mine) during the operation. Du Pont sent Worden's report to Washington along with one of his own in which he concluded that "This experiment also convinced me of another impression, firmly held and often expressed, that in all such operations to secure success troops are necessary."[11]

Once again, this was not what Welles wanted to hear. The Navy Secretary was so invested in the success of the monitors, both politically and psychologically, that he drew quite a different lesson from the experiment at Fort McAllister: Monitors had slugged it out with a southern fort for four hours and come away virtually undamaged. So what if they had limited offensive power? They could snap their fingers at any shore batteries in Charleston, pass them unharmed, and threaten the city itself with slow but inevitable destruction. Welles continued to hope and expect that Du Pont would be able to force his way into Charleston with a fleet of monitors and do so without any reliance on the army.

MEANWHILE, the Confederates inside Charleston were not idle. Pierre G. T. Beauregard took over command of the Charleston defenses from Pemberton in September 1862. It was a bit of a come down for the man who had become a national hero after Bull Run in the first summer of the war and who had commanded the Confederacy's western army after Shiloh, but it turned out to be an ideal appointment for the mercurial Creole. Appointing a four-star general to command the defense of Charleston demonstrated that the Confederate government considered its defense important, and Beauregard soon showed a capacity for both defensive organization and the ability to inspire the citizens.

Beauregard's naval counterpart in Charleston was Commodore Duncan N. Ingraham, a native South Carolinian and a veteran of fifty years of service in the Old Navy. Ingraham had little to work with at the outset of the campaign, but almost at once he initiated a program to build some ironclads of his own. The initial impetus for ironclad construction came from the citizens of Charleston. Prompted by a public plea in the newspaper, citizens sent in pledges and contributions. So many were received that the editor of the *Charleston Courier* had to apologize for not being able to print the names of all the contributors. Soon afterward, news arrived that the Confederate government had appropriated funds to build an ironclad at Charleston, and so, in the end, two of them were built: one paid for by the government and called "the State gunboat," and another by subscription, mostly from Ladies Aid societies, and hence called "the Ladies gunboat."[12]

The builders had the usual problems with the availability of construction materials, exacerbated on this occasion by the army's refusal to release the railroad cars necessary to transport the iron armor. Nevertheless, by the fall of 1862, both ships were in the water and on the way to completion. Smaller clones of the CSS *Virginia*, they were casemate ironclads 150 feet long. The "Ladies Boat" became CSS *Palmetto State* (4 guns), and the "State gunboat" became CSS *Chicora* (6 guns).* The guns in the bow and stern were mounted on pivots so they could fire not only directly ahead (or astern), but also to either side. By the end of the year, both ships were ready for service, and in January, while Du Pont was testing the monitors against Fort McAllister, Ingraham decided to test his own ironclads in an attack on the Union blockading fleet off Charleston.[13]

Before he could do so, the Confederates defending the Stono River achieved a surprise victory by capturing the Union gunboat *Isaac Smith* on January 29, 1863. Erecting masked batteries on both sides of the river, the Confederates allowed the *Isaac Smith* to steam past the first set of batteries, then opened fire with the second, catching the *Isaac Smith* in a crossfire. "I saw immediately that we were trapped," reported the *Isaac Smith*'s captain, Acting Lieutenant F. S. Conover. He sought to extricate himself, but a shot from one of the rebel guns knocked out the engine, and the *Isaac Smith* lost power. Unwilling to watch as his ship and crew were massacred, Conover deemed it his duty to surrender.[14] The Confederates took possession of the *Isaac Smith*, and after lightening her draft by taking off her guns, towed her through Wappoo Cut into Charleston Harbor and turned her into a Confederate guard boat, which they renamed the *Stono*.†

Hoping for a similar success, the very next morning (January 30, 1863) the *Palmetto State* and *Chicora* crept out of the harbor to attack the Union blockading fleet. The two rebel ironclads were painted a blue-gray to blend with the sea, and a thick haze on the water helped

---

*The Confederates later built two more ironclads in Charleston. They were the *Charleston* (10 guns), laid down in 1864 and which became the flagship of the squadron, and the *Columbia* (6 guns), which was laid down in 1865. Neither saw active service against the enemy.

†The *Stono* was wrecked off Sullivan's Island on June 5, 1863, while trying to run the blockade.

The Confederate ironclads CSS *Palmetto State* and CSS *Chicora* are depicted here in a painting by Conrad Wise Chapman. Note the spar torpedo projecting from the bow of the *Palmetto State* (right). These two ironclads carried out a successful and controversial attack on the Union blockading squadron off Charleston on January 30, 1863. (Courtesy of the Naval Historical Center)

conceal their stealthy approach. Ingraham himself was on board the *Palmetto State*, and his goal was to destroy as many Union warships as he could.

Out on the blockade, the USS *Mercidita* was the designated guard ship for the night, and hence the one closest to shore. At 4:00 a.m., her commanding officer, Captain Henry Stellwagen, had just gone to bed, when he was awakened by the watch officer: A low steamer was close alongside! Pulling his pea coat on over his pajamas, Stellwagen rushed onto the deck. Once there, he hailed the dark shadow on the water.

"What steamer is that?" he shouted.

"This is the Confederate States steam ram. . . ."

Stellwagen didn't catch the name of the ship, but it hardly mattered. "Fire!" he shouted. But the *Palmetto State* was so close, and so low in the water, that the *Mercidita*'s guns would not depress enough to hit her. In seconds, the *Palmetto State* rammed the *Mercidita*, firing her bow gun as she struck. That shot penetrated the *Mercidita*'s port-side steam drum, which exploded instantly, filling the ship with scalding steam. Stellwagen received a flurry of reports from below: The engines were out; water was flooding in; and most urgently, "Vessel sinking fast." The *Palmetto State* backed out, and Ingraham shouted across the water to the wounded *Mercidita*: "Surrender or I'll sink you."

Stellwagen played for time: "I can make no resistance: my boiler is destroyed."

Ingraham was insistent: "Then do you surrender?"

Stellwagen hesitated only for a moment. "Yes," he called back. He ordered his executive officer, Lieutenant Commander Trevett Abbot, to take a boat over to the *Palmetto State* to make a formal surrender of the *Mercidita*. Fearing that his ship was about to sink, and that he did not have enough ship's boats to save the crew, Stellwagen told Abbot to ask Ingraham if he could take the *Mercidita*'s crew on board his ship.[15]

There was no room for so many men on the *Palmetto State*. Instead, Ingraham agreed to parole all of the *Mercidita*'s officers and men on the condition that Abbot pledged his "sacred word of honor" that neither he nor any of the ship's officers or men "would again take up arms against the Confederate States during the war" unless they were exchanged, the usual convention in such cases. Abbot agreed.[16]

While this drama played out, the *Chicora*, with John Randolph Tucker in command, attacked the Union ships *Quaker City* and *Keystone State*. Having lost the element of surprise after the *Palmetto State*'s attack on the *Mercidita*, the *Chicora* became the target of several Union broadsides, but the Union ordnance glanced harmlessly off the ironclad's casemate. After firing several shots into the *Quaker City*, the *Chicora* focused her attack on the *Keystone State*, which was soon on fire. As on the *Mercidita*, one of the rebel shots hit the boiler and knocked out the *Keystone State*'s port engine. Witnesses on the *Chicora* later testified that the *Keystone State* struck her flag, and Tucker claimed that he saw men on the *Keystone State*'s quarterdeck holding out their arms in a plea for mercy. Concluding that the *Keystone State* had struck, Tucker prepared to lower a boat to take his prize. But though the Union ship was badly wounded, her wounds were not fatal, and she limped off out of range with her one working paddlewheel. Eventually she was taken under tow by the USS *Memphis* and escaped to Port Royal. The *Chicora*, joined now by the *Palmetto State*, fired into several more vessels, but the Union ships were faster than the plodding ironclads, and they soon sped out of range. In the growing daylight, Ingraham decided that he had risked his unseaworthy vessels long enough in the open ocean, and he ordered them back into port.[17]

A number of controversies emerged from this attack. The first was Confederate fury that while both the *Mercidita* and the *Keystone State* had apparently surrendered, they had nevertheless fled the scene. Stellwagen himself honored his pledge, declaring to Du Pont that he could not accept any further orders because he and his officers had given their parole. But what about the ship? Confederates believed that the Union was honor bound to turn the *Mercidita* over to Confederate authorities, but a Union Court of Inquiry concluded self-servingly that Abbot's pledge of parole "did not include the vessel and its equipment." As for the *Keystone State*, her commander, William LeRoy, denied that he had struck his flag, and he rejected the charge that he had violated the laws of war. Du Pont concluded that LeRoy had fought his ship valiantly in an unequal contest and had made off simply because his ship was faster than his attacker.[18]

The other post-battle controversy concerned the continued legitimacy of the blockade itself. To Confederate eyes, the *Palmetto State* and the *Chicora* had driven the Union blockade fleet away from Charleston. After the battle, the British Consul in Charleston, Robert Bunch, went out in HMS *Petrel* to have a look and declared that no Union warships were in sight. Since there was no longer a "competent force" off the city to enforce the blockade, Beauregard declared that the blockade had been "broken." The legal significance of this assertion was that, once broken, a blockade had to be re-established by issuing another proclamation. Because that proclamation would have to make its way across the Atlantic, Charleston would presumably be open to trade during the several weeks that would take. The Confederate Secretary of State, Judah Benjamin, asserted this argument to the British Foreign Minister John Russell, but sympathetic as he was to the Confederacy, Russell was loath to weaken the law of blockade since the British relied so heavily on it during their wars with European foes. Still, along with the capture of the *Isaac Smith* the day before, the embarrassing defeat of the Union squadron off Charleston on January 30, 1863, gave the Confederate Navy one of its signal victories of the war.[19]

As humiliating as these events were to the Union navy, Du Pont saw a silver lining in them. He hoped that the brazenness of the rebel attack off Charleston might "open Mr. Fox's eyes" to the difficulties that a Union naval force would encounter in an attack on Charleston Harbor.[20]

It did nothing of the sort. If anything, the humiliations of that January 30 made Welles and Fox even more eager to seize Charleston and prevent any future such embarrassment. They tried to encourage Du Pont, telling him "the glorious achievements of our Navy, inaugurated by yourself [at Port Royal], give every reason to hope for a successful issue at this point, where rebellion first lighted the flames of civil war." Despite Du Pont's preference for a combined operation, they wanted him to act unilaterally without collaborating with, or even

This *Harper's Weekly* illustration depicts the attack by Du Pont's ironclad squadron against Fort Sumter on April 7, 1863. Though the monitors proved tough enough, absorbing more than 500 hits from the guns of the fort, their limited offensive capability left the fort barely damaged. (Courtesy of the Naval Historical Center)

informing, the army. Fox urged Du Pont "not to take these soldiers too closely into your counsels in a purely naval matter," and "not to let the army spoil it."[21]

THUS PRESSED, Du Pont issued orders to his captains for a naval attack on Charleston on April 7, 1863. Du Pont's nine ironclads, including the massive *New Ironsides*, carried a total of only thirty-two guns, though twenty-two of them were 11-inch Dahlgrens and seven others were enormous 15-inch guns. The Confederates had far more guns—seventy-six of them—but none as heavy as those in the Union fleet.

On the other hand, the Confederates had a lot of confidence in the obstructions they had placed in the harbor. These obstructions were modified several times, but at the time of Du Pont's attack they consisted principally of a heavy cable supported by barrel floats that were anchored to the bottom and supported a net and streaming lines that were designed to entangle a ship's propeller. Though only a few torpedoes (mines) had been sown in the harbor at this time, the Union navy commanders believed that the floating boom also marked a mine field, and to counter that presumed minefield, John Ericsson had designed a special iron-armored raft, 50 feet long and 27 feet wide, that the lead Union ship, the *Weehawken*, pushed in front of it. Nicknamed "the Devil," the raft had heavy chains with grappling hooks hanging down from it. The hooks were supposed to snag the mines, drag them up under the raft, and detonate them prematurely. The raft, however, proved almost as great a danger to the *Weehawken* as to the torpedoes. Its suspended chains and grapples became entangled with the *Weehawken*'s anchor chain and delayed the whole squadron for most of two hours. Then, while under way, the continuous bumping of the Weehawken's bow with the armored raft actually dented the *Weehawken*'s bow armor. Worst of all, the chains and grappling hooks threatened to entangle the whole apparatus in the buoys and impedimenta of the minefield and ensnare the *Weehawken* in the web of obstructions. As a result, the *Weehawken*'s captain, John Rodgers, "upon deliberate judgment" decided that it would be foolish "to entangle the vessel in obstructions which I did not think we could have passed through and in which we could have been caught."[22]

Instead of a bold dash into the harbor, therefore, the Union ironclads stopped opposite Fort Sumter and took it under fire. At a range that varied from 550 to 800 yards, the Union ironclads and the gunners in Fort Sumter loaded and fired as fast as they could, with heavy bolts and exploding shells impacting both the brick face of the fort's walls and the iron turrets of the monitors. In this exchange, the gunners in the fort had a number of advantages. One was that Du Pont's flagship, the deep-draft *New Ironsides*, had great difficulty maneuvering in the narrow channel, collided with two of the monitors, and finally dropped anchor to avoid going aground. As it happened, she anchored directly over a large Confederate mine, though the frustrated Confederate engineer on shore who tried to detonate the mine, found that the "confounded thing . . . would not go off." On the other hand, the *New Ironsides* was anchored so distant from Sumter that she fired instead on Fort Moultrie.[23]

That left the fight against Sumter to the seven monitors and the *Keokuk*, which for all their defensive prowess, carried only two guns each, and due to the difficulty of reloading their huge guns, they fired very slowly. Fort Sumter had more guns, and they not only fired faster, they were remarkably accurate. It soon became evident that at least some of the buoys across the harbor entrance were range markers. As soon as a monitor neared one, shell splashes erupted all around her, several hitting home. Confederate gunners fired a total of 2,209 shots, 520 of which (nearly 24 percent) struck their targets, which was excellent shooting given the technology. Union marksmanship was good, too, but the slow-firing Union monitors got off only 139 shots. Though nearly 40 percent of those shots hit the fort, they did not significantly reduce the fort's firepower.* The concussion from the explosion of those huge shells broke all the windows of the buildings in the fort and pitted the brick face of the walls, but they inflicted no serious damage. The monitors, on the other hand, suffered a great deal. The *Passaic* received two hits in quick succession very low on her turret, jamming

---

*Of those 2,206 shots, 868 came from Fort Moultrie and 810 from Fort Sumter. The rest came from smaller batteries around the harbor. By way of comparison, U.S. warships in the Battle of Manila Bay thirty-five years later fired 9,500 shells at the Spanish fleet and made only 123 hits (less than 2 percent). In fairness, it must be noted that the range at Manila Bay was much greater.

it so that it could not turn, and as a result she had to drop out of range and anchor. Other shells wrecked the steering on the *Nahant* so that she could not maneuver, and she, too, had to retire. The *Patapsco* was hit forty-seven times, the *Nantucket* fifty-one times, and the *Weehawken* fifty-three times. Worst hit of all was the experimental ironclad *Keokuk* with her two non-revolving towers, which was struck ninety times. Du Pont "soon became convinced of the utter impracticability of taking the city of Charleston by the force under my command," and he ordered his squadron to withdraw.[24]

When he gave that order, Du Pont had every intention of renewing the attack the next day, but the reports from his several captains that night convinced him that doing so would only "have converted a failure into a disaster." Indeed, after battling the rising waters overnight, the crew of the battered *Keokuk* abandoned ship and watched her sink in the shallow waters off Morris Island. (Eventually, the Confederates were able to salvage her two 11-inch guns.) Concluding that "Charleston can not be taken by a purely naval attack," Du Pont ordered his ironclads back to Port Royal for repair. Two of them had to be taken under tow, unable to make it under their own power.[25]

When he received the news, Welles was hugely disappointed, and he began to doubt Du Pont's willingness to take the fight to the enemy. Even after Du Pont submitted the reports of his ship commanders, all of whom testified to the wisdom of Du Pont's decision to terminate the assault, Welles remained skeptical. After reading them, Welles noted ruefully in his diary, "It is the recommendation of all, from the Admiral down, that no effort be made to do anything." It did not help Du Pont's case that a week after his failed attack on Charleston, David Dixon Porter successfully ran his river ironclads past Vicksburg. Very likely, this increased Welles' inclination to look upon Du Pont's decision to withdraw as mostly a matter of will.[26]

There was one bright spot for the Union navy off the South Atlantic coast that summer. In Savannah, Confederates tried to duplicate the success of the *Palmetto State* and *Chicora* with the ironclad *Atlanta*. This vessel had been built in Glasgow, Scotland, as the *Fingal*, and James D. Bulloch had used her to run a load of munitions into Savannah in November of 1861. Almost at once, however, the *Fingal* became trapped there when Union troops occupied Tybee Island in the Savannah River.

Newly promoted Rear Admiral John Adolphus Dahlgren is shown here with some of his officers and ship captains on the fantail of USS *Pembina*. Dahlgren had lobbied hard for a sea command and worked just as hard to reduce the Charleston forts, but Charleston proved defiantly resistant to the end. (Courtesy of the Naval Historical Center)

Confederate authorities therefore decided to convert her into an iron-clad and rechristened her *Atlanta*. As at Charleston, a disproportionate amount of effort and resources were committed to her conversion. Her engines were probably the best ever placed in a rebel ironclad, but a scarcity of armor plate meant that her builders had to use railroad iron to cover her reconstructed casemate. At 204 feet, she was longer than the two ironclads in Charleston, but she also drew more water, which would eventually prove fatal. Nevertheless, hopes were high in Savannah—and in Richmond—about her future success. The veteran Josiah Tattnall, who had been the last commander of the ill-fated *Virginia* (*Merrimack*), planned to take the *Atlanta* out of Wassaw Sound and attack the Union anchorage in Port Royal. Before he could attempt that, however, both he and Ingraham were relieved of their commands by Stephen Mallory. Having decided to rely on younger and more energetic commanders, Mallory replaced the 69-year-old Tattnall with the 43-year-old Commander William Webb, who had a reputation for aggressiveness—though some would have called it recklessness.[27]

Under Webb's command, the *Atlanta* sortied on July 15, 1863. Her great draft made it difficult for her to maneuver in the shallows of Wassaw Sound, and on July 17 she ran hard aground within sight of two Union monitors that Du Pont had sent to watch her, the *Weehawken* and the *Nahant*. The two Union monitors closed on the *Atlanta*, and the heavy bolts from their 15-inch guns easily punched through the jury-rigged railroad iron that made up the *Atlanta*'s armor. After receiving only five shots, Webb surrendered. After repairing her, the Federals took the *Atlanta* into the Union Navy, keeping her name. While Du Pont took some satisfaction in this little victory, Welles saw it as further evidence of the superiority and effectiveness of the monitor-type warship, and it fed his conviction that Du Pont underestimated their capability.

Du Pont himself contributed to this conclusion by his behavior in reaction to a critical article in the *Baltimore Sun*, which asserted that his attack on Charleston had failed not because of any weakness in the monitors, but because the operation had been entrusted to "incompetent hands." It was the Navy's Chief Engineer Alban Stimers, who, like Welles, was heavily invested in the success of the monitor type warship, who had fed those views to the reporter. When Du Pont learned about it, he ordered Stimers arrested. He should have left well enough alone, for the ensuing Court of Inquiry not only found Stimers innocent, it did so on the grounds that what he had said was mostly true.[28]

Following that humiliation, Du Pont must have appreciated that his career was all but over. He had already offered to resign if the Department found someone who could do what he had not—capture Charleston—and taking him up on that offer, Welles wrote him that because he had shown no enthusiasm for "a renewed attack on Charleston . . . the Department has concluded to relieve you of the command of the South Atlantic Blockading Squadron." There was some confusion about who was to succeed him. Foote was Welles' first choice, but Foote's failing health and subsequent death opened the field for the ordnance specialist John A. Dahlgren.[29]

THE THIRD PHASE of the Union effort to capture Charleston began on July 6, 1863, when Dahlgren took command of the South Atlantic

Blockading Squadron. It was two days after Lee began his retreat from Gettysburg in Pennsylvania and Pemberton surrendered the city of Vicksburg to U.S. Grant in Mississippi. Dahlgren was an ordnance expert who was a close friend of Abraham Lincoln, but he had little active service at sea. Critics of his appointment insisted that making him an admiral and appointing him to the command of a squadron was a violation of both the traditions of the sea and a disagreeable example of presidential favoritism. Aware of the criticism, Dahlgren undertook his new job with a dedication and a work ethic designed to silence the critics. He shifted his flag from the large and comfortable steam frigate *Wabash* to the cramped monitor *Catskill,* opened a close collaborative correspondence with his army counterpart, and reported to Washington daily.[30]

Dahlgren did not, however, seek to renew a "purely naval" attack on Charleston Harbor. Instead, he adopted the plan that Du Pont had long advocated: assisting the army in the capture of nearby islands from which Union artillery could silence Fort Sumter. This time the Navy Department did not insist on a *coup de main,* and Dahlgren embraced the plan suggested by the new Union army commander, Major General Quincy Adams Gillmore, in which Gillmore's soldiers would cross from Union-occupied Folly Island to Morris Island, then advance northward along that narrow spit of sand to Cummings Point. From there the army could bombard Fort Sumter to open the way for Dahlgren's monitors. Gillmore preferred the Morris Island route to renewing the effort to occupy James Island, because Morris Island was smaller and (he believed) less well defended. On the other hand, 2,500 yards south of the Cummings Point battery was another rebel fortification called Battery (or Fort) Wagner that straddled the narrow width of the island so that (as at Battery Lamar on James Island) the Union attack would be funneled into a restricted front. Because of that, the campaign for Morris Island became the longest and the bloodiest chapter of the Union siege of Charleston.

The Confederates had occupied Morris Island from the first days of the war. A Confederate battery on Cummings Point at the northern tip of Morris Island had repelled the *Star of the West* back in January of 1861, three months before the war had even begun. Since then, Confederate authorities had greatly expanded its defenses. Batteries on Cummings

Point, now called Fort Gregg, guarded the entrance to the harbor, while a new fortification that was eventually named Battery (or Fort) Wagner guarded its rear and became the target of Gillmore's soldiers.[31]

The Union campaign began on the night of July 9, 1863, when two thousand Union troops in small boats crossed Lighthouse Inlet from Folly Island to the southern tip of Morris Island under the protection of Dahlgren's monitors. The monitors fired their 11- and 15-inch shells into the ranks of the seven hundred Confederate defenders, and the bluecoats easily gained a foothold, capturing eleven enemy guns in the process. Then they moved northward, driving their foes, paralleled in their advance by the monitors offshore. Here was a genuine, and very effective, combined operation. The Union advance halted, however, when it came within artillery range of Battery Wagner.

Gillmore ordered an attack on Wagner for July 18. The peculiar geography of Morris Island meant that only a single regiment at a time could conduct the assault. Colonel Robert Gould Shaw requested the privilege of leading the attack for his 54th Massachusetts regiment composed of African-American soldiers. They attacked just at dusk, and most of the fighting took place in the dark. Dahlgren sought to assist the soldiers with gunfire support from offshore, but the navy gunners could only guess at the location of the front line by picking out the muzzle flashes in the dark. In the end, despite great heroism, the attack failed, and Gillmore, who was an engineer by training, decided that Wagner could be overcome only by a regular siege. The year before, Gillmore, then a mere captain, had supervised the bombardment of Fort Pulaski in the Savannah River. Now he sought to do much the same thing at Fort Wagner. Union engineers laid out siege lines, and throughout the rest of June and all of July, they sapped forward in the time-honored (and time-consuming) manner, moving closer and closer to the enemy. In the hottest part of the summer, Gillmore's mostly African-American soldiers toiled in the sandy soil of Morris Island plagued by insects and measuring their progress in yards. They even set up a long-range Parrott rifle in the swamp, as close as they could get to Charleston, in order to target the city itself. After constructing a platform composed of more than 13,000 sandbags, Union soldiers dragged an 8-ton Parrott rifle out to the site and set it up. Called the "swamp angel" it could fire all the way into the city.[32]

On August 17, 1863, almost exactly two months after the futile infantry assault, Union army and navy forces at Charleston began a coordinated bombardment of Battery Wagner and Fort Sumter that lasted a full week. Having assembled what a modern scholar has called "the war's largest concentration of heavy ordnance," the Union sent thousands of heavy shells raining down on the rebel forts. The rebels fired back, though they had no guns to match the size or effectiveness of the Union heavy rifled artillery. Even so, a shot from Fort Sumter struck the conning tower on the *Catskill* and jarred loose several bolts, which flew about the small space killing Dahlgren's flag captain, George Rodgers, who had asked Dahlgren for permission to resume command of his old ship for the attack.[33]

Dahlgren himself rode the monitor *Weehawken* and during this prolonged army-navy bombardment, he kept in touch with his army counterpart by flag signal. Their close cooperation was evident in the messages they sent to one another:

— "What do you think of our morning's work?"
— "Sumter appeared to be damaged a good deal. What is your opinion?"
— "One of my officers reports that the enemy are mounting a heavy gun on the sea face of Wagner."
— "I will send some monitors up to stop it as soon as they have had a little rest."[34]

Gillmore even began using cadmium lights to illuminate the targets at night, which made it difficult for the defenders to make repairs or to bring reinforcements in from Charleston by boat.

By August 21, the "swamp angel" was ready, and Gillmore sent Beauregard a message demanding the evacuation of both Morris Island and Fort Sumter on pain of having Charleston itself shelled. Receiving no reply by the stated deadline, he ordered the gun to open fire and the first shell crashed into Charleston just past 1:00 a.m. on August 22. Some of those shells contained "Greek fire," an incendiary substance designed to start fires. A year earlier during the campaign for Fredericksburg in Virginia, Ambrose Burnside had ordered his artillery to shell the houses along the Rappahannock River to prevent their use by rebel sharpshooters. At the time, Confederate authorities had loudly condemned the practice of deliberately targeting civilian homes as barbaric. Eight

After Dahlgren and Gillmore pounded Fort Sumter from August to December 1863, the fort was little more than rubble. This sketch of the fort's interior was made by Confederate Lieutenant John Key in December. Despite its condition and the removal of most of its heavy guns, it continued to hold out against Union efforts to capture it, including an amphibious assault in September. (Courtesy of the Naval Historical Center)

months later at Charleston, Gillmore argued—accurately—that the city was a legitimate target because it was in effect an armed camp, but it was evident to all that his actions were designed primarily to punish the city that many northerners held responsible for the war, to terrorize its citizens, and depress their morale. In that respect, the shells fired by the "swamp angel" foreshadowed the bombing of European cities by the U.S. Army Air Corps in World War II. The bombardment of Charleston was cut short, however, when the "swamp angel" burst on its 36th discharge.[35]

The shelling of Wagner and Sumter continued. Dahlgren's monitors were in action every day, firing at the forts and other targets of opportunity. The constant activity was wearing on the monitors: their stacks were perforated by shot holes, their iron gears rusted out, and their bottoms covered in masses of shaggy marine growth that slowed their speed to no more than 3 knots. Dahlgren had to send them back to Port Royal, two at a time, for a refit. The men began to wear down, too. Buttoned up inside iron ships during the hottest part of the year, they gave way to illness and exhaustion. William Whelan, the Union Chief of the Bureau of Medicine and Surgery, suggested that the men take a morning swim each day and drink iced tea in the afternoon. Dahlgren successfully petitioned the government to grant the monitor crews a 25 percent hardship duty pay increase. Dahlgren himself, who suffered terribly from seasickness, also began to wear down. When Gillmore came aboard the *Catskill* for a conference, Dahlgren was unable to rise from his bed to greet him.[36]

By the end of August, Wagner was all but silenced, and Sumter reduced to little more than a pile of rubble. Gillmore assumed that the army had done its job and that it was now time for the navy to take the bull by the horns. On September 1, four months after Du Pont's disastrous assault, the Union ironclads again took Fort Sumter under fire. They got off a total of 245 shots and remained largely unscathed, but Dahlgren insisted that he could not take his ironclads into the harbor so long as the network of obstructions and torpedoes clogged the ship channel. Somewhat disgruntled by the navy's timidity, Gillmore continued the siege of Battery Wagner, where his mostly African-American sappers worked closer and closer, yard by yard, to the outskirts of Battery Wagner itself. By September 5, the sappers had reached the outlines of Wagner, and Gillmore prepared an infantry assault. Accepting the reality of their circumstances, the Confederates evacuated Morris Island on the night of September 7. The rebel flag still flew above Fort Sumter, but its heavy guns had been either removed or rendered inoperable by the steady Union bombardment. Seeking to finalize the victory, Dahlgren sent a note to Sumter's commander, Major Stephen Elliott, Jr., demanding its surrender. A defiant Elliott told the messenger to "Inform Admiral Dahlgren that he may have Fort Sumter when he can take it and hold it."[37]

Convinced that this was nothing more than bravado, Dahlgren prepared to storm the fort with 500 sailors and marines collected from the various ships of his squadron. Packed into thirty small boats, they were to be towed toward the fort by the small steam tug *Daffodil*. Cut loose during the making tide, they would then row furiously toward the fort. When Dahlgren mentioned his plan to Gillmore, the general replied that he, too, was planning to launch a small boat attack from Morris Island, and suggested that the sailors and marines be put under his command for a joint attempt. This Dahlgren declined to do. Eager to seize the glory for the navy, and worried that the army might get in ahead of him, Dahlgren issued orders for the attack to take place that very night—September 8.

Dahlgren appointed the captain of the monitor *Patapsco*, Commander Thomas H. Stevens, to lead the attack. Stevens was startled by the order and protested that he had no experience with, or knowledge of, landing operations. Dahlgren dismissed his fears, assuring him that the fort had been effectively defeated by the bombardment, and that it was only necessary to go in and take possession. Two years later, defending himself against the charge that he had not pressed the attack with sufficient vigor, Stevens insisted that Dahlgren had told him: "There is nothing but a corporal's guard in the fort, all we have to do is to go and take possession." Whether or not Dahlgren used those exact words, it is evident that he underestimated both the capability and morale of the fort's defenders. As it happened, there were only 320 men inside the fort, but they were well supplied with small arms and hand grenades and supported by the guns of Fort Johnson and Fort Moultrie as well as the ironclad *Chicora*, which was anchored nearby.

Stevens supervised the collection of small boats from throughout the fleet, and at ten o'clock that night, they pushed off from the temporary flagship *Philadelphia*, forming themselves into a long string attached to the stern of the tug *Daffodil*. The tug steamed in toward the harbor, but then, unaccountably, it stopped, turned, and began to steam back out. Because there was no means of communication between the tug and the boats, the sailors and marines were confused. Were they to cast off now? Then the tug came about again. Amidst the confusion, most of the boats cast off and were carried in toward the fort by the making tide. A few others, wondering if the whole event had been called off, headed back to the *Philadelphia*.[38]

According to the plan, one division of boats was to make for the southeastern face of the fort as a diversion, while Stevens took the main body to the southern side. Once again, however, there was confusion. Some boats made straight for the fort, others stayed off and opened with small arms fire. The hundred or so men who made it ashore scrambled up the rubble in an attempt to reach the ramparts only to be pinned down by small arms fire from the defenders. Worse, the rebel gunners on the *Chicora* and those manning the artillery on James Island and Sullivan's Island also opened fire. They had previously sited their guns on the base of the fort, and now their shells exploded among the assaulting party. Watching all this, Stevens believed it would be suicide to proceed with the attack. As he wrote later, he had to decide "either to land and be captured or withdraw and save what we could." Abandoning to their fate the 125 or so men who had already landed, he ordered the rest of the boats to pull back for the squadron. Those left behind were taken prisoner.[39]

Dahlgren, of course, was disappointed. Watching from his flagship, he confided to his diary that it "did not look like a vigorous assault." Welles was disappointed, too, and eventually Stevens had to defend himself from charges that he had not pressed home the attack. Whether or not Stevens deserved his criticism, there were multiple flaws in both the planning and the execution of the assault. The first was Dahlgren's unwillingness to cooperate with the army. The close cooperation that had marked the joint conquest of Morris Island had given way over the course of the siege to the tradition of separate— and jealous—command systems. Dahlgren was no doubt aware that Welles had long hoped that the navy would gain public credit for the capture of Fort Sumter, and whether that was the decisive factor, he was unwilling to wait until Gillmore was ready to add the weight of his forces to the assault. Stevens complained that "there was a large detachment from the army in boats lying close to the fort, which retired without making any demonstration." For his part, Gillmore claimed his soldiers could not assist because their boats were trapped there by the low tide.[40]

Dahlgren's overconfidence was a product of his second mistake: his assumption that the defenders of Fort Sumter were so worn out by the constant bombardment that they would collapse before a concerted attack. Whether or not he actually told Stevens that Sumter was held by only a "corporal's guard," he clearly underestimated the determination of the defenders. His overconfidence also led him to assemble the attack in a hurry without allowing sufficient time for thorough discussion among the participants. Such coordination might have ensured that each officer knew what was expected of him. Finally, the lack of communication between the tug and the boats—and among the boats themselves—meant that instead of a coordinated assault, the Union volunteers arrived piecemeal, boat by boat.

With the failure of the amphibious assault on Fort Sumter, the active siege of Charleston entered yet another phase. The Union occupation of Cumming's Point and the virtual destruction of Fort Sumter had greatly reduced the value of Charleston as a haven for blockade-runners, and Welles was wary of risking his beloved monitors to another pummeling by the other forts that ringed the harbor. He declared, "The Department is disinclined to have its only ironclad squadron incur extreme risks when the substantial advantages have already been gained." To do so now, he acknowledged, would be "merely a point of honor." Consequently, even though Union forces controlled Morris Island, and Fort Sumter had been reduced to a pile of rubble, Charleston itself remained in Confederate hands.[41]

MORE THAN NECESSITY, it is desperation that is often the mother of invention, and inside Charleston Harbor, the Confederates experimented with ever more audacious forms of naval warfare to engage the huge and still growing Union fleet offshore. One innovation that showed particular promise was the spar torpedo. The invention of Army Captain Francis D. Lee of the Confederate engineer corps, the spar torpedo was an explosive device attached to the end of a 20- or 30-foot-long pole, which was itself attached to the bow of a small steamer, rowboat, or even a canoe, and driven into the side of a Union warship. On March 18, 1863, three weeks before the ironclad attack on Fort Sumter, Confederate Navy Lieutenant William T. Glassell set out from Charleston in a rowboat equipped with a spar torpedo hoping to sink one of the Union blockading vessels. Foolhardy as this sounds, he might have succeeded if one of the rowers had not panicked at the last minute and upset the whole mission. A month later, the Confederates planned an even more ambitious coordinated attack using a whole fleet of small boats. This time, the plan was undone when Du Pont withdrew his ships from Charleston following his unsuccessful assault. There were no more rowboat attacks on the Union blockaders that spring, but the idea of blowing up a large warship with a small boat armed only with a spar torpedo became a central feature of Confederate naval strategy in Charleston Harbor.[42]

That summer, the Charleston firm of John Fraser and Company, a branch of Fraser, Trenholm, and Company in Liverpool, offered a $100,000 bounty to anyone who could sink the *New Ironsides*, or $50,000 for sinking a monitor. In the hope of winning such a prize, a former blockade-runner named James Carlin, navigated a small steam ram called the *Torch* out of the harbor on August 20, 1863. The *Torch* was equipped with a spar torpedo, but it was characteristic of many such audacious Confederate efforts that the engines of the *Torch* failed and the small boat began taking on water so that Carlin was forced to call off the attack.[43]

In spite of these disappointments, the potential of spar torpedoes was effectively demonstrated that fall by a small boat that was built 30 miles up the Cooper River and transported down to Charleston by train. Named the *David* (which seemed appropriate given its mission), this small cigar-shaped vessel was only 54 feet long and 5.5 feet wide. She was designed to sit so low in the water that only her conning tower, smoke stack, and about ten feet of her rounded hull would show above the surface. Under the command of Lieutenant Glassell, who had first tried to attack the Union Navy in a rowboat, the *David* set out on October 5, 1863, to sink the *New Ironsides*.

On board the big Union ironclad, Acting Ensign Charles Howard had the watch, and when a lookout reported an object in the water, he called out: "What boat is that?" The curious object continued to approach without responding, and when it was only 40 yards away, Howard gave the order to fire into it with small arms. Glassell, who was in the conning tower of the *David*, responded by firing a double load of buckshot from a shotgun, mortally wounding Ensign Howard, and seconds later Glassell detonated the torpedo at the end of the spar.[44]

The explosion sent a geyser of water nearly a hundred feet into the air, caved in the side of the *New Ironsides*, broke several of her ribs, and shattered the stanchions that supported the engine room. The explosion was not fatal, however, because the torpedo struck next to the ship's coal bunker and the stored coal blunted the force of the explosion. Though crippled, the *New Ironsides* stayed afloat. The *David* was less fortunate. The force of the explosion jammed the steering gear of the tiny boat, and the geyser of water that cascaded down her stack put out her engines. Glassell believed his vessel was sinking and ordered

This photo of a David boat sitting high and dry alongside a wharf in Charleston shows its peculiar construction. Because it was steam powered it could not fully submerge, but its low profile allowed it to conduct stealth attacks with spar torpedoes on Union blockading vessels. (Courtesy of the Naval Historical Center)

abandon ship. Everyone but the pilot (who could not swim) jumped over the side; Glassell and another man were soon taken prisoner. But the *David* did not sink. Instead it drifted away from the *New Ironsides*, and the engineer, James Tomb, climbed back on board. Assisted by the non-swimming pilot, he managed to get the engines going again, and eventually the *David* made it safely back to port.[45]

As for Glassell, Dahlgren ordered him clapped into irons, and he was eventually taken to New York to be put on trial for conducting an illegal form of warfare. It never came to that, however, since the Union, too, was experimenting with torpedo boats, and in the end he was exchanged for Lieutenant Conover who had been captured in the *Isaac Smith* the previous January. The attack impressed and alarmed the Union high command, and Dahlgren wrote to Welles of the torpedo boats that their "rapidity of movement, control of direction, and precise explosion indicate, I think, the introduction of the torpedo element as a means of certain warfare."[46]

Beauregard agreed. Once a strong advocate of ironclads, the rebel commander had decided that the loss of the *Atlanta* the previous spring had proved that Confederate ironclads could not compete with Union monitors. Because the monitors were "invulnerable to shots above water beyond 800 yards," Beauregard now decided that "they should be attacked below water." He therefore advocated a whole fleet of torpedo boats. Naturally prone to exaggeration, he prophesied, "Half a dozen of these steamers would raise the blockade of our Atlantic and Gulf coasts, and enable us to recover the navigation of the Mississippi River." At Charleston, Savannah, and even Augusta, new "David boats," as they came to be called, were laid down, and as many as a dozen of them (the precise number is uncertain) were eventually completed. There was bickering between the Confederate army and navy, and between the ordnance and engineering branches, about who was in charge of the program, and as always, finding reliable engines for them was an industrial bottleneck. These problems meant that despite their early promise, and despite Beauregard's prediction, the David boats did not succeed in changing the balance of power off Charleston Harbor.[47]

They did, however, cause the Union blockaders many anxious nights. Dahlgren reorganized the blockade to account for the Davids, and developed a number of counter-measures, including placing floating booms around some ships and calling for his captains to maintain a constant vigil. Interestingly, he suggested to Welles that the best countermeasure would be the construction of some Union torpedo boats whose mission it would be to attack and destroy the Davids. Though this was not done at Charleston, in the ensuing decades many such vessels were built. They were called "torpedo boat destroyers," a designation eventually shortened to "destroyers"—a class of warship still in use today.[48]

Even more revolutionary and audacious than the David boats was the subsequently famous *H. L. Hunley*, which American sailors identified as the "Diver," and many in Charleston called the "Fishboat." The brain child of a New Orleans entrepreneur named Horace L. Hunley, it was a true submarine. Because it had no engine, it could remain fully submerged as long as the air held out, which was several hours. It was propelled by eight men seated along one side of the boat who worked a crankshaft that turned a propeller. Hunley's vision was to attack an enemy ship by diving under the hull of the target vessel while towing a torpedo at the end of a 150-foot tether. The submarine would surface on the opposite side of the target and pull the torpedo into her hull.

Unlike the Confederate ironclads or the David boats, the *Hunley* was constructed in New Orleans not as part of a Confederate naval effort, but as a privateer. After the fall of New Orleans, she was shipped by rail to Mobile and eventually to Charleston. There, Beauregard decided that she was too valuable to leave in the hands of amateurs, and (like the *Manassas* at New Orleans) she was seized by the government. Beauregard put her under the command of Confederate Navy Lieutenant John Payne. Almost at once, the Fishboat proved unlucky when, approaching the dock on August 29, 1863, Payne inadvertently stepped on the lever controlling the dive fins while the hatches were open. The boat nosed downward, and water cascaded into her. Payne and two others escaped; five others went down with the boat.[49]

After that disaster, Horace Hunley came from Mobile to try his hand in refitting and testing the vessel, though technically he was not in "command," for he was not a military officer. Hunley brought with him Army First Lieutenant George Dixon of the 21st Alabama regiment, who had worked on the boat in Mobile. It was Hunley, however, who was in charge of the Fishboat on October 15, 1863 when she went out to make a practice run at the CSS *Indian Chief*, which it was using as a target vessel. The *Hunley* submerged as planned and passed under the target. But she never surfaced. Speculation at the time and since has been that Hunley himself had opened the sea cock in the forward part of the boat and failed to close it in the complete darkness that was produced when the boat nosed downward. Hunley's body was discovered with his head in the forward hatchway, and with his hand over his head as if he had been trying to push open the hatch cover that he had unbolted. The last minutes of the crew as the water rose about them in complete darkness can only be imagined.[50]

Salvaged again from the bottom of Charleston Harbor and rechristened the *H. L. Hunley* after her martyred inventor, the Fishboat was refitted once more and given to the command of Lieutenant Dixon, who managed to gather yet a third crew of volunteers from the *Indian Chief*. (It was during this refit, in December of 1863, that the southern painter Conrad

Wise Chapman, produced the only known contemporary image of the *Hunley*.) Once Dixon took command, he jettisoned Horace Hunley's notion of dragging a torpedo at the end of a long tow rope and adopted the system used by the David boats of a spar torpedo attached to the bow. That meant it would not be necessary to submerge completely during the attack; the *Hunley* would function essentially as a David boat, but with a lower silhouette and with muscle power instead of steam power for propulsion.

Under Dixon's command, the *H. L. Hunley* made her way out of the harbor on the night of February 17, 1864, and set a course toward the closest Union warship, the USS *Housatonic*, several miles offshore. Acting Master John Crosby was the officer of the deck on the *Housatonic* that night, and at about 8:45 p.m., he noticed something in the water only about 100 yards away. The two hatches of the *Hunley* (which Crosby called "protuberances") were just visible, and they made "a slight ripple in the water" as the object moved toward the *Housatonic* about at "3 or 4 knots." It looked, Crosby said later, like "a plank moving in the water," though he also noticed a "glimmer of light" from the forward protuberance. Having been warned to keep a sharp eye out for David boats, Crosby immediately ordered the anchor chain slipped, backed the engines, and called the crew to quarters. The captain of the *Housatonic*, Charles Pickering, rushed onto deck and saw an approaching object that "was shaped like a large whale boat, about two feet, more or less, under water." He ordered the ship to "Go astern faster." It was too late. The torpedo at the end of the *Hunley*'s spar exploded against the *Housatonic*'s hull just forward of the mizzenmast, and the ship began sinking immediately, going down stern first and heeling over to port before settling on the bottom with her weather deck about 15 feet below the surface. The crew scrambled up into the rigging and clung to it as the ship settled. Eventually they were rescued by the USS *Canandaigua*.[51]

The story of what happened to the *H. L. Hunley* is more of a mystery. For many years it was assumed that somehow the explosion of the torpedo had also destroyed the tiny submarine. But two facts contradicted such a scenario. No wreckage of the *Hunley* was found in the vicinity of the *Housatonic*, and, more conclusively, after the explosion, Dixon actually signaled news of his success to watchers on the shore. By prearrangement, Dixon was to show a blue light if the mission was successful, and a blue light was seen and acknowledged by Confederates on Sullivan's Island. It was also seen by men on board the USS *Canandaigua*. Clearly, then, the *Hunley* did not go down as a result of the initial explosion of her torpedo. Yet she never returned from her successful sortie, and her final hours have been the source of endless speculation.

Just over 130 years later, on May 3, 1995, divers employed by the adventure writer Clive Cussler found the *Hunley* lying upright and mostly undamaged on the Continental Shelf more than a quarter mile to *seaward* of where the *Housatonic* had gone down. Her final resting place suggests not only that the *Hunley* survived the explosion, but also that she made her way further offshore, perhaps to avoid the several vessels that rushed to the aid of the *Housatonic*. After the *Hunley* was raised and examined, the presence of calcium stalagmites inside the hull lent credence to the supposition that she submerged deliberately and remained watertight for years afterward. This seems to support the theory advanced by Brian Hicks and Schuyler Kropf in their book, *Raising the Hunley*, that Dixon took his boat to the bottom to wait there while the blockade vessels cleared the area, and the tide changed. It is possible that the scarring on the propeller cowling and her detached rudder were consequences of being struck by the *Canandaigua's* own propeller as that ship moved toward the scene. Or it may be that Dixon and the rest of the Hunley's crew simply waited in the dark for the tide to turn before beginning their return to port. If so, Hicks and Knopf speculate, they may have gotten "too comfortable" and died of anoxia, perhaps in their sleep.[52]

On the Union side, Dahlgren reported to Welles that the *Housatonic* had been sunk by a David boat, and he issued more orders about how to prevent a recurrence. Vessels on the inshore blockade were not to anchor but to remain in constant motion. If they did anchor, they were to set up "outriggers and hawsers stretched around with rope netting dropped in the water" and "use their utmost vigilance."[53]

In spite of the pyrrhic success of the *Hunley*, the Union noose around Charleston continued to tighten. By the end of 1864, only one channel into the harbor was open, and it was guarded around the clock by a score of Union warships. Blockade-running at Charleston all but ceased. So did Confederate counteroffensives. The *Hunley* was lost, the engines on the David boats were unreliable, and the vessels of the small Confederate ironclad fleet, also plagued by weak and unreliable engines, seldom got under way. When they did, they never ventured further than Fort Johnson halfway down the harbor. Though the rebel flag continued to fly defiantly from Fort Sumter, Fort Moultrie, and the Battery, for most practical purposes, the harbor at Charleston was closed.[54]

THERE WERE OTHER Union efforts to seize the forts that protected Charleston Harbor. In July 1864, and again in February of 1865, the Union army sought to return to James Island in order to seize Fort Johnson. As in the small boat attack on Fort Sumter, there was confusion, misunderstanding, and failure. The February assault, covered by naval gunfire from two Union monitors, secured a lodgment on the island and chased off some Confederate pickets, but after encountering resistance, the landing party fell back to Cole's Island near the mouth of the Stono River where the campaign had started nearly three years earlier.

Despite repeated and often heroic efforts to batter down the Confederate defenses, Charleston resisted every Union assault until the last days of the war. Only when William T. Sherman led his army from Atlanta to the sea did it become apparent that the fatal threat to Charleston was not from the sea but from the land. Once Sherman's army arrived at Savannah, it was clear that if the Confederates continued to hold on to Charleston, they would be cut off and the garrison captured. As devastating as the loss of Charleston would be to fading Confederate hopes, the loss of its defending army would be worse.[55]

Sherman had no intention of marching on Charleston, but he urged Dahlgren to "make as much impression on Charleston as [his] force permitted" to keep the enemy's attention focused there. In pursuit of that, Dahlgren sent his inshore ironclads to reinvestigate the line of obstructions across the harbor entrance in preparation for another assault. On January 15, 1865, the monitor *Patapsco* was supervising several small boats that were engaged in surveying the channel when "there was a shock, a sound of explosion, [and] a cloud of smoke on the port side." The *Patapsco* had struck a mine and "in less than half a minute," she was sinking fast, her deck already under water. Thirty seconds later the ship slipped under the surface, taking 62 officers and men down with her.[56]

In spite of that, the writing was clearly on the wall for the defenders of Charleston, and on the night of February 17, 1865, Confederate forces quietly prepared to evacuate the city and its protecting forts. The crews of the three rebel ironclads—*Charleston, Chicora,* and *Palmetto State*—set fire to their ships, which subsequently exploded, one by one. (Witnesses later claimed that the cloud of smoke from the *Palmetto State* formed itself into the shape of a Palmetto tree.) Ashore, the soldiers laid powder trains to the magazines and marched out of the forts leaving their flags flying. Explosions resounded all around the harbor. At daylight the next morning, the monitor USS *Canonicus* crept slowly in toward the harbor. Approaching within range of Fort Moultrie, Lieutenant Commander George Belknap fired two shells toward the fort. For the first time in three years, there was no reply.[57]

THERE WAS ONE MORE POSTSCRIPT. On Good Friday, April 14, 1865, Union officials staged a ceremony to mark the raising of the American flag over the ruins of what had been Fort Sumter. A crowd of dignitaries, including the Reverend Henry Ward Beecher, was on hand to witness the solemn event. Robert Anderson, the Union officer who had surrendered the fort in 1861, was there to raise the same flag that he had lowered exactly four years earlier. Even as officials prepared to begin the ceremony, however, astonishing news arrived: Lee had surrendered his army in Virginia! The news created a sensation. Now the raising of the flag over Fort Sumter would mark not only the redemption of Union honor, but the end of the war. After an invocation by the army chaplain, Anderson made a short speech and raised the tattered flag to the top of the pole. From the partially restored ramparts, Union artillery began a one hundred gun salute, and all around the harbor, the guns of Dahlgren's warships added their voice to the thundering cacophony. Once the echoes had faded, and the smoke settled, Beecher ascended the platform to give the principal oration, a lengthy and appropriately florid speech, which ended with a call for national reunion and forgiveness. "The moment their willing hand drops the musket and they return to their allegiance," Beecher intoned, "then stretch out your own honest right hand to greet them."[58]

That night in Ford's Theatre, John Wilkes Booth shot Abraham Lincoln to death.

6

The End Game

Mobile, Wilmington, and the Cruise of the *Shenandoah*

BY THE LATE SUMMER OF 1864, as Grant and Lee fought their bloody and relentless way from Cold Harbor to Petersburg, and Sherman closed in on Atlanta, only a few southern ports remained open to Confederate blockade-runners. The two most important were Mobile, Alabama, and Wilmington, North Carolina. Both cities commanded special interest and effort from Union naval officials, and both were stages for dramatic—even iconic—moments in the naval history of the Civil War. At Mobile, Farragut famously damned the torpedoes and ran his fleet into the harbor exactly as Welles had repeatedly urged Du Pont to do at Charleston. And at Wilmington, after one aborted effort, the rebel citadel of Fort Fisher finally fell to a genuine combined operation as navy vessels pounded it with gunfire while soldiers stormed its walls. In both cases, the defenders relied primarily on coastal forts to fend off naval attacks; in both cases, the outcome illuminated not only the enhanced capability of modern naval weaponry against such forts, but also the overwhelming superiority of Union naval forces over their Confederate counterparts. Meanwhile on the high seas, the Confederate flag continued to induce fear in the hearts of Yankee merchants as the CSS *Shenandoah* carried on the commerce raiding strategy of an increasingly beleaguered Confederacy.

MOBILE BAY is a large, enclosed body of water that thrusts into the Alabama Gulf coastline like a spearhead. The city of Mobile is located near the tip of the spear, some 30 miles north of the entrance to the bay, and it was important because by late 1863 it was the only Gulf coast city still under Confederate control that had railroad connections to the rest of the South. The entrance to the bay was constricted by narrow spits of land that arched together like collarbones to form a natural barrier broken only by a 3-mile-wide gap, and guarding that gap were two forts: Fort Morgan on the eastern headland at Mobile Point and Fort Gaines on Big Dauphin Island. Just as Fort Sumter and Fort Moultrie constituted a gauntlet for Du Pont's (and later Dahlgren's) ships at Charleston, these forts at Mobile made a daunting barrier for the fleet of Rear Admiral David Glasgow Farragut.

Fort Morgan was the more dangerous of the two. Like Fort Sumter, it had been built as part of the Third System of American coastal defense forts in the 1820s and 30s, and, like Sumter, its thick walls protected covered casemates that were connected by brick archways. Unlike Sumter, its star-shaped footprint reflected the style of the great French engineer Vauban who had designed fortifications for Louis XIV in the late seventeenth century. It mounted more than forty heavy guns, most of them 32-pounders, but boasted as well a few 8-inch Brooke rifles and 10-inch Columbiads, and those guns frowned over that three-mile-wide ship channel. Moreover, because much of the western portion of the channel was crowded with underwater torpedoes and obstructions, ships entering or leaving the bay had to keep to the right of the opening and pass directly under the guns of Fort Morgan. Finally, by 1864, the Confederates had vastly improved types of torpedoes, and though there were still occasional duds when the casing leaked or the fuse failed, they were far more reliable than those of 1862. Indeed, the presence of effective torpedoes at Mobile Bay would be a key element of the confrontation that took place there in August 1864.[1]

In addition to the forts and the torpedoes, the Confederates also had a naval force in Mobile Bay. The commander of that force was Admiral Franklin Buchanan who had commanded the ironclad CSS *Virginia* during its initial sortie back in March of 1862. Badly wounded on that occasion, he had spent several months recuperating before Mallory sent him south to Mobile in August of 1862 with orders to construct and

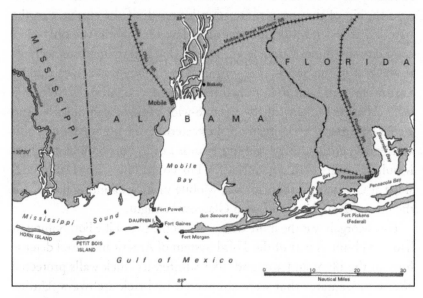

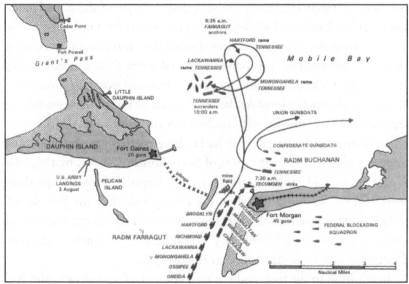

FARRAGUT'S ATTACK ON MOBILE BAY, AUGUST 5, 1864. Map by Bill Clipson, reprinted with permission from *The Naval Institute Historical Atlas of the U.S. Navy* by Craig L. Symonds, © 1995.

command an ironclad squadron there. Buchanan inherited one ironclad upon his arrival: the converted side-wheel steamer *Baltic*, which
had been purchased and armed by the State of Alabama and turned
over to the navy just prior to Buchanan's arrival. But the *Baltic* was
a disaster of a vessel: slow, unreliable, and almost as great a danger to
her crew as to the enemy. Within a year, Buchanan would order her
decommissioned in order to use her iron for other projects. Nor could
Buchanan convert existing ships into ironclads (as had been done with
the *Merrimack/Virginia*), for there were no appropriate vessels available
for conversion in Mobile Bay. Instead, he had to build an ironclad fleet
from scratch, and, as elsewhere throughout the South, that proved a
daunting endeavor.[2]

In the hope of assembling an ironclad squadron, the Confederates
laid down three ships in Selma, Alabama, 200 miles up the Tombigbee
River from Mobile, and a fourth at Montgomery. But as usual the
Confederacy's strategic vision was greater than its resources. There
was simply not enough iron plate, heavy guns, and especially marine
engines to build four new ironclads. Two of the vessels built at Selma—
Huntsville and *Tuscaloosa*—were so underpowered they could barely
move and had to be relegated to the status of floating batteries. The
large side-wheel steamer constructed at Montgomery—named the
Nashville—was so huge there simply wasn't enough iron plate to cover
her massive superstructure. In the end, the Confederates had only
enough material resources to build one ironclad. That one was the
screw-driven casemate ironclad CSS *Tennessee*.[3]

Launched at Selma in February of 1863, the wooden shell of the
Tennessee was floated downriver to Mobile to receive her armor, her
engines, and her guns. At 209 feet, she was 60 feet shorter than the
Virginia, and 60 feet longer than the *Chicora* and the *Palmetto State*
at Charleston. Her oak and pine casemate was 2 feet thick, and over
the top of that, workers layered on 5 inches of iron armor (6 on the
forward shield). Like most southern ironclads, her weak point was her
engine plant, which was cannibalized from the Yazoo River steamer
Alonzo Child and hopelessly inadequate for a large ironclad. The ship's
battery was another problem. There were plenty of 32-pound smoothbores available, but such weapons were useless against enemy ironclads.
What Buchanan needed were 9- or 10-inch rifled guns, but there were

none were to be had. In the end the *Tennessee* was armed with a battery of 7-inch and 6.4-inch double-banded Brooke rifles forged at Selma by the man who had succeeded Buchanan as captain of the *Virginia*, Catesby ap Roger Jones. Attaching the iron armor to the *Tennessee's* casemate also proved difficult. Since she was already afloat when she received her battery and her armor, the workmen had to attach some of the armor plate below the waterline on each side. This was accomplished by careening the ship over onto one side while half-submerged workmen bolted the iron plate to her hull.[4]

Obtaining a crew was another problem. The Confederacy was short of manpower everywhere, and there were simply not enough men available unless they could be drawn from the army. Confederate army commanders, however, were equally strapped for manpower and unwilling to give up their men unless explicitly ordered to do so. Not until February of 1864 did the Confederate War Secretary James Seddon direct the local army commander to give Buchanan the men he needed. Even then, they were a mixed lot. Only six of the 143 crewmen on the *Tennessee* were rated as "seamen," another three were rated "ordinary seamen," and the rest as landsmen or firemen (coal heavers). Sixty percent of them (88 of 143) were foreign born, with most of those coming from Ireland. Nevertheless, Buchanan was determined to whip them into shape. "I have some hard characters to deal with," he wrote to John K. Mitchell, the Chief of the Bureau of Order and Detail in Richmond, "and I am determined that they shall not violate orders as they please."[5]

By June of 1864, Buchanan at last had a fully operational, armed and armored warship ready for battle in Mobile Bay. His first instinct was to steam out of the bay and attack Farragut's blockading squadron of wooden ships off the coast, but counseled by the pilots that the *Tennessee* was unlikely to survive the heavier chop in the open Gulf waters beyond Mobile Point, he reluctantly accepted the fact that he would have to wait for Farragut to make the first move.

FARRAGUT WAS PERFECTLY WILLING to make the first move. Indeed, he had expected to do so as early as May 1864 when the *Tennessee* was still being completed. As part of Ulysses S. Grant's grand strategic plan, Farragut, in cooperation with an army commanded by Nathaniel P. Banks, was to attack Mobile in May of 1864 while Meade assailed Lee in Virginia, and Sherman attacked Joseph E. Johnston in Georgia. Banks, however, got sidetracked into an expedition up the Red River in Louisiana, and the assault on Mobile had to be delayed. Farragut was willing to tackle the place on his own, but aware that the enemy had at least one ironclad inside the bay (perhaps several of them), he was compelled to wait for the Navy Department to send him some monitors to deal with it. To supply this need, Welles ordered the double-turreted river monitors *Chickasaw* and *Winnebago*, each of them boasting four 11-inch guns, from New Orleans, and two new *Canonicus*-class single-turreted monitors, *Manhattan* and *Tecumseh*, which carried enormous 15-inch guns, from New York.

By the end of July, all but the *Tecumseh* had arrived, and Farragut was growing impatient. A Union army force of two thousand men commanded by Major General Gordon Granger was to land on Big Dauphin Island on August 3 to assault Fort Gaines, and Farragut did not want it said that the navy had been tardy. With or without the *Tecumseh*, he was determined to make his move on August 5, but as it happened, she arrived at 5:30 p.m. on August 4 towed by the USS *Bienville*.[6]

Farragut met with his captains and appraised them of his plan for the attack. The ships would be arrayed in two columns for the run into the bay, he told them. The column on the right, nearest Fort Morgan, would be composed of the four ironclads with the newly arrived *Tecumseh* in the lead. To the left, and slightly behind these behemoths, Farragut arranged his wooden ships "in couples," lashed together with the smaller vessels to port (farthest from Fort Morgan). The bigger wooden ships could thus employ their broadsides against Fort Morgan during the run through the channel while simultaneously shielding the smaller vessels, and if one of the pair were damaged, the other could tow it to safety. Farragut had planned to lead this column himself in the *Hartford*, lashed to the smaller *Metacomet*, which was under the command of James Jouett. At the last minute, however, his captains talked him out of it on the grounds that if he were killed or injured, it might throw the whole attack into confusion. Instead, therefore, the screw frigate *Brooklyn* would lead the column of wooden ships, with the smaller *Octorora* lashed to her port side. Farragut in the *Hartford* would go second. There was no need to fight it out with Fort Morgan the way Du Pont had attempted to slug it out with Sumter because unlike Charleston Harbor, Mobile Bay was big enough that once the Union ships were through the pass, they would be out of range of the forts. Farragut therefore planned to run his ships past the forts and into the bay while suffering as little damage as possible. One other element of his plan deserves mention here for it played a role in the battle to come: Because the army force on Big Dauphin Island was to cooperate in the attack, a pair of army signalmen was placed on board each vessel in order to speed communication.[7]

Each ship, each captain, had a specific mission. The two *Canonicus*-class monitors were to deal with the CSS *Tennessee* and, in particular, keep her away from the wooden ships. The two river monitors were to engage the water batteries at the foot of Fort Morgan. While they exchanged fire with the fort, the wooden ships, led by the *Brooklyn*, were to dash through the entrance as quickly as possible and into the bay. The unknown factor in all this was the torpedo field, marked by a channel buoy to show its easternmost limit. Unlike Charleston, where the South had sought to use torpedoes as offensive weapons, Buchanan had not bothered with them at Mobile except as defensive barriers. Old sea dog that he was, Buchanan believed that trying to sink ships offshore with spar torpedoes attached to small craft was a crack-brained notion. To his friend John Mitchell, he wrote, "I have little faith in those things." That is probably why he did not object when Horace Hunley's submarine was loaded onto a railroad flatcar for shipment to Charleston. Buchanan did, however, invest heavily in defensive torpedoes, and by the end of July more than 180 of them had been placed in the westernmost part of the ship channel, offset from one another in a checkerboard pattern so that there was no clear passage through the field. Aware of that, Farragut ordered his captains to "take care to pass to the eastward of the easternmost buoy" to avoid entering the mine field.[8]

The ships of the Union flotilla were ready before dawn, and by 5:30 they were under way. August 5 dawned cloudy "with very little sun" and gentle winds from the southwest. As Farragut's two columns of ships neared the entrance to the bay, the *Tecumseh* fired first, sending a 15-inch shell toward Fort Morgan. The fort responded with an 8-inch shell from a Brooke rifle. The firing soon became general, and smoke began to fill the narrow channel combining with the morning mist to obscure visibility. The Confederates had the early advantage not only because the guns in Fort Morgan were elevated, but also because the *Tennessee* could fire down the length of the Union column with her broadside, and the Union ships could reply only with their bow guns. In the parlance of nineteenth-century naval battles, the *Tennessee* capped Farragut's "T."[9]

Peering through the narrow slit in the pilothouse of the *Tecumseh*, Captain Tunis A. M. Craven focused on the movements of the *Tennessee*, which was his special objective, and he began to edge over to the left in order to close with her. That put the column of ironclads directly ahead of the column of paired wooden ships. Leading that column was James Alden in the *Brooklyn*, and the movement of the *Tecumseh* put him in a tight spot. If he also moved left to give the ironclads the right of way, he would be forced into the minefield; if he stayed east of the buoy to stay out of the minefield, he would run up the backs of the ironclads. At about the same time, he spied "a row of suspicious-looking buoys . . . directly under our bows." Torpedoes! With nowhere to go, Alden stopped.[10]

Behind him, the other ships, too, came to a halt to avoid running up on one another. Farragut immediately signaled Alden by flag hoist to "Go ahead." Alden ordered his army signal team to answer by wig wag, which was faster and more specific than flag hoist, especially amidst the smoke that was now filling the channel. On the *Hartford*, however, Farragut had ordered the army signal officers below, and now he had to send for them to decipher the message. Minutes passed before Farragut learned Alden's response: "The monitors are right ahead. We cannot go on without passing them. What shall we do?" Farragut again responded by telling everyone to "Go ahead." The worst possible circumstance was for the whole attack to come to a dead stop under the guns of Fort Morgan.[11]

Meanwhile, on board the *Tecumseh*, Craven was still focused on the *Tennessee*, now only 600 yards ahead, when a muffled thump shook the big ironclad, and within seconds she began to nose downward and list badly to starboard. The big monitor rolled over onto her starboard side, her bow plunged downward, her stern rose up out of the water with the brass propeller still turning in the air, and then she shot downward "like an arrow twanged from the bow," according to one witness.[12] In less than a minute the water where she had been was empty save for a handful of survivors struggling to avoid begin sucked down by the vortex.*

By now, Farragut had climbed into the rigging of the *Hartford* in order to be able to see over the smoke. Worried that he might fall from his perch, his flag captain, Percival Drayton, sent a sailor up with a line to secure him there. At first, Farragut waved him away, but then seeing the wisdom of it, he passed the line around his waist and allowed the sailor the tie him into the rigging. The sight of the *Tecumseh* going down must have been heart-stopping, but there was simply no option now but to forge ahead. He sent a small boat being towed by the *Metacomet* to pick up survivors from the *Tecumseh*, but ordered the *Hartford* to continue. Another message arrived from Alden: "Our best monitor has been sunk." Farragut hardly needed Alden to tell him this, and his orders to Alden remained the same: "Go ahead." Instead the *Brooklyn* began to back down. The whole movement was collapsing into confusion and disorder.

This is when Farragut took matters in hand and ordered the pilot on the *Hartford* to take the flagship out of line, and pass the *Brooklyn* on its port side. That would take the *Hartford*—and the *Metacomet*, still lashed alongside—directly through the minefield, but there was no other option. As the *Hartford* passed the *Brooklyn*, Farragut called over to Alden to ask him what was the problem, to which Alden shouted back "Torpedoes!" According to tradition, this is when Farragut replied: "Damn the torpedoes!" Over the years, several versions of this have emerged into the popular culture. The most famous is "Damn the torpedoes, full speed ahead." A more likely version is "Damn the torpedoes. Four bells, Captain Drayton. Go ahead, Jouett, full speed." Whatever his precise words, his meaning was unmistakable.[13]

As the screw sloop steamed slowly through the minefield, with Farragut still in the rigging, the sailors on the *Hartford* all but held their

---

*As the *Tecumseh* was sinking, both Captain Craven and the ship's pilot, John Collins, made their way from the pilothouse down into the turret, by then abandoned. They reached the bottom of the ladder to the outside at the same time. According to Collins, Craven stepped aside, saying, "After you, pilot," allowing Collins to scramble to safely. Craven never made it.

collective breath. Many expected momentarily to hear that muffled thump that indicated they had hit a torpedo. "Some of us expected every moment to feel the shock of an explosion," one recalled, "we imagined that we heard some caps [fuses] explode." But the expected explosion never came. Instead the *Hartford* passed safely through the minefield, followed by the rest of the fleet, each ship following carefully in the wake of the flagship. By 8:30, Farragut's entire squadron had passed the forts, survived the mine field, and was well inside Mobile Bay.[14]

Buchanan directed the *Tennessee* to steam directly for the Union flagship as she exited the minefield, and at near point blank range the rebel ironclad fired a 7-inch shell into the *Hartford*. It blew a huge hole in her side, killed ten men and wounded five, but struck too far above the waterline to sink her. Buchanan then sought to ram the *Hartford*, but the wooden sloop was twice as fast as the big ironclad and easily eluded her attack. Undeterred, Buchanan made several more runs at other Union ships as they passed into the bay, but she simply lacked the speed to catch them. Nor could the Union ships harm the *Tennessee* since the shells from the guns on the Federal warships glanced harmlessly off her casemate. One sailor on the *Brooklyn* noted that their shots "didn't seem to have any more effect on her than a bullet on the hide of an alligator."[15]

As the rest of the Union ships passed into the bay, the *Tennessee* fired into them as fast as the men could load. The *Kenebec*, *Onieda*, and *Ossipee* all suffered horribly while their return fire bounced off the casemate of the *Tennessee* "like peas from a shovel." Still, one by one the faster Union ships slipped past the lumbering *Tennessee* and made their way to safety several miles inside the bay. With no targets within range, Buchanan withdrew his big ironclad to the protection of Fort Morgan.[16]

The battle had opened that morning before either side had sent the hands to breakfast, and during this respite in the fighting, the men on both sides sat down to eat. Both Farragut and Buchanan planned to renew the battle. Strategically, Farragut had the stronger imperative. His squadron would not really command Mobile Bay until the *Tennessee* was neutralized; for his part, the longer Buchanan kept the *Tennessee* afloat as a force in being, the longer it would restrict Farragut's actions. Despite that, Buchanan was part of a culture where declining battle was an admission of weakness, and he decided that as soon as his men had eaten, he would take the *Tennessee* back out into the bay to renew the battle.

Farragut saw the *Tennessee* get under way again, and he wondered if Buchanan was going out of the harbor to attack those ships that had not yet entered. Rechecking her course, he exclaimed, "No! Bucks's coming here! Get under way at once; we must be ready for him!" He ordered Drayton to aim the *Hartford* directly at the *Tennessee*, and the two ships charged toward one another at a combined speed of 15 knots.[17]

Just as the Federal ships had been forced to run a gauntlet of forts to get into Mobile Bay, the *Tennessee* now had to run a gauntlet of Federal ships in her headlong attack. Aware that their guns had little effect on the big ironclad, the Federal captains tried to run her down. The screw sloop *Monongahela*, which had been fitted with an iron prow, was the first. She struck the *Tennessee* at an oblique angle, the blow sending the men on both ships sprawling to the deck and spinning the big iron-clad around "as upon a pivot." The iron prow of the *Monongahela* was "entirely carried away, together with the cutwater," but the armored shield of the *Tennessee* held firm. Buchanan's flag captain, James D. Johnston, was both relieved and a bit surprised. "We are all right!" he exclaimed. "They can never run us down now."[18]

Next the *Lackawanna* smashed into the *Tennessee*. The collision crushed in the stem of the *Lackawanna* and dented the side of the *Tennessee* starting a slow leak. Only feet apart, the men on the two ships screamed at one another. On the *Lackawanna*, the men threw a spittoon and a holystone at the rebel ram along with their insults. After the *Lackawanna* slipped astern of the *Tennessee*, the big monitor *Manhattan*, sister ship of the doomed *Tecumseh*, came up alongside. Lieutenant Arthur D. Wharton was peering out one of the *Tennessee*'s gunports when a "slowly revolving turret revealed the cavernous depths of a mammoth gun" only yards away. "Stand clear the port side!" he hollered jumping back, and a moment later a 440-pound iron bolt from one of the *Manhattan*'s 15-inch guns smashed into the casemate of the *Tennessee*. Unlike earlier shells from smaller Federal guns, this one broke through the 5 inches of iron and 2 feet of wood that made up the *Tennessee*'s casemate.[19]

This famous painting entitled *An August Morning with Farragut* by William M. Overend depicts the moment when the USS *Hartford*, with Farragut rather nonchalantly holding onto the lower rigging, scraped past Buchanan's *Tennessee* (seen dimly at right). Note the presence of a black sailor in the crew of the 9-inch Dahlgren gun in the foreground. (Courtesy of the Naval Historical Center)

Undaunted, Buchanan ordered Captain Johnston to steady up on a course to intercept the *Hartford*, and the two vessels continued to close one another. Had they met bows on, they might well have sunk one another, but at the last second, the helmsman on the *Tennessee* moved the wheel slightly to starboard and the two vessels scraped past each other, virtually touching, while gunners on both ships fired, and men screamed insults at one another. Unlikely as it seems, Percival Drayton later claimed that he saw the figure of Buchanan himself through an open gunport and, overcome with fury, threw his binoculars at him. The *Hartford's* 9-inch Dahlgren guns fired solid shot at the *Tennessee* "at a distance of perhaps not more than 8 feet" but without doing her any injury. On the *Tennessee*, only three guns bore on the *Hartford* and the primers on two of them failed, so that the Confederates got off only a single shot as the two ships passed, though that one shell exploded on the berth deck killing five men and wounding eight.[20]

In the melee that followed, the *Tennessee* was beset from all quarters. Her smokestack was completely perforated so that the fires would not draw; the steering chains that ran along the rear deck were severed so she would not steer; and several of the gunports had jammed shut after being struck by heavy shot, so that the guns could not fire. Buchanan himself was attempting to free one of the gunport covers when the ship was struck by a 15-inch bolt in his vicinity, hurling the Confederate admiral across the deck with a broken leg. "Well Johnston," Buchanan told his flag captain, "they have got me again." Johnston took command, but it was clear that the situation was hopeless, and after only a few more minutes, he surrendered.[21]

The defeat of the *Tennessee* meant that Farragut and his squadron controlled Mobile Bay. Cut off from its source of supply, Fort Morgan held out for three weeks before surrendering on August 23. The city itself held out until the end, but with the bay in Federal hands, Mobile became useless as a blockade-running port. The news triggered celebrations in Washington, and Lincoln ordered a 100-gun salute to honor Farragut's victory. Two days later, another 100-gun salute celebrated the fall of Atlanta. Now only Wilmington, North Carolina, held out as a major center for blockade-running.

LIKE CHARLESTON AND MOBILE, Wilmington was protected by a geography that made the city difficult to blockade and even more difficult to capture. It was removed some distance from the sea, occupying the eastern bank of the Cape Fear River, 25 miles upriver from its mouth, and a gauntlet of forts controlled access to the river: Forts Caswell and Holmes guarded Old Inlet at the river's mouth, and the even larger Fort Fisher guarded New Inlet where the Atlantic currents had worn a new entrance into the channel. Wilmington was invaluable to the Confederacy because (again like Mobile) it had direct rail communications to the rest of the Confederate South. The Wilmington & Weldon Railroad ran northward from the city to Weldon, North Carolina, where it connected with the Weldon & Petersburg Railroad into southeastern Virginia. By 1864, the Wilmington & Weldon Railroad had become one of the principal arteries of supply for the Army of Northern Virginia.

Most blockade-runners used New Inlet in their approach to the river, and as a result, it was Fort Fisher that was the key to rebel defenses at Wilmington. Unlike Fort Sumter and Fort Morgan, Fort Fisher was an earthwork fort, constructed during the war mostly by slaves who shoveled tons of sand and earth into an enormous two-sided field work a mile long and 24 feet high that was shaped like a giant number "7" with the longer side facing the Atlantic and the shorter side facing northward to guard against an overland attack. Twenty-two heavy seacoast guns studded its seaward face, and twenty-five more commanded its landward face. At the bottom of the "7," overlooking New Inlet itself, was a huge man-made conical mound, 60 feet high, topped with a beacon that blockade-runners used to calculate their final run into the river. The modern historian of the Wilmington campaign, Chris Fonvielle, labeled it "the mightiest fortress in America."[22]

Wilmington was a major blockade-running port, and attempting to shut it down consumed a disproportionate amount of Union naval assets. As many as thirty-five blockading warships patrolled the waters off the two entrances to the Cape Fear River, and in spite of that, dozens of blockade-runners still managed to sneak in and out with seeming impunity. For most of a year, the commander of the North Atlantic Blockading Squadron, Acting Rear Admiral Samuel Phillips Lee (a third cousin of Robert E. Lee), pressed Washington for permission to assault Fort Fisher in order to close down the port. His plan was to send one or two ironclad warships through New Inlet into the Cape Fear River so that they could shell the unprotected rear of Fort Fisher. Once Fort Fisher was neutralized, Lee planned to take his squadron through the inlet and upriver to Wilmington itself. But in 1862 and 1863, the Navy Department was sending all its ironclads to Du Pont for his attack on Charleston. Undeterred, Lee next proposed attacking Fort Fisher with a landing party put ashore north of the fort. The Navy Department found this idea even less palatable since it involved cooperation with the army, and neither Welles nor Fox was enthusiastic about such an operation.[23]

Not until the fall of 1864 did the Navy Department decide to make Wilmington the target of a concerted campaign. It was not so much because of the ongoing blockade-running. Rather it was because Sherman had decided to march his army northward from Savannah to Virginia and he wanted a reliable port en route that he could use either as a base of supply or, if need be, a refuge. Because of that, Grant added his voice to those urging an attack on Wilmington, and that shifted the strategic decision-making in Washington.

If Grant was now an advocate for an attack on Wilmington, he was less sure that Acting Rear Admiral Lee was the man for the job. He was disappointed with the way Lee had behaved during the recent ascent of the James River in the army's move toward Petersburg, and he let it be known that he would be happy with a change in command. Welles decided to bring Farragut from the Gulf of Mexico to command the North Atlantic Blockade Squadron and conduct the attack on Wilmington. But Farragut was happy where he was and asked to be excused. Instead, therefore, Welles sent for David Dixon Porter.*

The Union attack on Fort Fisher was to be another joint operation, and Porter's army counterpart was the politically astute but so far spectacularly unsuccessful Major General Benjamin F. Butler. The overall plan was for the navy to suppress the artillery fire from the fort, while an army landing party stormed the ramparts in much the same way that the army and navy had cooperated in the capture of Fort Wagner at Charleston. Butler proposed an additional element. He suggested to Fox that an old hulk stuffed with high explosives could be run up onto the beach next to Fort Fisher and detonated. The ensuing explosion would presumably destroy the fort entirely. Porter was enthusiastic; he may have hoped that the "powder boat," as it came to be called, plus a naval bombardment, would destroy Fort Fisher before the army arrived to claim the prize.

The original plan called for 300 tons of powder, half supplied by each service. The army came up with its 150 tons, but the navy offered a smaller amount of old and unreliable powder, and was late in delivering it. This postponed the scheduled attack for more than a week and meant that Butler's soldiers, already embarked in their transports, had to return to Beaufort, North Carolina, to resupply while they waited for the powder boat to arrive. Then when it did arrive, Porter decided to trigger it while Butler's men were still at Beaufort. Late on December 23, the USS *Louisiana*, loaded with 285 tons of black powder, was

---

*Porter and Lee essentially swapped positions: Porter took Lee's job as commander of the North Atlantic Blockading Squadron, and Lee headed west to assume command of the Mississippi River Squadron. Lee knew it was a kind of demotion, however, not only because he had hoped to command the attack on Wilmington but also because the Mississippi had by now become a strategic backwater.

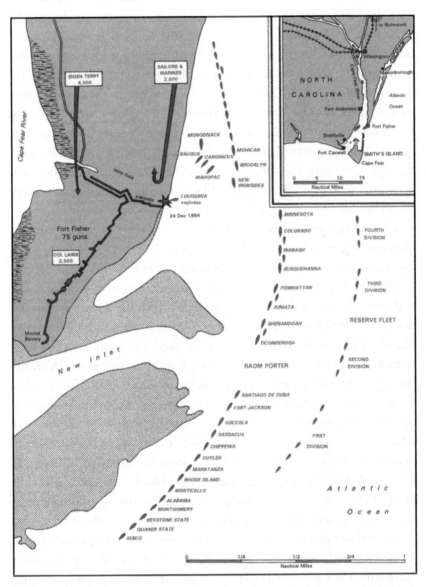

DAVID DIXON PORTER'S ATTACK ON THE WILMINGTON FORTS, FEBRUARY–MARCH 1865.
Map by Bill Clipson, reprinted with permission from *The Naval Institute Historical Atlas of the U.S. Navy* by Craig L. Symonds, © 1995.

towed into position and cast off just off the beach near Fort Fisher. Commander Alexander C. Rhind and his volunteer crew carefully navigated their way through the inshore obstructions, inadvertently aided by a blockade-runner that was making for New Inlet at the same time. In the dark of the night, Rhind had to guess at his location, and he dropped anchor when he believed he was 300 yards offshore (it was actually 500 yards). After setting the slow match, the crew escaped in a small boat. The *Louisiana* exploded at 1:35 a.m. on Christmas Eve morning. The results were disappointing. Not all of the powder ignited, and it merely blew up the ship without doing any meaningful damage to the fort. Colonel Charles Lamb, who commanded the fort's garrison, noted in his diary that "A blockader got aground near fort; set fire to herself and blew up."[24]

Though the powder boat had little impact on Fort Fisher, Porter's warships began their bombardment anyway. It is not clear what Porter expected them to accomplish. The army was still not at hand, so it is possible he hoped that he could demolish the fort with gunfire alone and gain a victory without having to share it with the army. For most of five hours, sixty-four ships mounting 630 heavy cannon hurled 10,000 rounds of high explosive ordnance at the sand and earth fort. The cannonade may well have been the largest naval gunfire assault in world history. "The roar of the cannon was something terrible," one sailor recalled. "Every particle of flesh upon one's bones seemed to be slipping off, eyes stinging, and we were almost blinded by powder, smoke, and refuse . . . , several men at my gun bled at the nose." Though Porter bragged to Welles that he silenced the forts in "about an hour and a half," and that "the forts are nearly demolished," the truth was that most of the navy shells flew long, well over the fort, or buried themselves in its 25-foot-thick sand walls without doing significant damage. Porter had not given his captains specific instructions regarding targets in the fort, and most gun captains simply aimed at the fort's flagpole. To be sure, the Confederate gun crews were driven temporarily into the bombproofs, but the fort itself was hardly "demolished." Porter later insisted that if the army had made a half-serious effort to seize the fort, it would have fallen easily into their laps, conveniently ignoring the fact that he had failed to wait for the army to be present before starting his bombardment.[25]

Butler, of course, was furious. He brought his transports up to Fort Fisher from Beaufort for a landing the next morning (Christmas Day). Not surprisingly, there was a greater sense of rivalry than cooperation between the two services. Porter's fleet renewed its bombardment, expending another 10,000 shells, which again caused most of the defenders to keep their heads down, but Major General Geoffrey Weitzel, who went ashore with the landing party, did not like the look of Fort Fisher's northern face where the fort appeared undamaged and the guns were still operational. Though a party of Federal skirmishers reached the northeast bastion of the fort, and one officer actually managed to grab a Confederate flag from a downed flagstaff, the main body never mounted a serious attack. Porter insisted it was simply for lack of trying. Butler himself did not go ashore, and Porter went alongside the general's command ship to insist that there were no Confederates within 5 miles of the fort. "You have nothing to do but to land and take possession of it," he shouted across ship to ship. Porter was wrong in that, of course, but his belief that it was true colored both his reports to Washington and his subsequent relationship with Butler.[26]

This first assault on Fort Fisher ended with the Union forces in retreat and the commanders of the army and navy elements bickering in language that might have led to duels in the pre-war years. Both Porter and Butler excoriated one another in their reports to the respective Secretaries. Porter wrote to Welles that Fort Fisher "could have been taken on Christmas with 500 men," but for the "cowardice" of the army. He even wrote to Grant to tell him "never send a boy on a man's errand." Butler wrote to Stanton that Porter's ships had completely failed to silence the guns of the fort, a claim which Porter called "a tissue of misstatements from beginning to end." Even after the war ended, the feud continued. The antagonism evident in the post-war memoirs of both Porter and Butler testifies to the bitterness of their relationship.[27]

It was evident that this partnership in command was a dismal failure, and that new commanders must be found if there were to be a second attempt. Porter urged Welles "not to withdraw a single ship" and try again but with a different general. "If this temporary failure succeeds in sending General Butler into private life, it is not to be regretted," he wrote. Grant, however, was as disappointed in Porter as he was in

This painting of the second bombardment of Fort Fisher on January 15, 1865, is by Ensign John Grattan, who served on Porter's staff. The Mound Battery, looking rather like a child's sand castle, is at left. (Courtesy of the Naval Historical Center)

Butler and wanted both men to be relieved. Porter got to keep his job only because Welles came to the defense of his mercurial admiral.[28]

Porter's new partner was Major General Alfred Terry, and Grant made it clear to Terry that once his soldiers were on the beach, they were not to stop until Fort Fisher was captured. He also urged Terry to establish and maintain good relations with the navy. "It is exceedingly desirable that the most complete understanding should exist between yourself and the naval commander."[29]

The second Union attack on Fort Fisher began on January 13, 1865. Fifty-nine ships, including four *Canonicus*-class monitors and the enormous *New Ironsides*, again hurled tons of high explosives at the sand fort, while Terry's 9,600 soldiers went ashore in surfboats 4 miles up the beach. Though Porter still insisted that the first bombardment had been entirely effective, he undermined that argument by completely changing his plan for the second bombardment. Whereas previously each ship had been directed simply to fire in the general direction of the fort using the flagpole as a guide, now each captain received a chart with red lines on it to indicate which section of the fort was to constitute his special target. Porter also ordered his ships to "Fire deliberately," and "to dismount the guns." Instead of firing as fast as they could load, the gunners watched the fall of each shot and adjusted for the next. It was not only a more carefully planned bombardment, it was also heavier. This time, the Navy fired nearly 20,000 shells into the fort.[30]

The other difference was the commitment of 2,261 sailors and marines to the land attack. Porter had several times insisted that if only he had been allowed to put his own forces ashore they would easily have captured the fort the first time when the army had balked. When he suggested to Terry the idea of putting a "boarding party" of sailors ashore to assist in the attack, the army general welcomed the idea, though his acquiescence may have been due in large part to his memory of Grant's orders to get along with the navy.

On Sunday, January 15, 1865, the Union Navy ships opened fire again, blanketing Fort Fisher with tons of explosives and solid shot. This time, the guns in the fort were silenced, one after the other; "only one heavy gun in the southern angle kept up its fire." Terry and his soldiers, plus Commander K. Randolph Breese who commanded the landing party of sailors and marines, got in position for the ground attack. At 3:30, Terry signaled Porter that he was ready, the navy lifted fire, and the attack began. Terry's soldiers focused on the western salient where Fort Fisher met the Cape Fear River while the sailors and Marines under Breese charged along the sandy beach toward the northeast salient near the coastline. The attack by sailors armed with pistols and cutlasses was ruthlessly shattered. Many were struck down as they crossed the open beach. Others fell as they attempted to scramble up the sloping earthen walls of the fort. Nearly three hundred were killed or wounded, and none managed to get inside the fort. Porter's notion that it was merely a matter of taking possession of an already defeated fort was thus revealed as vanity. Porter found another rationalization for failure. This time it was the marines who, he claimed, "were running away when the sailors were mounting the parapets."[31]

Though the sailors' attack failed, it did distract the fort's defenders from the real threat, which was Terry's 9,600 soldiers. They broke through the rebel defenders along the river front and charged into the fort. That did not end the battle, however. The Confederates fought bastion by bastion and yard by yard as they gave ground grudgingly.

Not until 9:00 that night, after almost six hours of fighting, and with 35 percent of the fort's garrison dead or wounded, did the fort's commander finally capitulate.

The fall of Fort Fisher closed the port of Wilmington as effectively as Farragut's charge into Mobile Bay closed that port. Only Galveston, Texas, which had no rail connection with much of the Confederacy, was still open to blockade-runners. For all practical purposes, the Confederacy was now cut off from overseas supply and support. Within weeks, Robert E. Lee would be forced from his defensive lines around Richmond and Petersburg and begin his retreat westward toward Appomattox Court House. Even then, however, the Confederate flag continued to fly defiantly on the high seas aboard the raider CSS *Shenandoah*.

THE CRUISE OF THE *SHENANDOAH* is one of the great sea tales of the Civil War. Built as the merchant steamer *Sea King* on the River Clyde for the India trade (which meant that she was designed for long voyages), she had an iron frame and a teak hull. She was a very fast sailor and could also make 9 knots under steam. Bulloch purchased her in September 1864 and sent her off to Funchal in the Maderia Islands, where Lieutenant Commanding James Iredell Waddell assumed command and turned her into a cruiser. Her cruising ground was to be the northern Pacific where Bulloch ordered Waddell to attack and destroy the American whaling fleet. From Funchal, he was to make for the Cape of Good Hope, cross the Indian Ocean to Australia, and then sail north "visiting the Bonin Islands, Sea of Japan, Okhotsk Sea and North Pacific, [and] be in position about the 15th of September . . . to intercept the North Pacific Whaling fleet." The problem with this scenario is that by that date, the Confederacy would no longer exist, since five months before that, Lee would surrender at Appomattox, though of course neither Bulloch nor Waddell had any way of knowing this.[32]

The *Sea King* safely reached the Azores in mid-October 1864, and like Maffitt and Semmes before him, Waddell sought to entice as many members as he could of her English crew to enlist in the service of the Confederacy. Counting Waddell, there were twenty-four Confederate officers, and Waddell hoped to enlist as many as a hundred crewmen. He described "a brilliant dashing cruise," and offered high wages before asking them to "assist an oppressed and brave people in their resistance to a powerful and arrogant northern government." But despite the promise of high wages and Waddell's eloquence, only twenty-three men agreed, too few even to raise the anchor without the assistance of the officers. With such a tiny crew, it would be difficult, if not impossible, to mount the heavy guns into their carriages, cut the gunports, build the magazine below the waterline, and complete the many other modifications consequent to her conversion to a ship of war. To use the British phrase, the *Shenandoah* at the outset of her cruise was very much a "lash up." Nevertheless, she departed the Azores with her small crew and with her cannon still unmounted in October 1864, with stores for fifteen months.[33]

Despite being unable to fire her big guns, the *Shenandoah* took her first prize on October 30. It was the bark *Alina* out of Searsport, Maine, bound for Buenos Aires with a cargo of railroad iron. It is noteworthy that while the South was starved for iron of any kind, forced to rip up railroads to armor its warships, the Union states continued to *export* iron to other countries. Waddell appropriated much of the *Alina*'s equipment, including her new block and tackle, desperately needed to secure his own big guns, before scuttling her. For most of the *Shenandoah*'s captures, the officers and crew helped themselves to whatever of value could be salvaged, including on one occasion 2,000 pounds of canned tomatoes, before sending the prize to the bottom. Waddell also managed to recruit five members of the *Alina*'s crew to join the *Shenandoah*. This, too, became a regular practice until finally the rebel raider had a crew large enough to man the sails and the guns at the same time. Waddell and the *Shenandoah* made five more captures during the next two weeks as the rebel raider worked her way southward, passing the bulge of Brazil near Bahia, then turning eastward along the latitude of the Roaring 40s, and passing into the Indian Ocean pushed on by "a fine cracking breeze."[34]

The *Shenandoah* reached Australia on January 26, 1865. As she entered the port of Melbourne, small boats filled with cheering and enthusiastic citizens crowded around her. If the reception was warming, the latest war news was more mixed. Waddell and his men learned of the Confederate victory at Cold Harbor and the seizure of the CSS *Florida* in the neutral port of Bahia, which the Shenandoah's crew considered "disgraceful." They also learned of Lincoln's re-election, a fact that meant there was to be "no end to the war." The *Shenandoah*'s arrival caused a sensation in Melbourne as crowds thronged to the harbor to see the Confederate ship. Entrepreneurial boatmen in the harbor charged a shilling for a round trip out to see the ship, and thousands came aboard—"a perfect mass of human beings," one crewman wrote in his diary. Amidst the confusion, the prisoners from the *Shenandoah*'s several prizes took the opportunity to go ashore, as did a number of her crew.[35]

On the official front, relations were a bit more formal and guarded. Waddell requested permission to make minor repairs, re-coal and resupply, as was permitted under the neutrality laws. His ship's propeller shaft was bent and the bearing cracked so that she would have to be drydocked to effect the repairs. Waddell also asked permission

The CSS *Shenandoah*, shown here under bare poles among the ice of the North Pacific, fired the last shots of the Civil War. This painting is based on an engraving that first appeared in the *Illustrated London News*. (Courtesy of the Naval Historical Center)

to land his prisoners in Melbourne (though most of them had already gone ashore on their own), and he informed the Commissioner of Customs, James Francis, that in addition to "fresh meat, vegetables, and bread," he needed "brandy, rum, champagne, port, sherry, beer, [and] porter."[36]

The more important issue was whether the *Shenandoah* was even entitled to treatment as a belligerent vessel, or whether she represented a violation of British law. Several of the *Shenandoah*'s liberated prisoners testified to government authorities that the *Shenandoah* was, in fact, the former *Sea King* out of Liverpool, and that she had been armed on the high seas with guns and equipment brought out by another vessel from England. Under such circumstances, she represented a clear violation of the Foreign Enlistment Act and might legally be seized. The British governor, Sir Charles Darling, preferred not to get in the middle of such a question, and stalled for time while granting permission for the *Shenandoah* to go into dry dock to fix her propeller and cracked bearing.[37]

There was some squabbling about the crew as well. Waddell had been short-handed from the day he took command, and he had recruited twenty-some "volunteers" from his several prizes en route to Melbourne. Now fourteen of them took the opportunity to desert. Waddell asked the cooperation of the authorities to reclaim them, but Darling was consistent in not wanting to get involved, and insisted that rounding up Waddell's errant crew members was beyond his jurisdiction. On the other hand, when one of these deserters testified that a local man named "Charley" had secretly boarded the *Shenandoah* in Melbourne and planned to join her crew in violation of the Foreign Enlistment Act, Darling demanded that Waddell allow his ship to be searched to find him. Waddell testified that no such person was on board his ship and that he would not allow a search since that would be a surrender of sovereignty. To compel a search, Darling issued an order halting all work on the ship and sent armed policemen to surround her where she lay in dry dock. A tense standoff ensued. In fact, despite Waddell's protestations, "Charley" *was* on board. He was a cook whose actual name was James Davidson. When in the midst of the standoff, he and three others decided to flee the ship, they were caught and arrested by government authorities. Darling had caught Waddell in a lie, or at least a serious error, but unwilling to exacerbate the crisis further, he simply declared that since "Charley" had been apprehended, work on the *Shenandoah* could resume.[38]

The *Shenandoah* completed its repairs and departed Melbourne in mid-February. On the question of unauthorized crewmen, however, Waddell had the last laugh. After the *Shenandoah* left port, forty-two men were "found" to have stowed away. Fourteen of them crawled out of the hollow iron bowsprit of the *Shenandoah*. Though Waddell claimed to have been "astonished" by their sudden appearance, it is hard to see how so many men could have gotten aboard without collusion by someone in authority on the ship. Waddell shipped thirty-four of the stowaways as sailors and eight others as marines. The new recruits more than doubled the size of the *Shenandoah*'s crew and without them, Waddell would have been hard pressed to man his ship at all.[39]

After her adventure in Melbourne, the *Shenandoah* headed into the South Pacific where Waddell encountered a string of bad luck. Forewarned of the *Shenandoah*'s presence by the American consul at Melbourne, U.S. shipping had fled the area so that no prizes were available, and a series of fierce storms battered the rebel raider as she struggled northward. Then on April Fool's day, she found and captured three American brigs that were anchored off the idyllic island of Pohnpei in Micronesia. On that same day, nearly halfway around the world near Petersburg, Virginia, Federal troops broke through Lee's lines at Five Forks, the event which prompted Lee's decision to evacuate the Richmond-Petersburg lines and begin his retreat to Appomattox. By the time the *Shenandoah* left Micronesia and sailed north to begin her assault on the American whaling fleet in the Pacific, Lee had surrendered.

After a brief visit to the Sea of Okhotsk, where the ship and her crew battled ice storms and fog, the *Shenandoah* entered the Bering Sea in mid-June. There the pickings were plentiful, and the *Shenandoah* captured one Union whaling ship after another, burning most of them and using the others as cartels for the prisoners. Newspapers that were found on board one of the whaling ships reported that Charleston and Richmond had fallen to the Yankees. On another, the ship's captain declared unequivocally that the war was over, that Lee had surrendered his army. Waddell demanded proof, but the whaling boat skipper

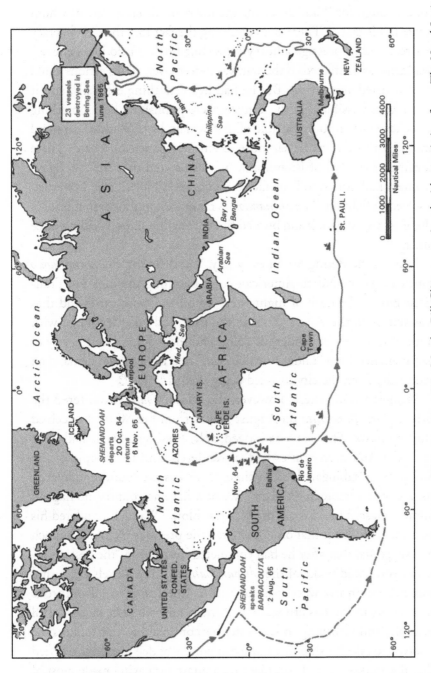

CRUISE OF THE CSS *SHENANDOAH*, OCTOBER 1864–NOVEMBER 1865. Map by Bill Clipson, reprinted with permission from *The Naval Institute Historical Atlas of the U.S. Navy* by Craig L. Symonds, © 1995.

could only reply that he had heard it in San Francisco. That was not good enough for Waddell, or the members of his crew, one of whom wrote in his diary, "There is no doubting the fact that the Confederacy has received in prestige a heavy blow, but further I do not believe." Waddell was conflicted. If the war was indeed over, all his actions could be construed as piratical. But he had heard nothing officially, and it was always possible that the Yankees were publishing lies, something he believed them to be capable of. A few days later, Waddell captured another prize that had even more recent newspapers on board. These confirmed the fall of Richmond, but also stated that the rebel government had moved to Danville, Virginia, and that Jefferson Davis had resolved to fight on. The *Shenandoah*'s rampage continued. In four days (June 25–28), she took and burned fifteen whaling ships, bonding three others.[40]

Leaving the Bering Sea in early July, Waddell took the *Shenandoah* south along the North American coast planning to enter San Francisco Bay in the dark of night, steal up on the Union ironclad that was stationed there, board her in the dark and take her. Then with both of those vessels under his command, he would place the city of San Francisco itself "under contribution," that is, he would demand an indemnity from the city to avoid being shelled.[41]

While en route there, however, the *Shenandoah* encountered the British bark *Baracouta* on August 2, and from her Waddell received chilling news. The war was indeed over, President Davis had been captured, southern armies had surrendered, and the people of the South were "subjugated." This time, there was no doubting the facts. As one officer wrote in his diary, "We now have no country, no flag, no home." Describing this as "the bitterest blow," Waddell pondered his next move. In his initial orders, written the previous October, Bulloch had suggested that after he had completed his mission "the best disposition you could make of the *Shenandoah* would be to sell her, either somewhere on the west coast of South America or to adventurous speculators in the Eastern seas." Uncertain now whether that was still possible, and unwilling to surrender his command to the Yankees, he resolved to take his ship to a European port. Waddell may have worried that the Yankees would consider him a pirate for having made most of his captures after the war had ended. In any case, he ordered the guns dismounted and struck below, pointed his ship southward, and began a 17,000-mile voyage back to her port of origin.[42]

The *Shenandoah* passed Cape Horn in mid-September and turned north. Six members of the crew, fearful of being caught by a Federal steamer during the long run back to England and hanged as pirates, petitioned him "to land us at the nearest and most convenient port," and ten others urged him to take the ship to Cape Town. Waddell's officers supported him in his decision to return to Liverpool, and in a testimony to Waddell's leadership, the rest of the crew, some 71 persons, signed another petition expressing confidence in whatever decision he made. Discipline held, and so did Waddell's luck. Though several ships were sighted en route to England, none pursued the now-disarmed *Shenandoah*, and on November 6, 1865, after a round-the-world cruise of 58,000 miles, during which she captured thirty-eight prizes, she dropped anchor in the Mersey River near the British ship-of-the-line HMS *Donegal*. Waddell distributed the prize money that had been taken before the end of the war to the members of the crew, put the rest of it ($820.28) in a bag and gave it to the paymaster of the *Donegal*. After four more days in a kind of legal twilight, the officers and men of the *Shenandoah* were released unconditionally, and the Civil War at sea came to an end.[43]

IT WAS OVER. After four years, tens of millions of dollars, and at least 620,000 American lives, the southern bid for independence had ended, and the nation was whole again. It had been primarily a land war in which more than three million armed men fought each other across half a continent in bloody battles from Shiloh to Gettysburg, and from Chickamauga to Charleston. As tragic as it was, it was the price of national unity, and of all American wars perhaps the most necessary. It was also the nation's first modern war: the first to employ the railroad, the telegraph, and the rifled musket; the first to feature massed artillery barrages and trench warfare; the first where the strength of the national economy was as important as the national will because the materials of war—uniforms, guns, bullets, canteens, railroad rails and telegraph wire, even rations—were mass produced in factories. This affected not only the nature of the war, but also the structure of American society in the years that followed. Though some historians shrink from the phrase "total war" and have instead adopted the historian Mark Grimsley's phrase "hard war" to describe the broadened use of violence against civilian targets especially after 1863, the Civil War was as close as this nation has ever come to experiencing total war. A greater percentage of Americans fought in it than in either of the world wars, and a far greater percentage were killed or wounded. Had post-traumatic stress disorder been a recognized ailment in the nineteenth century, it would likely have affected most of a generation. Then, too, save for a few forays by the British in 1814, the Civil War was also the only conflict in which hostile armies marched across much of the American countryside. It was the only war in which American farms, factories, and whole metropolitan areas became deliberate targets of hostile armies. And while both of the world wars ushered in important and transformative changes in American society, no war wrought greater social and economic change than the one fought between 1861 and 1865. To be sure, the social revolution was not complete—the slaves did not become genuinely free in any important meaning of that term for a hundred years or more. But the overall impact was nonetheless revolutionary.

At sea, too, the industrial transformation of the nineteenth century dictated a new kind of war, one dominated by steam engines, iron armor, explosive shells fired from rifled guns of unprecedented size, and torpedo boats. The blockade was the North's single greatest commitment to the naval war, and it absorbed huge resources of both materiel and manpower. For all the frustration inherent in trying to stop the scores of small, fast blockade-runners that continually passed through the blockade, it was an important contribution to the Union war effort, for even if it failed to bring the South to its knees, it contributed to an early and growing sense of isolation and eventually depression, both economic and psychological, in the South.

As the underdog in the naval war, the South was initially more creative, producing armored warships, underwater torpedoes, even a submarine. But it could not produce those things in the kind of quantity that the North could, and the North's ability to produce scores of monitors, hundreds of conventional warships, thousands of cannon, and to spend millions of dollars, meant that the South fought the naval war at a tremendous disadvantage, one it could never overcome. Instead the South relied on the traditional naval weapons of the weaker power: commerce raiders to savage the enemy's merchant marine and forts to defend its rivers and coastline.

The Confederacy's commerce raiders from the *Sumter* to the *Shenandoah* collectively devastated American shipping, and had an effect on the war that was disproportionate to their numbers, but in the end they could not be decisive. Similarly, the forts that the South either inherited or constructed could slow, but in the end could not stop, the Federal war machine. From Fort Henry and Fort Donelson in the West, to Fort Morgan and Fort Fisher along the coast, the new technology of naval war allowed the Union to prevail, overwhelming the defenses with gunfire (as at Fort Henry and Port Royal), running past them to render them helpless (as at New Orleans and Mobile), or besieging them with naval and land forces (as at Vicksburg and Charleston). What the new technology demonstrated was that large, well-sited fortifications, considered the most important objectives in western warfare for a thousand years, had been rendered if not obsolete, then at least outdated. Only Fort Sumter, that symbol of resistance and rebellion, stood up to the unprecedented pounding of the Union army and navy and remained defiant to the end, even if by then it consisted of no more than a pile of brick dust.

Naval forces did not determine the outcome of the Civil War; the North would have won the war even without naval supremacy so long as the Lincoln administration maintained the political support of the northern public. But naval forces affected its trajectory and very likely its length, and that, in the end, was important enough.

NOTES

Abbreviations Used in Notes

B&L   Robert U. Johnson and Clarence C. Buel, eds., *Battles and Leaders of the Civil War*. New York: The Century Company, 1887–88.

OR   *Rebellion Records. Official Records of the Union and Confederate Armies in the War of the Rebellion*. Washington, DC: Government Printing Office, 1880–1901. All references are to series I unless otherwise indicated.

ORN   *Official Records of the Union and Confederate Navies in the War of the Rebellion*. Washington, DC: Government Printing Office, 1894–1922. All references are to series I unless otherwise indicated.

Chapter 1

1. Alvah F. Hunter, *A Year on a Monitor and the Destruction of Fort Sumter*, ed. by Craig L. Symonds (Columbia: University of South Carolina Press, 1987), 9.

2. Thomas C. Cochran and William Miller, *The Age of Enterprise: A Social History of Industrial America* (New York: Harper & Row, 1942, 1961); David R. Meyer, *The Roots of American Industrialization* (Baltimore, MD: Johns Hopkins University Press, 2003), 225; Daniel Walker Howe, *What Hath God Wrought: The Transformation of America, 1815–1845* (New York: Oxford University Press, 2007).

3. Spencer Tucker, *Arming the Fleet: U.S. Navy Ordnance in the Muzzle-Loading Era* (Annapolis, MD: Naval Institute Press, 1989), 156–57.

4. K. Jack Bauer, *Surfboats and Horse Marines: U.S. Naval Operations in the Mexican War, 1846–48* (Annapolis, MD: Naval Institute Press, 1969), 28–29, 124; Kurt Hackemer, *The U.S. Navy and the Origins of the Military Industrial Complex* (Annapolis, MD: Naval Institute Press, 2001), 17.

5. Frank M. Bennett, *The Steam Navy of the United States* (Pittsburgh: Warren & Co., 1896), 112–13.

6. The statistics on the cruise of the *Susquehanna* are from the *Susquehanna's* log book, U.S. Naval Academy Special Collections, Nimitz Library.

7. Bennett, *Steam Navy of the United States*, 48–54.

8. *Navy Register*, 1860; Lincoln to Welles, March 18, 1861, and Welles to Lincoln, March 20, 1861, both in Abraham Lincoln Papers, Library of Congress, series I.

9. There is some controversy about whether the 1854 sloop is simply a modification of the 1797 frigate. Part of the confusion stems from the fact that the Congressional authorization called for a repair of the older ship, not a new construction. Geoffrey M. Footner in his book *USS Constellation: From Frigate to Sloop of War* (Annapolis, MD: Naval Institute Press, 2003) argues that the sloop is merely a restructuring of the older vessel. In the end, however, the sloop is so different from the original frigate, and used so few timbers from it, that it is more accurate to call it a completely new vessel. See Dana M. Wegner, *Fouled Anchors: The Constellation Question Answered* (Bethesda, MD: David Taylor Research Center, 1991).

10. Hackemer, *The U.S. Navy and the Origins of the Military Industrial Complex*, 23–24, 41–45; Tucker, *Arming the Fleet*, 206; Donald Canney, *Mr. Lincoln's Navy*, 65–67.

11. Canney, *Mr. Lincoln's Navy*, 65–67.

12. For information about the politics of these appropriations see Hackemer, *The U.S. Navy and the Origins of the Military Industrial Complex*, 59–66. For design characteristics of the *Merrimack*-class frigates see Canney, *Mr. Lincoln's Navy*, 56–69.

13. Bennett, *Steam Navy of the United States*, 169–74; Tucker, *Arming the Fleet*, 173–74; Canney, *Mr. Lincoln's Navy*, 60–62.

14. Hackemer, *The U.S. Navy and the Origins of the Military Industrial Complex*, 59; Canney, *Mr. Lincoln's Navy*, 60–62.

15. Tucker, *Arming the Fleet*, 176–82; Eugene Canfield, *Civil War Naval Ordnance* (Washington, DC: Naval History Division, 1969), 3–5.

16. Canfield, *Civil War Naval Ordnance*, 5–8.

17. Tucker, *Arming the Fleet*, 203–6; Canfield, *Civil War Naval Ordnance*, 23. See also Robert J. Schneller, *A Quest for Glory: A Biography of Rear Admiral John A. Dahlgren* (Annapolis, MD: Naval Institute Press, 1966).

18. Tucker, *Arming the Fleet*, 228–33; Canfield, *Civil War Naval Ordnance*, 5–8.

19. Tucker, *Arming the Fleet*, 68–70.

20. J. Thomas Scharf, *The Confederate States Navy* (New York: Rogers & Sherwood, 1887), 1:31, 33.

21. Report of the Committee on Naval Affairs (Confederate), February 21, 1861, ORN, series II, 2:41–42.

22. Maury to Ballard, October 22, 1861, ORN, II, 2:101. Also ORN, I:751.

23. Davis, *Duel Between the First Ironclads*, 7; Craig L. Symonds, *Lincoln and His Admirals: Abraham Lincoln, the U.S. Navy, and the Civil War* (New York: Oxford University Press, 2008), 51–52.

24. Tucker, *Arming the Fleet*, 217.

25. Raimondo Luraghi, *A History of the Confederate Navy* (Annapolis, MD: Naval Institute Press, 1996), 42–45.

26. James I. Waddell, *C.S.S. Shenandoah: The Memoirs of Lieutenant Commanding James I. Waddell*, ed. by James D. Horan (New York: Crown Publishers, 1960), 79; William Dudley, *Going South: U.S. Navy Officer Resignations and Dismissals On the Eve of the Civil War* (Washington, DC: Naval Historical Foundation, 1981). Thanks also to Wayne Hseih at the U.S. Naval Academy who shared with me his research on officer resignations.

27. Joseph T. Durkin, *Confederate Navy Chief: Stephen R. Mallory* (Columbia: University of South Carolina Press, 1987).

28. Joseph T. Durkin, *Stephen R. Mallory: Confederate Navy Chief* (Chapel Hill: University of North Carolina Press, 1954), 130–56.

29. Mallory to C. M. Conrad, May 10, 1861, ORN, series II, 2:69.

30. John M. Brooke, "The Plan and Construction of the 'Merrimac,'" B, 1:715–16; Craig L. Symonds and Harold Holzer, "Who Designed CSS *Virginia?" MHQ: The Quarterly Journal of Military History* 16 (Autumn, 2003): 6–14.

31. Ibid.

32. Ibid.

33. John Niven, *Gideon Welles: Lincoln's Secretary of the Navy* (New York: Oxford University Press, 1973); Symonds, *Lincoln and His Admirals*, 5–6.

34. Undated Bushnell letter from 1877 printed in B&L, 1:748–50.

35. Ibid., 1:748.

36. John V. Quarstein, *C. S. S. Virginia: Mistress of Hampton Roads* (Appomattox, VA: H.E. Howard, 2000).

37. Craig L. Symonds, *Confederate Admiral: The Life and Wars of Franklin Buchanan* (Annapolis, MD: Naval Institute Press, 1999), 138; Welles to Edger Welles, May 19, 1861, Welles Papers, LC (reel 19).

38. Eugenius Jack, *Memoirs of E.A. Jack, Steam Engineer, CSS Virginia*, ed. by Alan B. Flanders and Neale O. Westfall (White Stone, VA: Brandylane Publishers, 1998), 14.

39. William C. Davis, *Duel Between the First Ironclads* (Baton Rouge: Louisiana State University Press, 1975), 87–88.

40. The best general history of this fight is still William C. Davis, *Duel Between the First Ironclads* (Baton Rouge: Louisiana State University Press, 1975). See also Craig L. Symonds, *Decision at Sea: Five Naval Battles that Shaped American History* (New York: Oxford University Press, 2005), 111–12.

41. Symonds, *Confederate Admiral*, 166–69; Symonds, *Decision at Sea*, 114–16.
42. Davis, *Duel Between the First Ironclads*; Symonds, *Decision at Sea*, 81–138.
43. William F. Keeler, *Aboard the USS Monitor, 1862*, ed. by Robert W. Daly (Annapolis, MD: Naval Institute Press, 1964), 38.
44. Ibid., 63.
45. William H. Roberts, *Civil War Ironclads: The U.S. Navy and Industrial Mobilization* (Baltimore, MD: Johns Hopkins University Press, 2002), 34–39.
46. William N. Still, Jr., *Iron Afloat: The Story of the Confederate Armorclads* (Columbia: University of South Carolina Press, 1971), 136–38; Bern Anderson, *By Sea and By River* (New York: Knopf, 1962), 166–67.
47. Canney, *Mr. Lincoln's Navy*, 72–73.
48. Roberts, *Civil War Ironclads*, 3.
49. Still, *Iron Afloat*, 89–90.
50. Still, *Iron Afloat*, 81–82, 227; John Coski, *Capital Navy: The Men, Ships, and Operations of the James River Squadron* (Campbell, CA: Savas Woodbury, 1996, 82.
51. Coski, *Capital Navy*, 165–66; Luraghi, *Confederate Navy*, 288–89.
52. *New York Tribune* (reprinted in *Washington Constitution*, January 24, 1861); Report of the Committee on Naval Affairs, January 1859, quoted in Hackemer, *The U.S. Navy and the Origins of the Military Industrial Complex*, 68; Samuel R. Bright, Jr., "Confederate Coast Defense" (Ph.D. dissertation, Duke University, 1961), 1–2.

Chapter 2

1. Abstract log of the *Niagara*, ORN, 4:206; Craig L. Symonds, *Lincoln and His Admirals: Abraham Lincoln, the U.S. Navy, and the Civil War* (New York: Oxford University Press, 2008), 37–38.
2. Lincoln's Blockade Proclamation is in Roy P. Basler, ed., *The Collected Works of Abraham Lincoln* (New Brunswick, NJ: Rutgers University Press, 1953), 4:338–39; Stephen R. Wise, *Lifeline of the Confederacy: Blockade-Running During the Civil War* (Columbia: University of South Carolina Press, 1988), 8, 226; William N. Still, Jr., "A Naval Sieve," *Naval War College Review* (May-June 1983), 45; Raimondo Luraghi, *A History of the Confederate Navy* (Annapolis, MD: Naval Institute Press, 1996), 286.
3. David Surdam, *Northern Naval Superiority and the Economics of the American Civil War* (Columbia: University of South Carolina Press, 2001).
4. G. J. Marcus, *The Age of Nelson: The Royal Navy, 1793–1815* (New York: The Viking Press, 1971).
5. Blockade Proclamation, in Basler, ed., *Collected Works*, 4:339.
6. John G. Nicolay and John Hay, *Abraham Lincoln, A History* (New York: The Century Company, 1904), 4:270–75.
7. Lord Lyons to Lord John Russell, March 26 and April 9, 1861, both in Charles F. Adams, "The British Proclamation of May 1861," *Massachusetts*

Historical Society Proceedings (October 1914–June 1915), 48:222, 224; Seward to Charles F. Adams, May 21, 1861, in Basler, ed., *Collected Works*, 4:378–79. See also Symonds, *Lincoln and His Admirals*, 40, 42–43.

8. Symonds, *Lincoln and His Admirals*, 56; Donald Canney, *Mr. Lincoln's Navy*, (Annapolis, MD: Naval Institute Press, 1998), 62.

9. William H. Roberts, *Now for the Contest: Coastal and Oceanic Naval Operations in the Civil War* (Lincoln: University of Nebraska Press, 2004), 18–19; E. A. (Bud) Livingston, *President Lincoln's Third Largest City* (New York: E. A. Livingston, 1994), 101.

10. Symonds, *Lincoln and His Admirals*, 57–58.

11. Stephen R. Wise has called this "the first modern blockade." Wise, *Lifeline of the Confederacy*, 24.

12. Kevin Weddle, *Lincoln's Tragic Admiral: The Life of Samuel Francis Du Pont* (Charlottesville: University of Virginia Press, 2005), 4–105.

13. Ibid., 106–24.

14. Du Pont to Sophie Du Pont, October 23, 1861, in John D. Hayes, ed., *Samuel Francis Du Pont, A Selection from His Civil War Letters* (Ithaca, NY: Cornell University Press, 1969), 1:181.

15. Du Pont to Sophie Du Pont, August 7 and September 4, 1861, both in Hayes, ed., *Samuel Francis Du Pont Letters*, 1:129, 142–43; Du Pont to Henry Du Pont, October 15, 1861, ibid., 1:165.

16. Du Pont to Sophie Du Pont, September 17, 1861, and Du Pont to Henry Du Pont, October 15, 1861, both in Hayes, ed., *Samuel Francis Du Pont Letters*, 1:149, 165.

17. John D. Hayes, ed., "The Battle of Port Royal, S.C. from the Journal of John Sanford Barnes, October 8 to November 9, 1861," *The New-York Historical Society Quarterly* (October 1961), 45:379; Du Pont to Sophie Du Pont, October 26, 1861, in Hayes, ed., Samuel Francis Du Pont Letters, 1:185.

18. Du Pont to Sophie Du Pont, July 26, 1861, in Hayes, ed., *Samuel Francis Du Pont Letters*, 1:113.

19. Du Pont to Sophie Du Pont, November 2, 1861, in Hayes, ed., *Samuel Francis Du Pont Letters*, 1:206.

20. John Sanford Barnes in Hayes, "Battle of Port Royal," 380; Du Pont to Sophie Du Pont, November 2, 1861, in Hayes, ed., *Samuel Francis Du Pont Letters*, 1:206–7.

21. Du Pont to Sophie Du Pont, November 2, 1861, in Hayes, ed., *Samuel Francis Du Pont Letters*, 1:205, 207.

22. Hayes, ed., "The Battle of Port Royal," 387.

23. Ibid., 391.

24. Du Pont to Welles, November 11, 1861, ORN, 12:262–65.

25. Lee to Samuel Cooper, January 8, 1862, Clifford Dowdey and Louis H. Manarin, eds., *The Wartime Papers of Robert E. Lee* (Boston: Little Brown, 1961), 101.

26. Craig L. Symonds, ed., *Charleston Blockade: The Civil War Journals of John B. Marchand, 1861–1862* (Newport, RI: The Naval War College Press, 1976), 136, 138.

27. Ibid. (entry of June 23, 1862), 222–23.

28. Ibid.

29. Ibid., 224; Du Pont to Welles, June 27, 1862, ORN, 13:134–35.

30. Du Pont to Welles, April 23, 1862, ORN, 12:773.

31. Alvah H. Hunter, *A Year on a Monitor and the Destruction of Fort Sumter*, ed. by Craig L. Symonds (Columbia: University of South Carolina Press, 1987), 93.

32. Quoted in Surdam, *Northern Naval Superiority*, 206.

33. Wise, *Lifeline of the Confederacy*, 120.

34. Thomas E. Taylor, *Running the Blockade: A Personal Narrative of Adventures, Risks, and Escapes during the American Civil War* (London: John Murray, 1912), 49.

35. Ibid., 49, 50.

36. Ibid., 53–54.

37. *New York Herald*, November 25, 1863.

38. Ibid.

39. J. Thomas Scharf, *History of the Confederate States Navy from Its Organization to the Surrender of Its Last Vessel* (New York: Rogers & Sherwood, 1887), 2:483.

40. Wise, *Lifeline of the Confederacy*, 145–46; Gordon B. McKinney, *Zeb Vance: North Carolina's Civil War Governor and Gilded Age Political Leader* (Chapel Hill: University of North Carolina Press, 2004), 138–39.

41. Scharf, *History of the Confederate States Navy*, 2:484; "An Act to Prohibit the Importation of Luxuries or of Articles not Necessary or of Common Use," *Confederate Imprints, 1861–1865* (New Haven, CT: Research Publications, 1974), 10–11. See also Mark Thornton and Robert B. Ekelund, Jr., *Tariffs, Blockades, and Inflation: The Economics of the Civil War* (Wilmington, DE: Scholarly Resources, 2004), 50–51.

42. Wise, *Lifeline of the Confederacy*, 158; Thornton and Ekelund, *Tariffs, Blockades and Inflation*, 49–50; Weaver to Rowan, March 25, 1864, and Rowan to Welles, March 24, 1864, both in ORN, 15:374–76.

43. Luraghi, *A History of the Confederate Navy*, 284–86; Wise, *Lifeline of the Confederacy*, 144–52.

44. Luraghi, *A History of the Confederate Navy*, 286.

45. Wise, *Lifeline of the Confederacy*, 221–26.

46. Ibid., 226.

47. Richard D. Goff, *Confederate Supply* (Durham, NC: Duke University Press, 1969), 247; Luraghi, *A History of the Confederate Navy*, 286; Surdam, *Northern Naval Superiority*, 80, 207.

48. Thornton and Ekelund, *Tariffs, Blockades, and Inflation*, 47.

49. Hay diary entry of September 25, 1864, Michael Burlingame and John R. T. Ettlinger, eds., *Inside Lincoln's White House: The Complete Civil War Diary of John Hay* (Carbondale: Southern Illinois University Press, 1997), 219.

50. Wise, *Lifeline of the Confederacy*, 222; Surdam, *Northern Naval Superiority*, 145, 149, 207; Luraghi, *A History of the Confederate Navy*, 286. See the tables in Wise, *Lifeline of the Confederacy*, 229. Curiously, some 278,617 bales of cotton were exported from *northern* cities in the year before the war, including 23,225 from Boston, which rivals the total exports from southern cities in 1864. See Thornton and Ekelund, *Tariffs, Blockades, and Inflation*, 48.

51. See the table in Wise, *Lifeline of the Confederacy*, 250.

52. Robert M. Browning, Jr., *Success is All That Was Expected: The South Atlantic Blockading Squadron during the Civil War* (Washington, DC: Brassey's Inc., 2002), 317, 344.

53. Roberts, *Now For the Contest*, 164.

Chapter 3

1. The escape of the Sumter is described in Raphael Semmes, *Memoirs of Service Afloat* (Baltimore, MD: Kelly, Piet, 1869, reprint 1987), 114–18.

2. Semmes, *Service Afloat*, 129.

3. J. Thomas Scharf, *The Confederate States Navy* (Salem, NH: Ayer Company, 1988), 53ff. The quotation is from p. 68.

4. Craig L. Symonds, *Lincoln and His Admirals: Abraham Lincoln, the U.S. Navy, and the Civil War* (New York: Oxford University Press, 2008), 42.

5. Proclamation of a Blockade, April 19, 1861, in Abraham Lincoln, *The Collected Works of Abraham Lincoln*, ed. by Roy P. Basler (New Brunswick, NJ: Rutgers University Press, 1953), 4:339.

6. Scharf, *The Confederate Navy*, 54.

7. Parrott to Stringham, June 5, 1861, and Stringham to Welles, June 6, 1861, both in ORN, 1:28–29. See also Mark A. Weitz, *The Confederacy on Trial: The Piracy and Sequestration Cases of 1861* (Lawrence: University of Kansas Press, 2005).

8. Scharf, *The Confederate Navy*, 53–93; Bern Anderson, *By Sea and By River: The Naval History of the Civil War* (New York: Knopf, 1962), 43–45.

9. James I. Waddell, *C.S.S. Shenandoah: The Memoirs of Lieutenant Commanding James I. Waddell*, ed. by James D. Horan (New York: Crown Publishers, Inc., 1960), 81; Semmes, *Service Afloat*, 167.

10. Semmes to the Military Governor of Cadiz, January 5, 1862, quoted in Semmes, *Service Afloat*, 298.

11. Semmes, *Service Afloat*, 310–11.

12. Ibid., 329–45.

13. James D. Bulloch, *The Secret Service of the Confederate States in Europe* (New York: Thomas Yoseloff, 1959), 41, 54; Coy F. Cross, II, *Lincoln's Man in Liverpool: Consul Dudley and the Legal Battle to Stop Confederate*

Warships (DeKalb: Northern Illinois University Press, 2007), 18–23; James Tertius de Kay, *The Rebel Raiders: The Astonishing History of the Confederacy's Secret Navy* (New York: Ballantine, 2002), 16.

14. Bulloch, *Secret Service*, 58, 65–67; Cross, *Lincoln's Man in Liverpool*, 37–70.
15. Ibid., 56.
16. Helm to Benjamin, September 3, 1862, ORN, 1:760–61.
17. Preble to Farragut, September 4, 1862, ORN, 1:432.
18. Bulloch, *Secret Service*, 173; Preble to Farragut, September 4, 1862, ORN, 1:432.
19. Farragut to Welles, September 8, 1862, and Welles to Preble, September 20, 1862, both in ORN, 1:432–32, 434. See also Symonds, *Lincoln and His Admirals*, 260–61.
20. Mallory to Maffitt, October 25, 1862, ORN, 1:762; Abstract journal of the CSS *Florida*, ORN, 2:674.
21. Abstract journal of the CSS *Florida*, ORN, 2:674.
22. Ibid., 675.
23. Ibid.
24. Maffitt to Mallory, September 1863, ORN, 2:659–60.
25. Cross, *Lincoln's Man in Liverpool*, 38.
26. Bulloch, *Secret Service*, 233; Semmes, *Service Afloat*, 403.
27. Bulloch, *Secret Service*, 235.
28. James T. de Kay makes the case that it was Russell who tipped Bulloch to the fact that the *Alabama* was about to be seized. De Kay, *The Rebel Raiders*, 72–76.
29. Bulloch, *Secret Service*, 240–41.
30. Semmes, *Service Afloat*, 410–13.
31. Ibid., 423–24.
32. Ibid., 492.
33. Stephen Fox, *Wolf of the Deep: Raphael Semmes and the Notorious Confederate Raider CSS Alabama* (New York: Alfred A. Knopf, 2007), 73–75.
34. Fox, *Wolf of the Deep*, 79–82.
35. *New York Herald*, October 9, 1863; Semmes, *Service Afloat*, 521.
36. The *Boston Post* is quoted in Fox, *Wolf of the Deep*, 98.
37. Semmes, *Service Afloat*, 510–16.
38. Blake to Welles, January 21, 1863, ORN, 2:18–20; Semmes, *Service Afloat*, 543–47; de Kay, *The Rebel Raiders*, 141.
39. Welles' Report is dated December 7, 1863, and is in House Executive Document No. 1, 38th Congress, 1st session, v–vi, xxiv.
40. The Yankee prisoner is quoted in de Kay, *Rebel Raiders*, 177.
41. Semmes, *Service Afloat*, 745, 752.
42. Ibid., 749; de Kay, *Rebel Raiders*, 192.
43. John McIntosh Kell, *Recollections of a Naval Life* (Washington, DC: The Neale Company, 1900), 244.
44. Semmes, *Service Afloat*, 752; Kell, *Recollections of a Naval Life*, 247.

45. Abstract log of the USS *Kearsarge* in ORN, 3:64–65; Winslow to Welles, June 19, 1864, ORN, 3:59.

46. Kell, *Recollections of a Naval Life*, 248.

47. Ibid., 249.

48. Winslow to Welles, June 21, 1864, ORN, 3:60–61; Kell to "My Dear H," June 20, 1864, in Kell, *Recollections of a Naval Life*, 253.

49. Abstract log of the CSS *Florida*, ORN, 3:645; Morris to Mallory, February 29, 1864, ORN, 2:665.

50. Abstract log of the CSS *Florida*, ORN, 3:646; Morris to Mallory, July 13, 1864, ORN, 3:623–24.

51. Abstract log of the USS *Wachusett*, ORN, 3:257; Collins to Welles, October 31, 1864, ORN, 3:255–56.

52. Finding of the Court of Inquiry, undated, ORN, 3:280.

53. Welles to Collins, October 17, 1866, ORN, 3:269.

54. George W. Dalzell, *The Flight from the Flag: The Continuing Effect of the Civil War upon the American Carrying Trade* (Chapel Hill: University of North Carolina Press, 1940), 174–81, 189–92.

55. Ibid., 238–48; *New York Herald*, November 18, 1863.

56. *New York Sun*, March 25, 1865, quoted in Emerson David Fite, *Social and Industrial Conditions in the North during the Civil War* (New York: Frederick Ungar Publishing, 1963), 150–51.

57. Dalzell, *Flight from the Flag*, 231–36.

Chapter 4

1. Rodgers to Welles, June 8 and September 7, 1861, ORN, 22:283, 318–20.

2. Rodgers to Welles, August 22, 1861, ORN, 22:302–3.

3. Ibid.; Rodgers to Fremont, August 22, 1861, ORN, 22:302–4.

4. See, for example, Steven E. Woodworth, *Decision in the Heartland: The Civil War in the West* (Westport, CT: Praeger, 2008).

5. Daniel E. Sutherland, *Fredericksburg and Chancellorsville: The Dare Mark Campaign* (Lincoln: University of Nebraska Press, 1998).

6. Welles to Rodgers, May 16, 1861, ORN, 22:280.

7. Welles to Rodgers, June 17, 1861, and Rodgers to Welles, August 9, 1861, both in ORN, 22:287, 297–98.

8. Bern Anderson, *By Sea and by River: The Naval History of the Civil War* (New York: Alfred A. Knopf, 1962), 41–43; B. Franklin Cooling, *Forts Henry and Donelson: The Key to the Confederate Heartland* (Knoxville: University of Tennessee Press, 1987), 23–27; Gary Joiner, *Mr. Lincoln's Brown Water Navy* (Lanham, MD: Rowan & Littlefield, 2007), 17–21; John D. Milligan, *Gunboats Down the Mississippi* (Annapolis, MD: Naval Institute Press, 1965), 15–25.

9. Joiner, *Lincoln's Brown Water Navy*, 21–29; Milligan, *Gunboats Down the Mississippi*, 6, 21–23, 28–29, 85.

10. Welles to Rodgers, August 30, 1861, ORN, 22:307.

11. Jefferson Davis, *Rise and Fall of the Confederate Government* (New York: DaCapo, 1990), 2:20.

12. "Investigation of Navy Department," February 26, 1863, ORN, series II, 1:780.

13. William N. Still, Jr., *Iron Afloat: The Story of the Confederate Armorclads* (Nashville, TN: Vanderbilt University Press, 1971, reprint Columbia: South Carolina University Press, 1985), 41–42; Maurice Melson, "Shipbuilding," in William N. Still, Jr., ed., *The Confederate Navy: The Ships, Men and Organization* (Annapolis, MD: Naval Institute Press, 1997), 101–3.

14. Walke to Foote, November 9, 1861, ORN, 22:401.

15. Cooling, *Forts Henry and Donelson*, 74–79; Joiner, *Lincoln's Brown Water Navy*, 39; Milligan, *Gunboats Down the Mississippi*, 37–39.

16. Cooling, *Forts Henry and Donelson*, 101–6; Milligan, *Gunboats Down the Mississippi*, 40–41.

17. Foote to Welles, February 6 and 7, 1862, both in ORN, 22:537–39; Cooling, *Forts Henry and Donelson*, 106–21; Milligan, *Gunboats Down the Mississippi*, 40–41.

18. Foote to Welles, February 7, 1862, ORN, 22:537–39.

19. Jay Slagle, *Ironclad Captain: Seth Ledyard Phelps and the U.S. Navy, 1841–1864* (Kent, OH: Kent State University Press, 1996), 162–73.

20. A. S. Johnston to Judah P. Benjamin, February 8, 1862, ORN, 22:563.

21. Halleck to Foote, February 11, 1862, Grant to Foote, February 10, 1862, and Foote to Halleck, February 11, 1862, all in OR, 7:603–4, 600, 604.

22. Cooling, *Forts Henry and Donelson*, 142–43, 153; Milligan, *Gunboats Down the Mississippi*, 44–46.

23. Walke to Foote, and Foote to Welles, both dated February 15, 1862, ORN, 22:590–91, 584–85; Cooling, *Forts Henry and Donelson*, 153–57.

24. Cooling, *Forts Henry and Donelson*, 128–34.

25. Gant to Buckner, February 16, 1862, OR, 7:161; Cooling, *Forts Henry and Donelson*, 200–23.

26. Larry J. Daniel, *Shiloh: The Battle That Changed the Civil War* (New York: Simon & Schuster, 1997), 265; Milligan, *Gunboats Down the Mississippi*, 60–61.

27. Foote to Welles, April 6, 1862, ORN, 22:712–13; Joiner, *Lincoln's Brown Water Navy*, 61–62.

28. "Investigation of Navy Department," February 26, 1863, ORN, series II, 1:781–83.

29. Charles L. Dufour, *The Night the War Was Lost* (Garden City, NY: Doubleday, 1960), 187–205; Chester Hearn, *The Capture of New Orleans, 1862* (Baton Rouge: Louisiana State University Press, 1995), 152–53.

30. Fox to Porter, February 24, 1862, David Dixon Porter Papers, Library of Congress, box 17; Porter to Fox, March 28, and April 8, 1962, both in Robert Means Thompson and Richard Wainwright, eds. *The Confidential Correspondence of Gustavus Vasa Fox* (Freeport, NY: Books for Libraries, 1920, 1972), 2:91, 98.

31. Dufour, *The Night the War Was Lost*, 219–39.
32. Farragut to Welles, May 6, 1862, 18:157; Hearn, *The Capture of New Orleans*, 227.
33. Craven to Farragut, April 26, 1862, ORN, 18:182–83; Hearn, *The Capture of New Orleans*, 218–34.
34. Farragut to Welles, May 6, 1862, ORN, 18:156–57.
35. Dufour, *The Night the War Was Lost*, 299–315.
36. Farragut to Welles, May 6, 1862, ORN, 18:158.
37. Dufour, *The Night the War Was Lost*, 331–54.
38. Slagle, *Ironclad Captain*, 219–22; Milligan, *Gunboats Down the Mississippi*, 65–67.
39. Chester Hearn, *Ellet's Brigade: The Strangest Outfit of All* (Baton Rouge: Louisiana State University Press, 2000), 11–25.
40. Ibid., 29.
41. Ibid., 29–37.
42. Isaac N. Brown, "The Confederate Gun-Boat 'Arkansas,'" B&L, 3:572.
43. Ibid., 575–76; Walke to Farragut, July 15, 1862, and Farragut to Welles, July 17, 1862, both in ORN, 19:41, 4.
44. Brown, "The Confederate Gun-Boat 'Arkansas,'" B&L, 3:578.
45. Porter to Welles, April 17, 1862, ORN, 24:552–53.
46. Gideon Welles, *The Diary of Gideon Welles: Secretary of the Navy Under Lincoln and Johnson* (entry of July 7, 1863). Edited by Howard K. Beale (New York: W.W. Norton, 1960), 1:364; Lincoln to Conkling, August 26, 1863, *Collected Works of Abraham Lincoln*, ed. by Roy P. Basler (New Brunswick, NJ: Rutgers University Press, 1953–55), 6:409.

Chapter 5

1. Nickels to Parrott, May 13, 1862, ORN, 12:822.
2. Marchand to Du Pont, May 19, 1862, ORN, 13:13–14.
3. Du Pont to Ammen, May 22, 1862, ORN, 12:807.
4. *New York Tribune*, June 9, 1862; Fox to Du Pont, June 3, 1863, Gustavus V. Fox, *Confidential Correspondence of Gustavus Vasa Fox*, ed. by Robert M. Thompson and Richard Wainwright (Freeport, NY: Books for Libraries, 1920, 1972), 1:126.
5. Fox to Du Pont, June 3, 1862, Fox, *Confidential Correspondence*, 1:126; Salmon P. Chase, *Inside Lincoln's Cabinet: The Civil War Diaries of Salmon P. Chase*, ed. by David Donald (New York: Longmans, Green, 1954), 138 (entry of September 13, 1862).
6. Patrick Brennan, *Secessionville: Assault on Charleston* (Campbell, CA: Savas Publishing Company, 1996), 33.
7. Lincoln's Announcement, dated May 9, 1862, is in Roy P. Basler, ed., *The Collected Works of Abraham Lincoln* (New Brunswick, NJ: Rutgers University Press, 1953–55), 5:222.
8. Hunter to Benham, June 10, 1862, OR, 14:46; Brennan, *Secessionville*, 138–39.

9. E. Milby Burton, *The Siege of Charleston, 1861–1865* (Columbia, SC: University of South Carolina Press, 1970), 104, 108–9; Brennan, *Secessionville*, 309.

10. Fox to Du Pont, May 12, 1862, Fox, *Confidential Correspondence*, 1:119; Du Pont to Sophie Du Pont, May 29, 1862, in John D. Hayes, ed., *Samuel F. Du Pont, A Selection from His Civil War Letters* (Ithaca, NY: Cornell University Press, 1969), 2:79. Hereafter *Du Pont Letters*.

11. Worden to Du Pont, January 27, 1863, and Du Pont to Welles, January 28, 1863, both in ORN, 13:543–45.

12. Burton, *Siege of Charleston*, 124; William N. Still, Jr., *Iron Afloat: The Story of the Confederate Armorclads* (Nashville: Vanderbilt University Press, 1971; reprinted, Columbia, SC: University of South Carolina Press, 1985), 81–83.

13. Robert Holcombe, "Types of Ships," in *The Confederate Navy*, ed. by William N. Still, Jr. (Annapolis, MD: Naval Institute Press, 1997), 54; Still, *Iron Afloat*, 81–82.

14. Conover to Welles, May 7, 1863, ORN, 13:563–64.

15. Stellwagen to Du Pont, January 31, 1863, ORN, 13:579–80.

16. Abbott to Stellwagen, January 31, 1863, ORN, 13:580–81.

17. Tucker to Ingraham, January 31, 1863, with enclosure, and Le Roy to Du Pont, January 31, 1863, both in ORN, 13:581–82, 619–20.

18. Du Pont to Welles, February 18, 1863, and Du Pont to Le Roy, February 6, 1863, both in ORN, 13:612–13.

19. Burton, *Siege of Charleston*, 120–23, 129–30.

20. Du Pont to Sophie Du Pont, February 1, 1863, *Du Pont Letters*, 2:407.

21. Fox to Du Pont, February 16, 1863, Du Pont Letters, 2:443–45; Fox to Du Pont, February 20 and 26, 1863, in Fox, *Confidential Correspondence*, 1:181, 185.

22. Rodgers to Du Pont, April 8, 1863, RON, 14:12; John Johnson, *The Defense of Charleston Harbor* (Charleston, SC: Walker, Evans, Cogswell, 1890), 20. The "Devil" is described in Echols to Harris, April 9, 1863, ORN, 14:89, and a drawing of it is on p. 93. The Devil became detached during the battle and later washed up on Morris Island.

23. Burton, *Siege of Charleston*, 138.

24. See the tables in Johnson, *Defense of Charleston Harbor*, 58–59. "Abstract of Expenditure of Ammunition," ORN, 14:27; Echols to Harris, April 9, 1863, and Du Pont to Welles, April 15, 1863, both in ORN, 14:87, 6.

25. Du Pont to Welles, April 8, 1863, ORN, 14:3–4.

26. Gideon Welles, *Diary of Gideon Welles: Secretary of the Navy Under Lincoln and Johnson*, ed. by Howard K. Beale (New York: W.W. Norton, 1960), 1:276 (entry of April 20, 1863).

27. Still, *Iron Afloat*, 129–35.

28. Craig Symonds, *Lincoln and His Admirals: Abraham Lincoln, the U.S. Navy, and the Civil War* (New York: Oxford University Press, 2008), 265–67.

29. Welles to Du Pont, June 3, 1863, ORN, 14:230; Kevin J. Weddle, *Lincoln's Tragic Admiral: The Life of Samuel Francis Du Pont* (Charlottesville: University of Virginia Press, 2005), 187–207.
30. Symonds, *Lincoln and His Admirals*, 242.
31. Steven R. Wise, *Gate of Hell: Campaign for Charleston Harbor, 1863* (Columbia: University of South Carolina Press, 1994), 17.
32. Ibid., 169–70.
33. Ibid., 161–62.
34. The signal communications are in ORN, 14:450–51. See also Symonds, *Lincoln and His Admirals*, 246.
35. Wise, *Gate of Hell*, 169–75.
36. John A. Dahlgren, *Memoir of John A. Dahlgren, Rear Admiral United States Navy, by his Widow, Madelaine Vinson Dahlgren* (New York: Charles L. Webster, 1891), 410–12 (entry of September 2, 1863).
37. Gillmore's report is in OR, 28(2):344. See also Wise, *Gate of Hell*, 180–204.
38. Stevens to Welles, September 28, 1865, ORN, 14:633.
39. Forrest to Stevens, August 10, 1865, ORN, 14:634.
40. The excerpt from Dahlgren's diary is in ORN, 14:636; Stevens to Welles, September 28, 1863, ORN, 14:633.
41. Welles to Dahlgren, October 9, 1863, ORN, 15:26–27.
42. Thomas J. Scharf, *The Confederate States Navy* (New York: Rogers and Sherwood, 1887), 754; Burton, *Siege of Charleston*, 214–15.
43. Burton, *Siege of Charleston*, 216–17.
44. Rowan to Dahlgren, October 6, 1863, and Dahlgren to Welles, October 7, 1863, both in ORN, 15:10–11, 12; Burton, *Siege of Charleston*, 220–21.
45. Rowan to Dahlgren, October 6, 1863, ORN, 15:12–13.
46. Confidential Report of John A. Dahlgren, October 7, 1863, ORN, 15:13.
47. Beauregard letter dated November 14, 1863, ORN, 15:695.
48. Dahlgren to Welles, January 13, 1864, ORN, 15:238–39.
49. Mark K. Regan, *The Hunley* (Orangeburg, SC: Sandlapper Publishing Co., 2005), 69–70.
50. Extract from Journal of Operations, October 15, 1863, ORN, 15:692; Regan, *The Hunley*, 94–105.
51. Higginson to Dahlgren, February 18, 1864, ORN, 15:328; Proceedings of the Court of Enquiry, March 7, 1864, ORN, 15:332–33; Pickering's testimony is in Regan, *The Hunley*, 199–200.
52. Brian Hicks and Schuyler Kropf, *Raising the Hunley: The Remarkable History and Recovery of the Lost Confederate Submarine* (New York: Ballantine Books, 2002), 245–49.
53. Dahlgren's order, dated February 19, 1864, is in ORN, 15:330–31.
54. Dahlgren to Welles, September 25, 1864, ORN, 15:689.
55. Burton, *Siege of Charleston*, 55.
56. Dahlgren to Welles, January 16, 1865, ORN, 16:171–74.

57. Burton, *Siege of Charleston*, 321; Belknap to Dahlgren, February 19, 1865, ORN, 16:258–59.

58. Debby Applegate, *The Most Famous Man in America: The Biography of Henry Ward Beecher* (New York: Doubleday, 2006), 11.

Chapter 6

1. Arthur Bergeron, *Confederate Mobile* (Jackson: University Press of Mississippi, 1991), 4–5; Earl W. Fornell, "Mobile During the Blockade," *Alabama Historical Quarterly* 23 (Spring 1961): 29–43.

2. Craig L. Symonds, *Confederate Admiral: The Life and Wars of Franklin Buchanan* (Annapolis, MD: Naval Institute Press, 1999), 184.

3. Ibid., 190.

4. Ibid., 192–99.

5. "Descriptive List of the Crew of the Confederate States Steamer Tennessee," no date, Museum of the Confederacy; Buchanan to Mitchell, October 17, 1863, Buchanan Letters, Virginia Historical Society, Richmond; Symonds, *Confederate Admiral*, 200.

6. Jack Friend, *West Wind, Flood Tide: The Battle of Mobile Bay* (Annapolis, MD: Naval Institute Press, 2004). 153–60.

7. Farragut's General Order No. 10, July 12, 1864, ORN, 21:397–98.

8. Buchanan to Mitchell, October 17, 1863, Buchanan Letters, Virginia Historical Society, Richmond; Farragut's General Orders No. 11, July 29, 1864, ORN, 21:398.

9. Friend, *West Wind, Flood Tide*, 165–66; Farragut's General Order No. 10, July 12, 1864, and Farragut to Welles, August 5, 1864, both in ORN, 21:397–98, 405–6.

10. Alden to Farragut, August 6, 1864, ORN, 21:445.

11. Alden to Farragut, August 5, 1864, OR, 52(1):575.

12. Friend, *West Wind, Flood Tide*, 181.

13. Two of the most widely read histories of the U.S. Navy report that Farragut said: "Damn the torpedoes! Full steam ahead!" A third renders it as "Damn the torpedoes, full *speed* ahead." See E. B. Potter et al., *Sea Power: A Naval History* (Annapolis, MD: Naval Institute Press, 1981), 148; Kenneth J. Hagan, *This People's Navy: The Making of American Sea Power* (New York: The Free Press, 1991), 171; and Nathan Miller, *The U.S. Navy: A History* (New York: William Morrow, 1990), 138.

14. Quoted in Friend, *West Wind, Flood Tide*, 189.

15. Drayton to Farragut, August 6, 1864, ORN, 21:425; "Hav" to his mother, August 6, 1864, Collection of Nancy Lloyd, Baltimore, and quoted in Symonds, *Confederate Admiral*, 213.

16. Quoted in Friend, *West Wind, Flood Tide*, 213.

17. J. Crittenden Watson, "The Lashing of Admiral Farragut in the Rigging," *Battles and Leaders of the Civil War*, ed. by Robert U. Johnson and Clarence C. Buel (New York: Century, 1888), 4:407.

18. Batcheller to Strong, August 5, 1864, ORN, 21:473; Chester Hearn, *Mobile Bay and the Mobile Campaign: The Last Great Battles of the Civil War* (Jefferson, NC: McFarland, 1998), 103; Friend, *West Wind, Flood Tide*, 196–97; Daniel B. Conrad, "Capture of the C.S. Ram *Tennessee* in Mobile Bay, August, 1864," *Southern Historical Society Papers* (1891), 19:75–76.

19. Marchand to Farragut, August 5, 1864, ORN, 21:466; Foxhall Parker, "The Battle of Mobile Bay," *Papers of the Military Historical Society of Massachusetts* (1902), 12:35; Symonds, *Confederate Admiral*, 217.

20. Drayton to Farragut, August 6, 1864, ORN, 21:427; Symonds, *Confederate Admiral*, 217.

21. Symonds, *Confederate Admiral*, 218.

22. The notion of Fort Fisher representing a giant numeral "7" is from Chris Fonvielle, whose book *The Wilmington Campaign: Last Rays of Departing Hope* (Campbell, CA: Savas Publishing, 1997) is the definitive source.

23. Lee to Fox, December 14, 1862, Gustavus V. Fox, *Confidential Correspondence of Gustavus Vasa Fox*, ed. by Robert Means Thompson and Richard Wainwright (Freeport, NY: Books for Libraries, 1920), 2:242; Symonds, *Lincoln and His Admirals: Abraham Lincoln, the U.S. Navy, and the Civil War* (New York: Oxford University Press, 2008), 316.

24. Abstract log of the USS *Kansas*, ORN, 11:245; Ari Hoogenboom, *Gustavus Vasa Fox of the Union Navy* (Baltimore, MD: Johns Hopkins, 2008), 256–58.

25. The anonymous sailor is quoted in Fonvielle, *The Wilmington Campaign*, 133; Porter to Welles, December 24, 1864, ORN, 11:253.

26. Benjamin F. Butler, *Butler's Book* (Boston: A. M. Thayer & Co., 1892), 796.

27. Porter to Welles, December 29, 1864, and Porter to Grant, January 3, 1865, both in ORN, 11:263–65, 405; David Dixon Porter, *Naval History of the Civil War* (Boston: D. Appleton & Co., 1886), 606; Butler, *Butler's Book*, 791.

28. Porter to Welles, December 29, 1864, ORN, 11:264.

29. Fonvielle, *The Wilmington Campaign*, 201; Grant to Terry, January 3, 1865, OR, 46(2):25.

30. Parrott to Porter, no date, ORN, 11:462–63; Porter's General Order No. 78, January 2, 1865, ORN, 11:426.

31. Porter to Welles, January 14, 1865, ORN, 11:433; Fonvielle, *The Wilmington Campaign*, 250–58; Hoogenboom, *Gustavus Vasa Fox*, 262.

32. Memorandum dated August 19, 1864, in Bulloch to Waddell, October 5, 1864, both in ORN, 3:749–55. See also James I. Waddell, *C.S.S. Shenandoah: The Memoirs of Lieutenant Commanding James I. Waddell*, ed. by James D. Horan (New York: Crown Publishers, 1960), 83.

33. Waddell, *C.S.S. Shenandoah*, 94.

34. Waddell to Bulloch, January 25, 1865, ORN, 3:760; Waddell, *C.S.S. Shenandoah*, 104–5, 107.

35. William C. Whipple, *The Voyage of the CSS Shenandoah: A Memorable Cruise*, ed. by D. Alan Harris and Anne B. Harris (Tuscaloosa: University of Alabama Press, 2005), 108, III (diary entries of January 25 and 20); Lynn Schooler, *The Last Shot: The Incredible Story of the CSS Shenandoah and the True Conclusion of the American Civil War* (New York: Harper/Collins, 2005), 127–28.

36. Waddell to Francis, January 30, 1865, ORN, 3:764.

37. Francis to Waddell, January 31, 1865, ORN, 3:764.

38. Schooler, *The Last Shot*, 139–44.

39. Waddell to Francis, February 14, 1865, ORN, 3:770–71; Waddell, *C.S.S Shenandoah*, 131–38; Abstract log of the *Shenandoah*, February 18, 1865, ORN, 3:788.

40. Whipple, *Voyage of the CSS Shenandoah*, 166 (diary entry of June 22); Waddell, *C.S.S. Shenandoah*, 163–67; Schooler, *The Last Shot*, 203–14. A list of the *Shenandoah*'s captures is in ORN, 3:792.

41. Waddell, *C.S.S. Shenandoah*, 175.

42. Whipple, *Voyage of the CSS Shenandoah*, 182 (diary entry of August 2); Bulloch to Waddell, October 5, 1864, ORN, 3:754.

43. The petitions, dated September 28, 1865, are in ORN, 3:779–83; Waddell, *C.S.S. Shenandoah*, 183.

BIBLIOGRAPHICAL ESSAY

THE BASIC SOURCE for the study of the Civil War at sea is the 30-volume *Official Records of the Union and Confederate Navies in the War of the Rebellion*. Though few would sit down to read this collection from front to back, it nevertheless can be read in great stretches. Having picked it up to consult a particular letter, I have often found myself reading page after page to follow the story as it was written by the participants. Similarly, the memoirs of the participants are a rich source not only of information but also for understanding the viewpoints of the combatants. Several of these are mentioned below.

As for secondary reading, after decades of neglect, the naval war has recently attracted a lot of serious scholarly attention, and there are now a number of excellent general histories. Joining old standards like Virgil Carrington Jones' 3-volume work *The Civil War at Sea* (New York: Holt, Rinehart and Winston, 1960–62) and Bern Anderson's *By Sea and By River* (New York: Knopf, 1962), are newer works that take advantage of newly discovered sources or offer a valuable reassessment. Among these are William M. Fowler, *Under Two Flags: The American Navy in the Civil War* (New York: W.W. Norton, 1990; available in paperback from the Naval Institute Press, 2001); Ivan Musicant's *Divided Waters: The Naval History of the Civil War* (New York: Harper/Collins, 1995); Spencer Tucker's *Blue and Gray Navies: The Civil War Afloat* (Annapolis, MD: Naval Institute Press, 2006); and James M. McPherson's *War on the Waters: The Union and Confederate Navies, 1861–1865* (Chapel Hill: University of North Carolina Press, 2012). A recent book that provides excellent insight into the Union's wartime Navy Department is Stephen R. Taaffe's *Commanding Lincoln's Navy: Union Naval Leadership during the Civil War* (Annapolis, MD: Naval Institute Press, 2009). Other books that provide particular insight on crucial aspects of the naval war include Michael Bennett's *Union Jacks: Yankee Sailors in the Civil War* (Chapel Hill: University of North Carolina Press, 2004); David G. Surdam, *Northern Naval Superiority and the Economics of the American Civil War* (Columbia: University of South Carolina Press, 2001); and Barbara Brooks Thompson,

Bluejackets and Contrabands: African Americans and the Union Navy (Lexington: University of Kentucky Press, 2009). I will include here, too, my own book, *Lincoln and His Admirals: Abraham Lincoln, the U.S. Navy, and the Civil War* (New York: Oxford University Press, 2008). Finally, Chester Hearn's several books on Civil War naval topics are both well researched and well written.

For works on the ships and the guns of the Civil War era, the standard work for many years was Frank Bennett, *The Steam Navy of the United States* (Pittsburgh: Warren & Co., 1896), supplemented by his *The Monitor and the Navy under Steam* (Boston: Houghton Mifflin, 1900). The first of these is a fat (953-page) volume by a naval engineer who occasionally lapses into lengthy digressions, but it remains the starting point for someone interested in the details of ship design, marine engineering, and ship performance in the nineteenth century. A shorter and more accessible book is *The Old Steam Navy: Frigates, Ships, and Gunboats, 1815–1885* (Annapolis, MD: Naval Institute Press, 1990) by Donald Canney, who also wrote *Lincoln's Navy: The Ships, Men, and Organization, 1861–1865* (Annapolis, MD: Naval Institute Press, 1998). A companion volume edited by Canney, *The Confederate Navy*, with an identical subtitle (Annapolis, MD: Naval Institute Press, 1997), is a collection of essays on various aspects of the rebel navy. Robert Gardiner edited the volume *Steam, Steel and Shellfire: The Steam Warship, 1815–1905* (Annapolis, MD: Naval Institute Press, 1992) from Conway's "History of the Ship" series.

For Union ironclads, see William H. Roberts' *Civil War Ironclads: The U.S. Navy and Industrial Mobilization* (Baltimore, MD: Johns Hopkins University Press, 2002), and for the Confederate effort see William N. Still, Jr.'s, classic *Iron Afloat: The Story of the Confederate Armorclads* (Nashville, TN: Vanderbilt University Press, 1971; reprint Columbia: University of South Carolina Press, 1985). William C. Davis's *Duel Between the First Ironclads* (Baton Rouge: Louisiana State University Press, 1975) is still the best general history of that iconic fight. For the history of the naval policy decision-making that surrounded the appropriations for these ships, see Kurt Hackemer's excellent book, *The U.S. Navy and the Origins of the Military Industrial Complex* (Annapolis, MD: Naval Institute Press, 2001).

On the blockade see Robert M. Browning, Jr.'s, two books, *From Cape Charles to Cape Fear: The North Atlantic Blockading Squadron during the Civil War* (Tuscaloosa: University of Alabama Press, 1993) and *Success Is All that Was Expected: The South Atlantic Blockading Squadron during the Civil War* (Dulles, VA: Brassey's, 2004), and William H. Roberts' shorter but essential book, *Now for the Contest: Coastal and Oceanic Naval Operations in the Civil War* (Lincoln: University of Nebraska Press, 2004). For blockade-running see Stephen A. Wise, *Lifeline of the Confederacy: Blockade-Running during the Civil War* (Columbia: University of South Carolina Press, 1988). The adventure of blockade-running is covered in a number of postwar memoirs including Thomas E. Taylor, *Running the Blockade: A Personal Narrative of Adventures, Risks, and Escapes during the American Civil War* (London: John Murray, 1912).

James Bulloch himself offers the most detailed picture of how he and others conjured the *Florida* and *Alabama* in the shipyards of Liverpool. In 1883 he published his memoir entitled *The Secret Service of the Confederate States in Europe*, and a modern edition is available from Thomas Yoseloff of New York (1959). Similarly, the best account of the cruise of the *Alabama* comes from the pen of her captain, Raphael Semmes. Though Semmes (like Bennett) is prone to long digressions, his narrative memoir is still lively reading, and, like Bulloch's memoir, it is available in a modern reprint: *Memoirs of Service Afloat during the War Between the States* (Secaucus, NJ: Blue & Gray Press, 1987). Two other books that provide firsthand accounts of life aboard the Confederacy's most famous rebel raider are John McIntosh Kell, *Recollections of a Naval Life* (Washington, DC: The Neale Co., 1900), and Arthur Sinclair, *Two Years on the Alabama* (Annapolis, MD: Naval Institute Press, 1895, 1989). The best general history of the construction of the rebel raiders is James Tertius de Kay, *The Rebel Raiders: The Astonishing History of the Confederacy's Secret Navy* (New York: Ballantine Books, 2002). For the Confederate privateers, the only book that deals fully with the subject is William M. Robinson, Jr., *The Confederate Privateers* (New Haven, CT: Yale University Press, 1928).

As noted in the text, the impact of the rebel raiders is discussed in detail by Robert Dalzell, whose book *The Flight from the Flag* (Chapel Hill: University of North Carolina Press, 1940) has become a classic. In it, Dalzell tried not only to illustrate the lasting impact of the rebel raiders on American trade, he also sought to craft a neo-Mahanian vision of the future in which the United States emerges as the dominant world power. That, plus the fall of France to the Nazis which took place as the book went to press, is why he views the decline of the American merchant marine with such alarm.

There are a number of excellent works on the river war. John D. Milligan's *Gunboats Down the Mississippi* (Annapolis, MD: Naval Institute Press, 1949, 1990), is old but still valuable. It should be supplemented by B. Frank Cooling's *Forts Henry and Donelson: The Key to the Confederate Heartland* (Knoxville: University of Tennessee Press, 1987), and Larry J. Daniel and Lynn N. Bock's *Island No. 10: Struggle for the Mississippi Valley* (Tuscaloosa: University of Alabama Press, 1996). Specialty works that cast light on the river war include two fine books by Chester Hearn, *The Capture of New Orleans, 1862* (Baton Rouge: Louisiana State University Press, 1995) and *Ellet's Brigade, The Strangest Outfit of All* (Baton Rouge: Louisiana State University Press, 2000). An excellent book that deserves more attention than it has received is Jay Slagle's *Ironclad Captain: Seth Ledyard Phelps and the U.S. Navy, 1841–1864* (Kent, OH: Kent State University Press, 1996), which is based on Phelps' private letters and exposes much about both the operational history and the internal politics of the Union Mississippi Squadron. For the Vicksburg campaign, the best one-volume work is Michael B. Ballard, *Vicksburg: The Campaign that Opened the Mississippi* (Chapel Hill: University of North Carolina Press, 2004), though *Vicksburg Is the Key: The Struggle for the Mississippi River* (Lincoln: University of Nebraska Press, 2003) by

William Shea and Terrence Winschel is also useful. For the truly ambitious, see Edwin C. Bearss, *The Campaign for Vicksburg*, 3 vols. (Dayton, OH: Morningside, 1985–86).

The only full-length book on Union combined operations is Rowena Reed's *Combined Operations in the Civil War* (Annapolis, MD: Naval Institute Press, 1978), which is marred by her inexplicable admiration for George B. McClellan. For a contrasting view see Craig L. Symonds, ed., *Union Combined Operations in the Civil War* (New York: Fordham University Press, 2009). There are several good histories of the siege of Charleston. A good place to start is E. Milby Burton's *The Siege of Charleston* (Columbia: University of South Carolina Press, 1970), which relies heavily on the *Official Records*, but which is both a bit pedantic and overwhelming sympathetic to the heroic defenders of the city. Steven Wise's *Gate of Hell: Campaign for Charleston Harbor, 1863* (Columbia: University of South Carolina Press, 1994) is better grounded in the sources, more balanced, and also has the advantage of being more readable. Two nineteenth-century volumes offer a number of insights, but should be used with caution: John Johnson's *The Defense of Charleston Harbor* (Charleston, SC: Walker, Evans and Cogswell, 1889) and Samuel Jones, *The Siege of Charleston* (New York: Neale Publishing Company, 1911). There has been a lot of interest since 1995 about the *H. L. Hunley*. The best books to consult are Mark K. Regan's *The Hunley* (Orangeburg, SC: Sandlapper Publishing Co., 2005) and Tom Chaffin's *The H. L. Hunley: the Secret Hope of the Confederacy* (New York: Hill & Wang), 2008). Brian Hicks and Schuyler Kropf detail the recovery of the *Hunley* in their book *Raising the Hunley* (New York: Ballantine Books, 2002).

The best book on Farragut's run into Mobile is Jack Friend's detailed and dramatic *West Wind, Flood Tide: The Battle of Mobile Bay* (Annapolis, MD: Naval Institute Press, 2004), and the best book on the capture of Wilmington is Chris Fonvielle's definitive study *The Wilmington Campaign: Last Rays of Departing Hope* (Campbell, CA: Savas Publishing, 1997). For more on the cruise of the *Shenandoah*, Waddell's own tale is printed in the *Official Records* (vol. 3, 792–836), and has been published separately as *C.S.S. Shenandoah: The Memoirs of Lieutenant Commanding James I. Waddell*, edited by James D. Horan (New York: Crown Publishing Co., 1960). A journal kept by William C. Whittle has been published as *The Voyage of the CSS Shenandoah, A Memorable Cruise*, edited by D, Alan Harris and Anne B. Harris (Tuscaloosa: University of Alabama Press, 2005). This story is well told by Tom Chaffin in *Sea of Gray: The Around the World Odyssey of the Confederate Raider Shenandoah* (New York: Hill & Wang, 2006), and by Lynn Schooler in *The Last Shot: The Incredible Story of the CSS Shenandoah and the True Conclusion of the American Civil War* (New York: Harper/Collins, 2005).

INDEX

Page numbers in **bold** indicate illustrations.